Asian Diaspora and East-West Modernity

Comparative Cultural Studies
Steven Tötösy de Zepetnek, Series Editor

The Purdue University Press monograph series of Books in Comparative Cultural Studies publishes single-authored and thematic collected volumes of new scholarship. Manuscripts are invited for publication in the series in fields of the study of culture, literature, the arts, media studies, communication studies, the history of ideas, etc., and related disciplines of the humanities and social sciences to the series editor via email at <clcweb@purdue.edu>. Comparative cultural studies is a contextual approach in the study of culture in a global and intercultural context and work with a plurality of methods and approaches; the theoretical and methodological framework of comparative cultural studies is built on tenets borrowed from the disciplines of cultural studies and comparative literature and from a range of thought including literary and culture theory, (radical) constructivism, communication theories, and systems theories; in comparative cultural studies focus is on theory and method as well as application. For a detailed description of the aims and scope of the series including the style guide of the series link to <http://docs.lib.purdue.edu/clcweblibrary/seriespurdueccs>. Manuscripts submitted to the series are peer reviewed followed by the usual standards of editing, copy editing, marketing, and distribution. The series is affiliated with *CLCWeb: Comparative Literature and Culture* (ISSN 1481-4374), the peer-reviewed, full-text, and open-access quarterly published by Purdue University Press at <http://docs.lib.purdue.edu/clcweb>.

Volumes in the Purdue series of Books in Comparative Cultural Studies include <http://www.thepress.purdue.edu/series/comparative-cultural-studies>

Sheng-mei Ma, *Asian Diaspora and East-West Modernity*
Irene Marques, *Transnational Discourses on Class, Gender, and Cultural Identity*
Comparative Hungarian Cultural Studies, Ed. Steven Tötösy de Zepetnek and Louise O. Vasvári
Hui Zou, *A Jesuit Garden in Beijing and Early Modern Chinese Culture*
Yi Zheng, *From Burke and Wordsworth to the Modern Sublime in Chinese Literature*
Agata Anna Lisiak, *Urban Cultures in (Post)Colonial Central Europe*
Representing Humanity in an Age of Terror, Ed. Sophia A. McClennen and Henry James Morello
Michael Goddard, *Gombrowicz, Polish Modernism, and the Subversion of Form*
Shakespeare in Hollywood, Asia, and Cyberspace, Ed. Alexander C.Y. Huang and Charles S. Ross
Gustav Shpet's Contribution to Philosophy and Cultural Theory, Ed. Galin Tihanov
Comparative Central European Holocaust Studies, Ed. Louise O. Vasvári and Steven Tötösy de Zepetnek
Marko Juvan, *History and Poetics of Intertextuality*
Thomas O. Beebee, *Nation and Region in Modern American and European Fiction*
Paolo Bartoloni, *On the Cultures of Exile, Translation, and Writing*
Justyna Sempruch, *Fantasies of Gender and the Witch in Feminist Theory and Literature*
Kimberly Chabot Davis, *Postmodern Texts and Emotional Audiences*
Philippe Codde, *The Jewish American Novel*
Deborah Streifford Reisinger, *Crime and Media in Contemporary France*
Imre Kertész and Holocaust Literature, Ed. Louise O. Vasvári and Steven Tötösy de Zepetnek
Camilla Fojas, *Cosmopolitanism in the Americas*
Comparative Cultural Studies and Michael Ondaatje's Writing, Ed. Steven Tötösy de Zepetnek
Jin Feng, *The New Woman in Early Twentieth-Century Chinese Fiction*
Comparative Cultural Studies and Latin America, Ed. Sophia A. McClennen and Earl E. Fitz
Sophia A. McClennen, *The Dialectics of Exile*

Asian Diaspora and East-West Modernity

Sheng-mei Ma

Purdue University Press
West Lafayette, Indiana

Printed in the United States of America.

Library of Congress Cataloging-in-Publication Data

Ma, Sheng-mei.

Asian Diaspora and East-West Modernity / by Sheng-mei Ma.

p. cm. -- (Comparative cultural studies)

Includes bibliographical references and index.

ISBN 978-1-55753-611-2 (pbk. : alk. paper) -- ISBN 978-1-61249-209-4 (epdf) -- ISBN 978-1-61249-208-7 (epub) 1. Asian diaspora. 2. East and West. 3. Popular culture--Asia. 4. Civilization, Modern. 5. American literature--Asian American authors--History and criticism. I. Title.

DS12.M3 2012

305.895--dc23

2011049171

Contents

Acknowledgments

Earlier versions of parts of some chapters have appeared in the following: chapter 1 in *Asian Gothic: Essays on Literature, Film and Anime*, ed. Andrew Nock Soon Ng, Jefferson, NC: McFarland, 2008, 187-209; chapter 2 in *Sun Yat-sen Journal of Humanities* 26 (Winter 2008): 17-32; chapter 5 in *Studies in Symbolic Interaction* 33 (2009): 149-63; chapter 6 in *Of Mice and Men: Animals in Human Signification*, ed. Vartan Messier and Nandita Batra, London: Cambridge Scholars Press, 2009, 152-77; chapter 7 in *Asian Cinema Studies* 17.2 (2006): 32-46.; chapter 8 in *Mechademia 4: War/Time* (2009): 183-96; chapter 10 in *China Rights Forum* 1 (2008): 121-26. All articles are reprinted by permission.

I am indebted to the following individuals, who made it possible for me to complete this book during the period leading up to my Chair Professorship at Taiwan's Providence University, 2012-13: Karin Wurst and David Prestel at my home institution, Michigan State University, Steven Tötösy de Zepetnek, I-Chun Wang, Fu-chang Wang, Kun Jong Lee, John Lent, and Patricia Haseltine. As always, I could not have accomplished this or any other project without the support of Lien Hsu and Roan Ma.

Introduction

Digging to China (or America)

Living is dying, an unscripted, unconscious rehearsal for the premiere of death—one show only for each individual serving the life sentence, cyclical reruns for collective humanity. In similar denial, modernity has dissociated itself from death and the other, death as the other. Modernity is a dream posited on the dialectical relation between self and other: industrialized West versus pre-industrial East at the turn of the last millennium; Chinese metropolises versus the rural hinterland at the turn of this millennium. In both and many more instances, the uneven development of technology results in a power binarism where the modern half in any pair is privileged. Modernity prevails because of its alleged immanence of rejuvenation, which is oftentimes but a time-space compression by virtue of advanced technology. As it is less time-consuming to traverse great distances and accomplish arduous tasks, we come to see each present moment as a new beginning rather than an extension of the past. Modernity, therefore, signifies the new in an absolute sense, which means death to the old; the lifeblood for the modern drains from bodies imagined to be unmodern. Since the old and traditional do not die absolutely, merely metaphorically, modernity is not so much a death sentence for "time past" as a death rehearsal inherent in "time present," not so much an execution as a stay of execution. Any such trial run for the ultimate finale or the apocalypse that modernity pretends to be must cast a deus ex machina of sorts, the nonself or the transcendent, to effect a decisive rupture. Hence, modernities, also known as death rehearsals, are born out of where self and other, East and West, living and nonliving, and other dualities intersect, such as in the daily routine in life, which is a barely noticeable process of dying, a steady digging of one's own grave. Beyond the personal level of aging, death rehearsal takes place on the collective and cultural level. Modernity with its Euro-American imperialist underpinnings has routinely propped itself up on the corpses of the other: Africa (Conrad's *Heart of Darkness* [1898]), Arabia (Joyce's "Araby," [1914], in addition to those detailed in Edward W. Said's *Orientalism* [1978]), and Asia (not detailed in Said, who focuses on Western representations of the Near East, which overlaps with Arabia). The Triple-A Club, if you will, provides key service to ensure the West's smooth motoring across, or into, the globe.

Dig a hole through the earth, Americans (i.e., US-Americans and Canadians) joke, and you come out on the other side, in China, presumably. Joking aside, the figure of speech suggests the Orientalist thrust that the Orient, crystallized by China, lies diametrically opposed to the Occident. While the modern West fashions its identity by putting an end to the old, its previous incarnation—an empty shell—is shed and transferred onto the Eastern other, an alterity validating and valorizing the West's metamorphosis. As Shu-mei Shih argues, China is part of the peripheral, "non-Western alterity that constituted Western modernism" (*The Lure of the Modern* 4). Modernity hence arises by vacating the Orient into a void, a state of being on the order of death. It is indeed ironic that in the name of digging to reach the other, the West fails to dig or comprehend the East, and the other way around, too, as implied by the parenthesis, "(or America)," in the introduction title. Amid this mutual misunderstanding, modernity flashes like lightning from culture clashes between West and East, sky and earth; modernity comes to manifest itself through the manna—technology and modernization—falling from the sky since the nineteenth century and the raw materials and human bodies vaporized from the earth. Both positive and negative forces are of course integral to the thunderbolt, which summons the genesis of light as well as scorches the earth. As modern colonialism lays waste much of the East, it quickens not only the awakening of life's futility but also new sprouts of human consciousness—such as alternative modernities—from the charred earth.

As the West digs in its Orient for sustenance, the consumed and the consuming unite as one. This impulse toward a mythical, oceanic wholeness underwrites much of apocalyptic modernism, whether in T.S. Eliot's "the fire and the rose" (*Four Quartets*) or in W.B. Yeats's "the dancer from the dance" ("Among School Children"). In *Totem and Taboo* (1913), Sigmund Freud hypothesizes that such "cannibalistic incorporation" lays the foundation for civilization—the Oedipus complex—and it continues in Freud's own time in the form of modernism. This paradox of self-expansion and self-annihilation is externalized as the double or doppelgänger. Freud theorizes in "The Uncanny" (1919) that "the 'double' was originally an insurance against the destruction of the ego, an 'energetic denial of the power of death' . . . and probably the 'immortal' soul was the first 'double' of the body" (235). In a circular, uroboros-like fashion, the Freudian double of a subterranean China (or America) digs into one's own subconscious dread of death, while its entombment symbolizes "intra-uterine existence" and the prelude to life (244). In Georges Bataille's mythopoeic *Death and Sensuality* (1962), this prenatal phase marks the end of the continuous oneness of death, from which and to which separate lives cleave, both in the sense of extricating from and clinging onto death. Deploying the concept of the abject, Julia Kristeva echoes both Freud and Bataille: "The time of abjection is double: a time of oblivion and thunder, of veiled infinity and the moment when revelation bursts forth" (*Powers of Horror* 9). Death crystallizes abjection shunned by all for its power to obliterate totally, but it also enlightens should one dare to face one's own repressions.

The ambiguity of digging suggests, on the one hand, intense living with deepening consciousness and, on the other, utter futility, since one is condemned to an ignoble end all the same. Even in a reverse scenario from Genesis, the first fratricide and illicit gravedigger wins eternal perdition, if not for the man, then for the name Cain (Genesis 4:10-11). Consequently, the ritual of digging spells one's own demise while intimating a magical rebirth, the ultimate metamorphosis of the great unknown, the hereafter, at the heart of any mythology, such as the Resurrection. Such transformation averts the need, as Max Horkheimer and Theodor W. Adorno maintain, "to conceive of death as absolute nothingness, since absolute nothingness is inconceivable" (215). Indeed, given that no one can survive the molten lava and intense heat of the earth's core, the West's burrowing through and emerging from the birth canal amounts to a suicidal interment. Orientalism intends not only to control the East but, subconsciously, to identify with and lose oneself in it. Orientalist politics of hegemony arrives with its deconstructive poetics, the materialistic, egotistic drive veiling a spiritual stirring almost like love. The parenthesis of "(or America)" in the introduction title highlights an introjected, centripetal arc of Orientalism, in spite of the Saidian thesis of its ulterior, expansionist character. Yet if the unidentified subject, that is, the mind's gravedigger, changes from America to China, the parenthesis brings out the parallel phenomenon of the East fantasizing the West. Forever toiling under the shadow of (neo)colonialism, Asian modernity has consistently assumed the form of a contest between tradition and Westernization. To construct modernity, Asians must journey to the West, at times via an imaginary transoceanic crossing. The double entendre of digging becomes, in the Asian experience, a reincarnation in the wake of a drowning en route. Whatever the metaphor of concomitant life and death—modernity's lightning, Orientalism's digging, or Asia's sinking—the going down into an insentient state connotes a rising of breath, an etherealizing of body. The power dynamic is conspicuously revealed when East-West modernity takes the shape of, in America and in English, a casual childish joke of "digging to China" and, in Asia and Asian diaspora, a gasping for air felt by people of Asian descent. This East-West power dynamic is one of the subjects of the Comparative Cultural Studies series, edited by Steven Tötösy de Zepetnek, which maps out theoretically, methodologically, and in application the framework of comparative cultural studies, a merger of tenets of the discipline of comparative literature and the field of cultural studies (see "From Comparative," "The New Humanities").

It would shed light on the cultural complexity of East-West to bring up a puerile homophone so obvious to bilingual speakers that no one sees it or deigns to give voice to it. In addition to being geographical-cultural markers, East-West, or *dongxi* in Mandarin, also means "thing or creature," referred to either with affection or contempt. *Dongxi* sounds like "don't see" and, indeed, bilingual scholars never bother to focus on this. On the contrary, I intend to vacillate between the "official" East-West and its shadow, this ghostly, repressed, unnameable thingie so close to the heart yet so uncanny. It is apt, at the outset, to remember (raise?) the dead—the dormant Chinese, Sanskrit, and other Asian languages—lying beneath these words in English.

"No eye, no ear, no nose, no tongue, no body, no mind," intones the ghost of Lama Norbu in Bernardo Bertolucci's *Little Buddha* (1993) to his three US-American and South Asian disciples, who are triplet reincarnations of his deceased master Lama Dorje. The Chinese actor Ying Ruocheng plays a Tibetan monk chanting in

English a Sanskrit text translated into *The Heart Sutra* by the Tang Dynasty Tripitaka of *The Journey to the West* fame. The mind-bending textual palimpsests shroud film viewers in sensory and psychic nonexistence, a common understanding of death. Yet to Buddhists, this nonexistence connotes the nirvana—true life once the self is released from the illusions of living. Turning away from his Marxist faith after the collapse of the Soviet Union in the late 1980s, the Italian filmmaker sees in Buddhism yet another totalizing narrative, a system of meaning through which humans define themselves, a definition that is near negation, a state of being that is a rehearsal for death. "No eye, no ear, no nose, no tongue" rids one of sensations; "no body" rids one of the seat of sensations; "no mind" rids one of oneself or consciousness. Drawing from Zen Buddhism à la D.T. Suzuki, Norman O. Brown agrees it is "to become empty, to become nothing . . . to have no self, to be of no mind, to be a dead man" (*Love's Body* 264). The Christian parallel to this death of human senses for a spiritual rebirth is baptism, Christ's immersion in the river to drown the old self, echoing the Styx in Greece's Hades and the *Tongtian* (Reaching Sky) River where Tripitaka discards his mortal frame in Wu Ch'eng-en's sixteenth-century novel *The Journey to the West*. Orientalism further enacts this paradox in the formulaic disorientation Western protagonists feel in the Orient, whether in E.M. Forster's Marabar Cave, Orson Welles's Beijing Opera in *The Lady from Shanghai*, or Roman Polanski's "Forget it, Jake! It's Chinatown" (see chapter 1 in Ma, *East-West Montage*, which contains a detailed analysis of both Welles's and Polanski's films). The Orient is depicted as overstimulating with totally incomprehensible visual, auditory, olfactory, tactile, and even gustatory sensations, which, in effect, shut down all discerning faculties, a deadening in preparation for the transcendent exit from Western selfhood. Lama Norbu's parting words, Brown's sixties variation, and the Orientalist flight amount to a denial of reality as the human body and mind perceive it. Just as the message in Bertolucci is delivered by a phantom whose physical form vanishes mid-sentence, with his voice trailing behind, so do all the new selves come into being against the disappearing other. Apparently, any ghost, particularly of the Asian strain, my own included, performing this disappearing act called modernity, arises from the schism between multiple sites in this global era, evidenced by tortuous mediations through several cultures, time periods, and languages in Bertolucci, Brown, and Orientalists.

Yet the very idea of Asia's ghost hinges on two controversial formulations: spectral presence and a construct called Asia. Indeed, some humans identify themselves as graced with an Asian soul, either bloodline or felt affiliation, like Caucasian youngsters tattooed with kanji; other ghosts are identified as such by the society, with or without their consent, like Japanese American internees in the 1940s. As a result, Asia's ghost is most diverse: it is an Asian in diaspora, the former self having gone down during the ocean crossing; it is Asia itself, torn asunder in the wind of modernity from the West; it is non-Asia, possessed by Orientalist phantasmagoria and global exigencies. Whereas death denotes the opposite to consciousness, the finality that is unknowing, the representations of death—Ingmar Bergman's character Death in *The Seventh Seal* (1957), Bertolucci's phantom monk, and the gallery of ghosts soon to be unveiled—are not death itself, as death lies beyond representations, but the danse macabre invoking loss, flirting with the other side. A void beyond human comprehension, death arises in imagination as a shadowy, ghostly population, the ancient mariner's never-ending ghost stories of pretend deaths.

A dead man writes no more, so let us forestall a bit longer to contemplate the possible moves on the Bergmanian chessboard. This book unfolds on a stage spanning East and West with a mixed cast of whites and Asians, of whites in yellowfaces and Asians in whitefaces. Drawing from Asian, Asian diaspora, and Orientalist discourse, encompassing Anglo-American, Asian American, and Asian literature as well as J-horror and manga, Chinese cinema and internet, and the Korean Wave, *Asian Diaspora* probes into the conjoinedness of West and East, of life and death, and of modernity's illusion and nothing's infinitude, rendering fluid the two hemispheres of the globe, the twin states of being and nonbeing, and things of value and nonentity. This book thus challenges the fossilized conceptualizations in area studies, ontology, and modernism.

In the first two chapters I trace the Asian pursuit of modernity into nothing, as embodied in horror film and the gaming motif in trans-Pacific literature and film. Chapter 1, "Asian Cell and Horror," probes into the ambiguity of the cell phone in Asian horror films. Incarcerated by the cell or prison house of Western modernity, Asians reach out through the invisible line of a cell phone or a film reel, spinning a web of contemporary horror and ghost stories, which further tightens the socio-pathological stranglehold. Chapter 2, "Asian Diaspora Does Vegas," explores the gaming motif in trans-Pacific literature and film, from the earliest wave of nineteenth-century Cantonese at the Gold Mountain, to the wave of wartime and postwar sojourners whose miserable lives gravitate toward gambling dens, to a classic in the contemporary Korean Wave with scenes set in Sin City. In chapters 3 through 8, I focus on souls trapped in the borderlands of East and West, the edges of humanity and meaning. That this aggregate of chapters is so bulky indicates that much of East-West comparative studies are stranded in between, where diasporic texts are plagued by uncertainty and exhaustion, knee-deep in the subterranean water, which, needless to say, crisscrosses East and West. In chapter 3, on children's and young adult books, I explore how loss has occasioned a revisualization of Asia in Allen Say and Kyoko Mori. Rather than an irredeemably negative concept, emptiness is the filmic negative to life's color photograph, with the potential of reanimation. In chapter 4, "A Child's Passing into Asian Diaspora," I analyze the paradox of passing. The ocean crossing for many an Asian child since the latter half of the twentieth century is tantamount to the passing or demise of the child's "old" self. Yet a child's passing may point as much to an adult's beginning as to a child's end. Passing means not only death but also a passage into, an adoption of, self-identity, exemplified by Asian American identity politics as in Chang-rae Lee and Kazuo Ishiguro. In chapter 5, "yEast for Modern Cannibals," I propose a table of three consisting of Anglo-America, Asia, and Asian America, with each guest drawn to the host of yEast, the construct of East, as the agent for selfhood. The feast of cannibals reveals a communal interest in modernity, which is but a veiled, sublimated form of monstrosity. In chapter 6,

"Bugman in Modernity," I detail how modern West and East come to see their self-image in bugman, the epistemological fusion of insect and human, in diametrically opposite ways: the West horrified by the metonymic grafting of insect body parts; the East escaping into a metaphoric substitution by insect. In chapter 7, "Kim Ki-duk's Nonperson Films," I delve into the extreme human condition of "nonperson" in this representative filmmaker of the Korean Wave. The state of nonperson does not simply equate dehumanization; rather, dehumanization must be taken to accentuate humanity, since only humans can be subject to it. Psychologically, nonpersonhood appears to be the way in Kim to shed human bondage. In chapter 8, I analyze three manga artists drawn to wartime Japan: Keiji Nakazawa in the 1970s, Osamu Tezuka in the 1980s, and Yoshinori Kobayashi at the turn of the century. Deflecting Japan's historical responsibility over the war, Nakazawa's *Barefoot Gen* mourns the atom bomb, Tazuka's *Adolf* indulges in an anti-Semitic Hitler myth, and Kobayashi's *On Taiwan* peddles his right-wing apologia for Japanese militarism.

In the final two chapters, I discuss the West's death-bound yet enlightening Orientalism and China's own schizophrenic split. In chapter 9, "Orientalism Goes to War in the Twentieth Century," I explore fictions and films featuring whites in war-ravaged Asia or amid Asian bellicosity. Western characters dangle between their power as colonial Gods and their paralysis, a death-like trance induced by armed conflict, the yellow peril, illegal substances, eroticism, or postmodern affectlessness. To achieve such a trance, Eastern props—locales, bodies, and as a discourse—are deployed narcissistically. The book concludes with chapter 10, "Hyperreal Beijing and the 2008 Olympics," a four-year occurrence blown all out of proportion by a China eager to demonstrate that it is no longer subpar in relation to the West. To make way for (post)modernist sports venues of steel and fiberglass, much of the Old Beijing was summarily demolished. The Chinese media has long flaunted the event as an unprecedented spectacle, from the Zhang Yimou-orchestrated opening ceremony to the competition itself. Beijing's single-minded, all-out wager on this contest between East and West resembles the endgame in chess, where players risk all to win. Official triumphalism, however, was persistently tweaked by sixth-generation filmmakers' lenses on what I call the "hyporeal," little people falling through the cracks of urbanization and modernization.

Walking the stylistic tightrope between research and poetry, critical analysis and intuition, or Forster's "the prose and the passion," in my four scholarly books in English I interrogate cultural marginality in terms of *Immigrant Subjectivities* (1998), *The Deathly Embrace* (2000), *East-West Montage* (2007), and *Diaspora Literature and Visual Culture* (2011). *Asian Diaspora* continues to restore affect and heart to diaspora in between East and West, at-homeness and exilic attrition. Diaspora, by definition, stems as much from socioeconomic, collective displacement as it points to emotional, visceral reaction; the study of diaspora, alas, has been bled dry by the vampire of theoretical abstractions and academic trendiness. Through scholarship and lyricism, I attempt to resuscitate Asian diaspora, pumping blood into the heart of twenty-first century globalization—East-West modernity.

Chapter One

Asian Cell and Horror

The human body is a cell, a prison house, from which the voice, the speaker of the mind, escapes through the invisible line of a cell phone, computer, or film reel. That umbilical cord to Western technology eases Asian subjects' atomization, but paradoxically implicates the cell, telephone, and computer user in a web of bondage, a pandemic of evil, as exemplified by Asian horror films and ghost stories such as *Ringu* (1998), *The Eye* (*Gin Gwai,* 2002), *Oldboy* (2003), *Ju-On* (2003), and many more. What connects such on-screen horror with the Asian audience and, increasingly, global cinema is a malaise of disconnect. For if the human body is graphed by the coordinates of the x-axis of time and the y-axis of space, then the z-coordinate of the mind ranges far from the two-dimensional plane of daily existence. Among other things, the mind dreams of renewal, of transformation from old to new, hence reversing the flow of time and rejecting the confines of space, albeit temporarily. Transformation is but change, the essence of life, speeded up, which would otherwise progress in a gradual and slow-paced manner. In the frenzy of modernization, Asia desires to fast forward alteration. A case in point: many Chinese believe that China has completely bypassed in recent decades the phase of household telephones in Western history, moving directly from no household phones to cell phones (Mendoza, "China: Mobile Superpower" 374). Yet such leapfrogs are so gigantic and swift that one feels torn, as if leaving behind one's heart, the thin thread of attachment ripped. Nostalgia for what one has lost invariably shadows forward-looking, even futuristic, sentiments, except melodramatic tears are now replaced by horrified screams. While reveling in the new, the self secretly conjures up the old, either female ghosts (*Ringu* and *The Eye*) or buried memories (*Oldboy).* The horror genre thus returns to modernity's repression, or Asia's ghost. To cast in the metaphor of human dichotomy again, the millennial Asia in the precocity of modernization acquires a mature, full-grown body, while the mind dangles between a wayward child and a traditional patriarch, between what is to come and what refuses to pass on, between, in Jagdish Bhagwati's words, the PC (personal computer) and the CP (Communist

Party) ("Made in China" 25). Far from Asia bashing, the figure of speech simply subscribes to the truism of the discrepancy between biological and psychological age. In such a schizophrenic divide, China's meteoric rise as the twenty-first century's factory is plagued by environmental devastation, a disparity between rich and poor, human rights abuses, gender inequity, minority repression, and a mishmash of childish willfulness and moribundity. This disconnect is not unique to Asia: rarely is the infrastructure or hardware of a developed, postmodern society supported by comparable software; egotism and self-interest rather than altruism and compassion appear to drive civilization. In the Asian horror genre, this disjunction finds a metonym in the cell phone, which echoes Forster's plea: "Only connect!" (*Howards End* 214).

The cell phone, in effect, becomes a surrogate or mirror image for the human body. The human body and mind contains a universe within, characterized by incalculable biochemical and biological linkages, which the Wachowski brothers visualize in *The Animatrix* (2003) in the image of transmission of points of light on a computer's circuit board. Stephen King dubs it "organic circuitry" of the brain in his 2006 sci-fi thriller *Cell* (158), hence erasing the romantic separation of the organic from the mechanic. Placed as it is, the body is the thinnest of placenta, porous to boot, that separates the universe within from the universe without, until death, some say, releases the one inside the placenta to merge with the one outside. Ditto the cell phone, whose plastic shell holds a constellation of networks whenever it reaches out to the cosmos beyond. Technology has indeed yoked infinity and infinitesimality: while its size continues to shrink, the cell dazzles in multitasking in telephone, text message, camera, internet access, daily planner, address book, calculator, timepiece, alarm clock, and whatnot, so much so that a cell user develops a near dependency. As a cell phone is misplaced, the user feels incapacitated without his or her familiar (soul?), stricken with grief. Consistent with Freud's insights in "Mourning and Melancholia," losing one's cell equals losing oneself, for the cell is the self, or dream self, which, despite its smallness, does big things.

Such an externalized dream self claims a virtual, at least auditory, community. As a cinematic device in Korean television serial dramas or the Korean Wave rippling throughout Asia and Asian diasporic communities, cell phones justify the ubiquity of shot-reverse shot editing. Wherever and whenever the characters happen to be, they are, by means of cells, perennially face to face, even intimate close-ups for each other and for the viewer. This no doubt reflects the wish fulfillment of the millennial Asian diaspora where fans frequently seek to reach characters of another culture, another language, and another time. Yet this essentially global, diasporic dream suggests that the cell user may shy away from being alone with him- or herself, placing such calls to virtual voices in place of actual voices from actual bodies, a symptom of deep-seated neurosis. That the virtual community is flimsy at best is born out by the recurring nadir in the Korean Wave. The dramatic felicity courtesy of cell phones routinely vanishes at the heart-wrenching moment for lovers when the "heart" or memory chip of the cell phone is removed by one party in an attempt to end the relationship. The "heartless" cell user formulaically turns depressed and catatonic, whereas the other user, agitated beyond words with each thwarted call and unanswered message, tries frantically to give his or her heart. The former is resigned to solitary confinement; the latter strives to break it.

Largely following this pattern, Daniel H. Byun's 2004 thriller *The Scarlet Letter* features a memorable reversal: an egomaniacal police officer talks to his lover, a blues singer played sultrily by Eun-ju Lee, on the cell as they thread past and greet guests, including each other, at a reception in honor of the officer's cellist wife, who has just completed her solo performance. The cell's dubious nature emerges unequivocally with this brilliant scene. The cell places the user in two communities, simultaneously, with respect to reception guests and to a disembodied voice. Parallel communications take place in a mutually exclusive fashion, unless the cell user chooses to relay the message. Yet this mediation is never transparent: in *The Scarlet Letter*, it is downright duplicitous. The officer's supposed dialogue may well be a monologue insofar as his wife is concerned, who is not privy to that low whispering in his ear. The suspicious wife wonders whether he responds to the "inner voice," oblivious to or because of the presence of the public. Among other attractions, the cell intrigue is no doubt one of the selling points to garner international distribution. An adept cross-cultural communicator, Byun fashions a tie-in between a Korean product and the global market. The commercial aspect notwithstanding, the match between the Christian paradigm and the Korean psyche of crime and punishment is well-nigh perfect: the namesake of Nathaniel Hawthorne's Puritan allegory; the opening epigraph of the original sin; and the refrain of guilt, confession, and repentance. The plot twists are somewhat contrived, though, in the relentless sensationalism—passion, murder, mercy killing, liaison, and lesbianism. Unknown to the officer, his lover and wife were once involved in a lesbian relationship; the triangular love is far more complicated than what he conceives. Straddling the genre of thriller, with scenes portraying carnal desire, and the genre of horror, particularly the two killings splattered with blood, Byun succeeds in flirting with the transgressive fringes of Korean sensibility.

One and one-half casualties, however, never return from his project of far-flung overreaching. Eun-ju Lee received scathing criticism for her daring performance baring her body as well as the character's mental instability. Compounded by family debts and personal problems, the 25-year-old Lee hanged herself on 22 February 2005, one in a rash of celebrity suicides in South Korea in recent years. Serendipitously, the double entendre of Asian cell for cell phone and prison cell converges in her final moments on screen. Her passionate lovemaking with the officer locks them in a car trunk, their death trap, perhaps a subconscious maneuver to possess him, even if it means twin suicide. As they wrestle in love and, subsequently, with death in the coffin of the trunk, his cell vibrates on the dashboard, his present wife and her ex-lover hoping in vain to reach them. Rather than an ascent to stardom, Lee's escape from Korean social roles into bluesy plumbing into Eros and Thanatos alienated her to the point that she parted from herself. Yet another casualty of sorts is Hyeon-a Seong, whose character beats her husband's head to a pulp with the statuette of the Virgin Mary. Seong used to have a beautiful round face, yet her cheeks are now shaved off by cosmetic surgery, popular in South Korea and neighboring countries, leaving a long, slender, and stylized Western face. Seong's "old" body embodies a cocoon, from which she emerges a butterfly in the image of the West. Successful self-transformation for Byun, Lee, and Seong involves the trapping of Western modernity, from the glamorous, Hollywood-inspired surface of the film and of the half-face to the explosion of pent-up Korean libido. A tinge of unease, nevertheless, haunts this flight from the cell of Asianness: Western opera, classical music, and blues punctuate transgressions against social mores and law, all unfolding within chic upscale apartments, and the Virgin Mary, of course, is the weapon of choice. In particular, a panning shot from the back at the two nude lovers recalls the traditional Korean ritual of the bridegroom carrying the bride on his back, which has become almost an obligatory scene marking the climax of love in contemporary Korean television serials. (Instead of the pop song lyric, "Sealed with a Kiss," Koreans seal their vow with a portage.) Avoiding frontal nudity, Lee sits on the poolside, her right knee drawn up, leaning on the back of the officer, who turns out to be standing in the pool and clipping her left toe nails. This tableau recreates, momentarily, the traditional ritual, which only accentuates the tragic trespasses of adultery and nudity. The longing to be one with the lover, with the West, and, paradoxically, with Koreanness is doomed from the start. The void left by Lee's nude body and Seong's round face is the true, Conradian "The Horror! The Horror!"—which is renamed and aestheticized as the genre of horror for mass entertainment.

While the cell phone and other vehicles of mobility or communication are designed to enable connectedness, alienation has always been a spell cast on modernization in the wake of the industrial revolution. For producers of modernity, as Karl Marx theorizes, labor in the modern era reifies laborers. Charlie Chaplin's worker character bears out Marxist prophecy in lapsing into a mere cog in the assembly line of *Modern Times* (1936). For the masses, the machine in the garden, in Leo Marx's terms, causes a disturbance to pastoral ties to nature and human nature. The engine to progress and the master narrative of modernity, reason, and science ameliorate as much as they estrange human life, in part because they suppress alternative discourses, such as religion, belief in the supernatural, and other myth-making efforts. Peter Brooks's pioneering *The Melodramatic Imagination* (1976) has maintained that melodrama and the Gothic give voice to what is repressed during the Enlightenment. Amid the rational and secular mid- to late-eighteenth century, the need for transcendence, for the supernatural, and for sentimental excesses is satisfied, Brooks asserts, by such genres. G. Richard Thompson agrees that "Gothic literature may be seen as expressive of an existential terror generated by a schism between a triumphantly secularized philosophy of evolving good and an abiding obsession with the Medieval conception of guilt-laden, sin-ridden man" (*The Gothic Imagination* 4-5). The Gothic tradition metamorphoses into horror and sci-fi in the modern West. Isabel Cristina Pinedo sees postmodern horror film as manifesting a general malaise, casting in doubt "temporal order and causal logic" (96). Almost nihilistic in its unremitting violence, the horror film exposes, maintains Pinedo, "the terror implicit in everyday life: the pain of loss, the enigma of death, the unpredictability of events" ("Postmodern Elements" 106). Such logic sees horror as a working out of modern and postmodern repressions. One figure associated with this angst is what Noel Carroll calls the "overreacher" or mad scientist, whose demise is invariably caused by the hubris of playing God. The scientist's will in this psychodrama within the West drives experiments, causing self-alienation in the end. Whereas science and technology inflate the ego unduly, infringing on the Creator's domain, they are seldom viewed as alien invasion from another part of the world. After all, the machine roaring across the idyllic countryside initiates the industrial revolution, part of the history of modern West. Likewise, the mad scientists—Drs. Faustus, Frankenstein, Jekyll, Moreau, Strangelove—are all part of "us." (The only doctor who is one of "them" is Dr. Fu Manchu, the archetype of the Yellow Peril, who, you will agree, does not belong here.) The ensuing colonialism of the East by the West comes about as a result of the differential pace of technological development. Accordingly, Asia is thrust into modernity, an awkward embrace even for Japan, perhaps the most successful of Asia's modernizing efforts. Japan, needless to say, is the only nation in the world with the bitter taste of atomic bombs, the "pinnacle" of modern science.

Ringu

Water exists in three states—solid ice, liquid water, or vaporized steam—and so does a telephone—transmitting, ringing, or dead. Any electronic device, for that matter, is either operating or not, with a brief moment of warm-up or wind-down between the two more durable states. In human terms, that sliver of space between living and dead is inhabited by shadows of ghosts. Even when humans are "solids," 60 percent of the human body consists of water. Even when humans are gone, they flow through loved ones' memories like currents of water. Despite its elusiveness, water or ghost (watery ghost in *Ringu*) is the secret of life, the hidden passage that either end goes through before reincarnation. *Ringu* fully deploys such symbolism of water, from the film's rain-soaked aura to the genesis of life in the ocean and in the oceanic womb. However, as the ghost in *Ringu* resides in the well, the vagina or birth canal turns out to issue death from the earth's womb of subterranean water. The telephone calls to the hotel guests staying right above the well in *Ringu* constitute a wicked umbilical cord from the ghost to her "stillborn." In such a grotesque reversal of life, the telephone ring symbolizes a Keatsian pregnant moment between connection and disconnection, or connection under erasure. In and of itself, every telephone connection is already a disconnection. While the telephone, especially the cell, demolishes all spatial and temporal prisons, it presupposes a dissociation of the physical body from its voice. Even on a Skype web cam, the split between the physical body and its image persists. The cell, pun intended, rarely captures a whole person—body and mind—as we would like it to, only parts, which, fetishistically, metamorphose into that person. Given that face-to-face communication often involves less than a whole person as well, since one may be distracted and not all there, the cell comes to encapsulate the wish to connect and the ultimate failure of doing so. This argument based on a hypothetical whole person begs the question of what a person is. In point of fact, one may well contend that only fragments of the self exist at any given moment, not unlike water under the proverbial bridge. That the bridge is fixed does not mean water or thoughts ever are. Short of an ontological thesis refuting the self altogether, I merely submit that the cell and other communication tools serve to highlight the limitation of contact.

The futility of "only connect" haunts even Walter Benjamin's utopian mechanical reproduction, the lynchpin of modernity. Benjamin celebrates the emancipatory potential of machine use, which evolves into Jean Baudrillard's postmodern simulacra, copies without an original. Benjamin and Baudrillard dispense with the question of the machine maker or of the original, relishing instead the horizontal or rhizome network. Their playful, quasi-apocalyptic stance posits, nonetheless, an originary absence, a void schizophrenically displaced onto popular culture, from Gothic monsters centuries ago to specters in contemporary horror. Rather than retracing human origin back to the Creator, as medieval predecessors used to do, horror films constitute a genealogy of evil parallel to the lost lineage. Yet horror hinges on the void of good, which evokes, like memory, mental images rendered powerful by virtue of their absence. For instance, the female ghost Sada (short for Sadako) at the core of *Ringu* comes from a mysterious origin, while her name (chastity, virginity, or virtue) implies an immaculate conception from the devil. Commercially, such a pan-Christian motif lends itself to Western remakes and global cinema. Conceptually, the perversion only comes into being vis-à-vis the existing Christian and Japanese orthodoxies. The failure to unite with a missing God prompts reaching back to origin of another kind. That Sada's story is told over and over again—from Koji Suzuki's 1991 misogynist, paranoid novel to Hideo Nakata's 1998 more politically correct *Ringu* to Gore Verbinski's 2002 remake *The Ring* to Nakata's Hollywood debut of the 2005 *The Ring Two* and to more—suggests the global audience's need to revisit primal fears, each remake harking back to antecedents, ultimately to the mystery of Sada or death. Similar to the symbiosis of good and evil, the mystery of death links inextricably with that of life, each deriving its meaning from the other.

Into this stormy marriage also go East and West. Since the Meiji Restoration of 1868, Japan has succeeded in mastering Western technology. The identity of the modern West is constructed on the basis of science and technology. Even technological glitches in Western horror films, such as those perpetrated by mad scientists, rarely discredit technology as a whole. In fact, technology often provides redemption for humanity in sci-fi postnuclear holocaust. (What Neo and Trinity need in order to rescue Morpheus is "Guns! Lots of guns!") On the contrary, in modern Japan, technology acquires a duality standing for, on the one hand, the essence of modernity of the self-anointed "Robot Kingdom," and for, on the other, a part of the self that points ambivalently to the Western other. A classic example comes from Junichiro Tanizaki's "Terror" (1913), which presciently opens with the protagonist's "railroad phobia" that comes to infect even nature itself, now transformed into industrial images of "blast furnace" and "movie screen." A doctor with a Western-style moustache remains blind to the protagonist's inner malaise and perceives only his strong physique. About to be conscripted into the military and the machinery of expansionism after a near century of Westernization, the terrified protagonist escapes into whiskey, a Western import. Western technology is a net that interpellates modern life so seamlessly that the net is invisible to the protagonist. Tanizaki pinpoints the Japanese "conundrum," to borrow from *The Ring*, of a highly developed nation ill at ease with its own technology, of ancient Japanese myths (re)possessing ordinary modernity.

Contextualized by this ambiguous relationship with Western technology, the director Hideo Nakata adroitly combines the technology of quotidian life with supernatural ghosts and ancient haunting. Before this point, the twins are usually separated. Alfred Hitchcock's *Dial M for Murder* (1954), for instance, features the telephone as a mere prop for malicious intent; the telephone does not embody, as it does in *Ringu*, malice itself. The other extreme manifests itself in *The Matrix,* where old-fashioned telephone landlines offer the escape routes for freedom fighters. By contrast, *Ringu* manages to vest in modern technology the Japanese tradition of female ghosts and repression—with classic long black hair, white gossamer gowns, and the setting of a drowning well. All three characteristics derive from traditional ghost stories. The long black hair reflects not only the long hair worn by East Asian women of old but also the fact that one's hair lives on after one is dead. In 1769, Uyeda Akinari thus gives the ghost of a faithful wife, "tousled hair tumbling down her back," in "Homecoming" (*Ugetsu Monogatari* 10), which inspires, together with Lafcadio Hearn's Orientalist *Kwaidan* (1904), "black hair" in Masaki Kobayash's avant-garde film, *Kwaidan* (1965). The white gossamer robe, on the other hand, has come to be a stylized feature of female ghosts, as Izumi Kyoka in "The Holy Man of Mount Koya" (1900) imagines one such waif in "gossamer gowns as sheer as butterfly wings" (59). Finally, drowning in the well and hanging account for most female suicides in traditional Asian texts. (This is echoed in Zhang Yimou's *Raise the Red Lantern* [1991]. Due to the location, Zhang changes the site of suicide from the family well in Su Tong's original story to a "hanging" room on the roof.) Whereas the three attributes delineate sharply the image of a ghost in stasis, motion picture requires movement. Sada and her spectral colleagues, consequently, move in an awkward and hopping gait, a stylization taken from the horror genre, especially Hollywood's slasher films and Hong Kong's zombie films of previous decades. More primeval and feral than the hopping ghosts, the animalistic phantom of *Ju-On* crawls exclusively.

Yet these female ghosts alone do not effect haunting; Sada, for one, is channeled through the use of modern everyday amenities, such as playing a videotape or receiving a telephone call, and screen image and lived experience is no longer kept apart. The passive images in Sada's home video memorialize past suffering, yet they actively foretell the future. Past and future are bound in the present viewing. The ruthless spread of evil finds its perfect metaphor in virus, both as an epidemic and as a computer bug, once again as a yoking of primitive life force and advanced technology. There is no way to resist the malevolence contained in the videotape; the only way to survive is to make a copy of the videotape and have someone else watch it. Koji Suzuki's novel likens this to chain letters, part of the urban legend, the reaching out from cells of anomie. In other words, the victim in *Ringu* survives by becoming the victimizer or at least the willing accomplice in a network of sin. The ring in the Japanese title and in Hollywood remakes refers to both the ever-expanding circle of membership of victim or victimizer and to the telephone call. The call arrives punctually at the end of the tape, delivering the ill tiding seven days hence, an inverse Genesis of horrid death marked by the silent scream from a mouth wide open and horrified eyes, always captured upside-down on a film negative, the antithesis to life's positive. In Verbinski's *The Ring*, the death mask resembles a scrambled face, the jumbled dots and lines on TV when reception is denied. This death mask symbolizes as much the haunting of a traditional ghost as the wrath of a tape for not having been mass produced. When a viewer falls short of spreading the message of misery, that viewer is erased like film negatives or reformatted by the image on the television screen that materializes into the ghost. Watching a tape is now the other way around; each audience is being watched by the sun-eye on the tape, the first recognizable image after the static and electronic noise. The circular shape of the sun-eye is associated with the circle of the well, with Sada's inverse, bloated fisheye that kills with a single look, and with the hollow sockets of the death's head that the protagonist Asakawa retrieves at the bottom of the well and embraces in a trance.

This horror scenario is by no means original. Indeed, *Ringu* succeeds because it taps into not only modern mass hysteria but also the horror formula of alien infection, as in David Cronenberg's *Videodrome* (1983) and *Shivers* (1975). The former focuses on a hallucinated TV producer with a slit in his stomach, which plays video cassettes; the latter features, in the words of Adam Lowenstein, "phallic/fecal-looking parasites that cause sexual dementia in their human hosts" (*Shocking Representation* 156). Nakata's relationship to the West is not restricted solely to the idiosyncratic and art-house Cronenberg. *Ringu* opens with a baseball game on TV, an American icon from the postwar occupation of Japan. The first casualty, the high school girl Tomoko, is taken unawares, since her parents are out enjoying an extra inning of the baseball game, an eerie association between the game broadcast on TV and the real life of the characters. The TV screen and the viewer's life are already wedded by means of Western symbols. In addition, Tomoko's death must be traced back to her stay seven days before at an Izu hotel's Western-style log cabin, where Tomoko and other victims watch the tape. The interior design of the cabin includes Western skylights, a sofa, a fireplace, and, of course, a television and VCR. Western food with knives and forks is served against a backdrop of tennis courts. Western sets complement body language and themes related to the West. At Tomoko's funeral, her cousin Yoichi keeps rubbing his forehead, evoking the cross on Ash Wednesday. Yoichi's mother, the journalist Asakawa, seeks help in solving the mystery from her ex-husband, Professor Ryuji Takayama, who is endowed with extrasensory perception, just like Sada and her mother. The study of ESP is closely associated with the turn-of-the-century spiritualism in the West, a revival of religiosity and the supernatural amid what was becoming the hegemony of science. Although Sada's powers come from ancient and unknown sources, the specific marker of ESP and science suggests an alliance with alien forces from outside Japan, accounting for Sada's wizardry in electronics.

Sada in *Ringu* places telephone calls only to the Izu hotel, right above the well in which she is drowned. The phone line connects the two realms of existence of the living and the dead, although Sada remains silent on the phone except for electronic noise, which is perhaps her voice after all. By contrast, the ghost Samara in Verbinski's *The Ring* can call a downtown Seattle apartment. Not only do her calls turn mobile in Western culture, but Samara becomes more vocal and whispers, "Seven days!" Samara is so prone to dialogue, in fact, that she leaves a message on the answering machine. The fundamental difference in where the calls are placed has to do with the Asian concept of bones. Sada unfailingly rings the hotel because, as Asakawa conjectures, that is where her bones lie. The *Ring*'s phone call, consistent with the American myth of mobility, is not bound by the location of the bones. The cell service allows, so to speak, more roaming in the US. Asakawa's realization sets in motion the alleged closure, that is, the finding and burying of Sada's bones in the well, which turns out not to appease the angry spirit, contrary to Asian folk beliefs over the burial of remains. As a consequence, Ryuji is killed when his deadline of seven days is up. Ryuji's tragic death arrives when he notices his female student's prank on the plus sign on his blackboard. He adds the vertical line to the minus to restore what is also the sign for the crucifix, inadvertently hailing the coming of the anti-Christ Sada from the TV. That vertical line completing the crucifix connects God on top, human in the center, and ghost at the bottom of the well. Ryuji surely does not intend to bring on his horrid demise, but as he is an ESP expert, there may be an eerie kinship between himself and Sada. The human yearning for attachment, through the physical line of the telephone, the invisible thread of human memory, or the trinity of God-human-devil, results in his death.

Ryuji is able to warn Asakawa posthumously to save their son Yoichi, who has watched the tape at the urging of Tomoko in a failed attempt to save herself. Ryuji's affinity with Sada is confirmed when the viewer realizes, with the wisdom of hindsight, that Ryuji appears in Sada's video as a hooded figure pointing to "COPY," capital letters in English printed on the spine of the cassette. Western images help damn some characters, yet Yoichi is saved by a message in English. The duality of the West resonates with that of the traditional Japanese family: the polarized East and West turn out to be alike in terms of the innate dualism within either one. The horror story stems from the erosion of the traditional family: a Dr. Ikuma, whom some suspect to be Sada's father, pushes Sada into the well and seals the mouth with a slab of stone. The horror continues in the broken family of Asakawa, Ryuji, and Yoichi. Ryuji, at one point, bemoans that he with his abnormal ESP gift and his estranged family should perish together, hence putting an end to the curse. Ironically, the curse must be honored should family be preserved. At the end of the film, Asakawa drives into an ominous rainstorm gathering in the horizon, with her tender voice-over asking her father "for a favor." As the tape and a spare VCR are in the passenger's seat, Asakawa is sure to ask her father to watch the copy in order to lift the curse from his grandson, a perverse sharing of gifts from the devil. That Asakawa would ask suggests at least a glimmer of hope for humanity in that the grandfather is likely to sacrifice himself out of love. But unless he stamps out the surge of evil with his own death, Sada's tape will never end. "She never sleeps!" as *The Ring* puts it: infection and pollution is one sure way to connect with fellow human beings.

Chanwook Park's Horror

Sada the Unmoved Mover dwells in the supernatural realm, contaminating the human world owing to her insatiable wrath. That Unmoved Mover is in turn conjured up by the creators and fans of horror. We will Sada into existence because hate and revenge are fundamental, although unseemly, emotions, which are then projected outward. The motives of the ghost stem squarely from the human psyche: vengeance evens the score between felt grievances in the past and violence in the present, seeking equilibrium between internal tension and the status quo. The lopsidedness within one's heart is cancelled out when transferred onto the society, particularly onto the torn bodies of adversaries. Revenge is human contact of the most naked kind, feasting on another's flesh and blood.

An Asian prison cell provides the set, literally and figuratively, for Chanwook Park's revenge trilogy—*Sympathy for Mr. Vengeance* (2002), *Oldboy* (2003), *Sympathy for Lady Vengeance* (2005)—and a short feature *Cut*, one of three marketed in the US as a packaged DVD entitled *Three Extremes* (2004), the other two shorts being Fruit Chan's *Dumplings* and Takashi Miike's *Box* (all three shorts endeavor to live up to the trilogy's English name, *Three Extremes*, probing into sadomasochism, cannibalism, incest, and other taboos at the margins of human sensibility). Park's avengers suffer kidnapping or incarceration, ranging in length from one deadly evening in *Cut* to thirteen-and-a-half years in *Lady Vengeance* to fifteen years in *Oldboy* to lifelong deafness and slavery in *Mr. Vengeance*, during which the prisoners are secreted away, their lives ingested and cannibalized by enemies with overwhelming material resources linked to Western modernity. Nursed in hate, the prisoners turned avengers embark upon a cycle of violence so horrific and indiscriminate that it amounts to endocannnibalism, the flesh-eating of one's own kind, and self-mutilation. The most tabooed form of this self-consumption is incest, which occurs in *Oldboy*, *Dumplings*, and *Box*. The thread running through incarceration, ingestion, and incest follows, cinematographically, the line of cell phone, computer, photographs, film reel—all modern conveniences that embody a primal loss—and it ends, ultimately, in the viewers' gaze. Like bodies in space and time, where Western modernity is, the Korean tradition is not. Postmodern and ethnic heterogeneity, hybridity, and multiplicity championed by Fredric Jameson, Lisa Lowe, and the like are intellectual theories that undo, in the hands of postmodernists, the myth of Classicism's Golden Age and, in the hands of ethnic scholars, area studies' melancholia and nostalgia. Such theorizing focuses more on white and Asian American conditions than on Asian and Asian diasporic ones. Whether postmodern universalist affectlessness or Asian American particularist identity politics, their playful or activist insistence on hybridity subscribes to only one side of the Janus-faced Asian modernity, the side that laughs or rages, whereas suppressed tears and horrified screams are exorcized and find accommodation in the horror genre. Ghosts and victims of violence thus lurk in Park's elaborate prison house of Western capitalism, framed by the lens of global cinema. On the other hand, reflecting ambivalence vis-à-vis the other, the avengers' nativist revolt proceeds under the auspices of Western, Chinese, or non-Korean tropes, most notably *Lady Vengeance*'s Virgin Mary and *Oldboy*'s Chinese fried dumplings, the "spiritual" food throughout their captivity and the key to their revenge. Jeeyoung Shin, in "Globalisation and New Korean Cinema," holds that "the hybrid nature of Korean cinema is a product of the localization of global media culture," echoing Jenny Kwok Wah Lau's idea of the new Asia in formation, displaying "multiple modernities" (57). Rather than remain content with a depthless postmodernist heterogeneous grab-bag, I analyze inherent contradictions of Asian globalization, evidenced in Park's work.

The earliest of Park's horror oeuvre, *Mr. Vengeance*, demonstrates the strongest ideological bent, whereas subsequent films turn to increasingly stylish, self-conscious, modernist visions of retribution. Yong-mi in *Mr. Vengeance* is a left-wing terrorist with lines such as "Movement of capital maximizes the value of money," "Dissolve the big business conglomerates," and "Expel the US imperialist army" ever ready on her tongue. Despite or because of Yong-mi's role, the film critic Chong Song-il is reported to have accused *Mr. Vengeance* of "skulking Stalinism" (qtd. in Kyu Hyun Kim, "Horror as Critique" 113). Kyu Hyun Kim goes on to defend the film as "less concerned with the evils of capitalist exploitation than with our refusal (or inability) to transcend our subjective perspectives and enter into communication with one another" (115). Nonetheless, the film balances its critique of social bondage and individual anomie. Yong-mi's boyfriend Ryu, a deaf and mute foundry worker, gives his own kidney to an organ-harvesting gang in exchange for a matching kidney for his ill sister. With different blood types, Ryu's organ would be rejected by his sister. This and all the other schemes go awry: Ryu is not only locked forever in a soundless and voiceless world but robbed of one of his vital organs. Ryu's disabilities, inborn or imposed, epitomizes Marxist theory on how capitalism drains laborers' lives like a vampire. Alienated by labor, Ryu is one of many walking corpses on the dim, deafening, and dehumanizing plant floor. When these workers emerge into the sunlit outdoors after their shift, they all look dazed, stumbling in exhaustion and half asleep, reminiscent of underground workers slouching out of the lift in Fritz Lang's *Metropolis* (1927). Social injustice compounds the customized cellblock each character is assigned. One striking scene shows four young males masturbating while eavesdropping on what they mistakenly believe to be a woman's prolonged orgasm. The camera then moves through the thin partition between the cells to reveal Ryu's sister crying out in pain and Ryu in an extreme close-up to the left of the frame slurping ramen noodles. Depth of field is deliberately eschewed; the blurred image of the sister tossing and moaning emphasizes the siblings' separation, despite their devotion. The eavesdroppers are trapped by their sexual fantasy, the sister by her illness, and Ryu by disabilities.

Barred from one another, characters seek connection through revenge, a veiled devouring of one another, evoking the mythical union of the oedipal complex within the digestive system postulated by Freud in *Totem and Taboo*. Witnessing a laid-off worker begging, and then mutilating himself in front of, two "captains of industry," Ryu decides to kidnap the capitalist Tong-jin's young daughter for ransom. Ryu's sister learns of the crime and commits suicide in shame. Burying her along a creek, the deaf Ryu is unaware of the cries for help of Tong-jin's daughter as she slowly drowns in the distance. Park's signature montage comes into play when the girl in the background splashes and howls, a blurred shot framed on the left by a close-up of Ryu. Despite following the kidnappers' instructions, transmitted through mail and text messages, in paying the ransom, Tong-jin does not get his daughter back. Bereaved, he avenges the death by electrocuting Yong-mi and slashing, drowning, and dismembering Ryu. The bloodbath is by no means cathartic, as Aristotle teaches us in *Poetics*; instead, it simply halts when all parties touched by the revenge perish. Tong-jin himself is stabbed to death by Yong-mi's fellow terrorists. The knife thrust into Tong-jin's heart fixes in place a propaganda leaflet, and Tong-jin, in his dying gasps, cranes his neck and squints hard to read what is in effect his own death certificate. The fade-out is punctuated by Tong-jin's unintelligible mumbling, which appears to be a senseless, farcical reading aloud of the leaflet, but it may well be a deathbed confession or an obituary for himself.

This hauntingly grotesque "closure" bears out Park's style of Gothic comic or gallows humor. Unequivocally, Western scholarship on such genres sheds light on this Korean filmmaker, since not only is Park's sensibility modernist in its jarring incongruities but also his products are internationalist from conception to distribution. Avril Horner and Sue Zlosnik define Gothic's comic turn as "a double remove, an inflection within an inflection since in the Gothic comic turn—as in the joke—terror is suspended and horror is held in abeyance. If, as Brooks suggests, melodrama and the Gothic gesture theatrically towards a lost transcendence, then it could be argued that the comic within the Gothic offers a position of detachment and skepticism towards such cultural nostalgia. . . . the beginning of a deconstructionist turn inherent within modernity. Such a perspective breaks the twinning of the Gothic and the psychoanalytical in a proto-deconstructive impulse" (3). They proceed to situate such comic turns in the tradition of "the grin of the skull beneath the skin. This aligns with graveyard or gallows humour and is expressed graphically by one of Gothic's famous characters, Van Helsing in *Dracula*, through the figure of 'King Laugh'" (15). As part of his Gothic comic, Park's stylish cinematography distances and frames violence in such a way that horror unfolds with clinical precision and ludic absurdity. As the massacre of the kidney-harvesting gang proceeds with a minimum soundtrack, viewers are offered a bizarre camera angle from under a steel staircase, inches above the ground, peeping in safety but threatened by the expanding pool of blood. Violence is doubly removed and rendered an aesthetic experience, as the bodies in pain, observed voyeuristically, utter no sound. Earlier, one gangster's rape of an unconscious girl is interrupted by Ryu coming down the staircase. The gangster turns and moves toward Ryu in baby steps, his pants wrapped around his ankles. The tracking shot of his plump shins in mincing steps tempers carnage with comic relief. Such montage-like incongruities are poised between laughter and terror. Still earlier in the film, Ryu wakes up naked, minus a kidney, gesticulating desperately on the roadside to hitch a ride, a scene straight out of supermarket tabloids, erstwhile Candid Camera, or today's YouTube. Dehumanization, in Park's hands, turns chillingly funny.

Rather than the generic divisions between the Gothic and the melodramatic advanced by Peter Brooks, Horner and Zlosnik, and other Western scholars, Park illustrates perhaps the quintessentially Korean sensibility in yoking the two. This wedding seems strange to the West that keeps apart the literary form channeling repressed passions and that channeling pathos or bathos. Put simply, the West sees the Gothic as releasing excess blood, the melodramatic excess tears. The Korean Wave follows no such breakdown, giving rise to episodes confusing to Western viewers. When Ryu cleans and tickles his naked sister, the scene evokes tenderness instead of incestuous impulse. When Ryu horse plays with the kidnapped girl by lifting her skirt, this inappropriate act of sexual harassment is meant to maximize the child's play. When the kidnappers jump rope with the kidnapped to the tune of a patriotic song about North and South Korea, the innocent fun may look incredulous to a Western audience paranoid about abductions and terrorism. But this scene, set at the playground, which enjoys an eternal return to nearly every show in the Korean Wave, professes a deep-seated Korean melancholia over the loss of innocence, amplified by the litany of the division of the motherland. The urge to restore to oneness can be psychologically regressive, culminating in the oedipal, incestuous complex. In one fell swoop in *Oldboy*, Park compresses all these impulses by grafting the horror of incest to melodrama. After fifteen years of incarceration, the protagonist Dae-su enjoys a sweet moment with his lover Mi-do, gently blowing dry her hair. Dae-su is soon to discover, however, Mi-do's identity as his long-lost daughter. But the film most eloquent in this juxtaposition of melodrama and horror is *Lady Vengeance*, which, true to its title, is the next of kin to *Mr. Vengeance.*

The refrain of innocence lost is shared by both films in the kidnapping and death of children. The villain Mr. Baek in *Lady Vengeance* teaches schoolchildren English. At gunpoint, he even serves as the English translator between Lady Vengeance, Lee Geum-ja, and her daughter, adopted by Australians. A Western language provides the cover for the child killer, but the West is a sanctuary as well. In addition, Geum-ja specializes in European pastries and cakes, the counterweight to or reiteration of the film's cannibalistic motif. Overwhelming Christian metaphors bedeck this drama of sin and redemption. Geum-ja is both an angel of compassion and a hell's angel, spending over a decade in prison plotting against Baek. In his capacity as the English instructor at various schools, Baek has murdered five children, and his victims' marble, Hello Kitty, and other mementos are stringed on his cell phone. The cell phone chain alone does not reanimate past crimes; Baek has videotapes documenting crying children in bondage before they meet their ends, which so shock and outrage the victims' parents that they decide to take justice into their own hands. The videotapes are unspooled to strangle Baek in a collective reprisal. The butchering of Baek should logically conclude the film, yet a melodramatic closure drags on, balancing blood with, for lack of a better word, sweets. A bittersweet scene at the delicatessen completes, so to speak, the group therapy, butchering knives now replaced by knives and forks in a celebration of the victims' lost birthdays. When the chandelier tinkles in the breeze, one bereaved parent alludes to France, where people believe that an angel passes through at each crystal clink. The parents look up, as if to witness their children's souls ascending. This sentimental ending can barely contain the nausea over the suspicion that the apparently chocolate cake they partake of in memory of their children is made with Baek's blood, collected in the previous scene and mysteriously unaccounted for. The strange looks when they taste the cake do little to dispel the doubt.

Based loosely on Japanese comics by Garon Tsuchiya and Nobuaki Minegishi, *Oldboy* ups the ante on transgressiveness by way of double incest and self-mutilation. The victim-turned-avenger Oh Dae-su has been imprisoned for fifteen years for an unknown offense, during which time he was repeatedly hypnotized and programmed to orchestrate his romance with Mi-do upon release. The confinement and incest are masterminded by Lee Woo-jin, whose own incestuous tryst with his sister Soo-ah at their Catholic high school, Evergreen, was witnessed by Dae-su. Dae-su blabbed the scene to his friend No Joo-hwan before moving away to Seoul. Haunted by gossips, Soo-ah drowned herself, after having taken a picture of herself for Woo-jin to remember her by. Grieved by the loss of his sister-lover and mother surrogate, Woo-jin returns from his study in the US a millionaire, prepared to destroy Dae-su. Dae-su learns of Mi-do's true identity from the family album Woo-jin presents him, an album that correlates the two-year-old Mi-do and the adult Mi-do. To prevent Woo-jin from revealing the horror to Mi-do, Dae-su cuts off his tongue since he, as Woo-jin accuses, "talks too much," silencing himself forever to buy Woo-jin's silence. This schematic sketch immediately brings to mind Greek tragedies where the oedipal complex, cannibalism, and self-flagellation find early expression. Searching in the other direction, into futuristic sci-fi, one sees a resemblance between Dae-su's cutting of the tongue and Neo's loss of his mouth. When Neo in Agent Smith's custody in *The Matrix* demands the right to make a phone call, his mouth is magically sealed with skin-colored slime. Undoubtedly, Dae-su's action of raw, realistic brutality fits squarely into horror, whereas Neo's belongs to the fantastic, insulated as it is by the genre of sci-fi. Neo's surreal, nightmarish experience continues when an electronic bug is planted through his navel and removed therefrom. By contrast, the schizophrenic Dae-su has a vision that ants troop out of his veins to cover his body. The bug in the sole of Dae-su's shoes may be more easily removed than Neo's internal bug, but the mind control over Dae-su is intact vis-à-vis a Neo "unplugged" and freed from the Matrix. That Dae-su's severed tongue is self-inflicted only accentuates his psychological turmoil, while Neo the Christ figure moves inexorably toward freedom. The tongueless Dae-su is no more prophetic than before, quite different from the sightless Neo with true insights in *The Matrix: Revolution* (2003).

Yet another key difference lies in the role of the telephone in Neo's apocalypse and Dae-su's anti-apocalypse. Whenever cornered, Neo and the Zion underground flee through the telephone line, turned into atoms by the Zion operator. Dae-su, on the other hand, remains in bondage, as Woo-jin says, "in the bigger prison." His isolation and anguish stem from the telephone and other vehicles of communication. He is abducted near a phone booth during a lull in the conversation with his daughter. Severed from human society, removed from the stream of time, Dae-su, for fifteen years, stares at the TV in his cell, a constant reminder of what he has lost. Upon his release, Dae-su is given a wallet full of money to tide him over in a capitalist society and a cell phone to "bond" with his captor. Dae-su pursues the villain with the aid of computer and instant messaging, getting so close that Woo-jin slashes the throat of one of his pursuers with a cracked CD, indeed a double-edged sword. Prior to cutting his own tongue, he called Mi-do to forbid her from opening the gift box with the "family album," which was a thread to the past that could strangulate. All such tools of communication are designed to shorten spatial and temporal distance. But time seems too persistent to be erased. The film resembles a fugue on time: the opening credits of melted timepieces in the style of Salvador Dali's 1931 *The Persistence of Memory*; the clock secured on a cartload of belongings when Dae-su moves to Seoul; the going away present of a wrist watch when Dae-su is released, a handcuff of time in the middle of tattooed lines all over his hands, one line for each year of incarceration; the five days from the first to the fifth of July for Dae-su to discover the truth; the subtle ticking of the clock in the background music.

Apparently, time lurches on without pause, mirrored in the ruthless stalking of the sinner. To exact punishment, Dae-su favors the hammer and his fists (this may have inspired the self-portrait of the 23-year-old Seung-hui Cho, who perpetrated the deadliest massacre on a university campus in US history. During the lull between his shooting rampages at Virginia Tech on 16 April 2007, Cho mailed a package to NBC News. One photograph in the package depicted him wielding a hammer with both hands. This appears to copycat the haunting promotional shot of the avenger in *Oldboy*). When Dae-su engages the gang in his former prison house, the fight unfolds, in a linear fashion, in the long, dimly lighted corridor like a side scroll video game. Even the trajectory of his hammer aiming at a guard's forehead is diagrammed, cartoon style, as a straight line, while it is bound to be an arch. Yet the flow of time is not unidirectional; it circles back, as if on a Möbius strip, around and around. Linearity bends backwards and is cyclical. Thus, the film opens with a twice-told shot of Dae-su holding onto the necktie of a man about to fall off a high-rise building. The refrain does little to lessen Dae-su's ambiguity: savior or murderer of the suicide in this scene; avenger or monster in the rest of the film. These lines of differences prop up the linear revenge plot, but the futility of revenge sabotages the forward thrust of human intention, inevitably turned inward against oneself. Woo-jin, despite his wealth, is a sick and twisted man, an Evergreen boy whose maturing and psychic growth are arrested by the trauma of losing his sister-mother. His infantile regressiveness evinces itself when he latches onto Soo-ah's nipple in a semblance of suckling. Moreover, the groping of her thighs and the removal of her panties connote the desire to return to the womb. The past revisits Dae-su in similar tropes of homecoming to the lost maternity, rendering him yet another oxymoronic Evergreen "oldboy." Sitting idly in a salon in a green shower cap, Dae-su listens to a high school classmate reminiscing. He drops his gaze at the classmate's exposed knees, suddenly awakened by the ring of the salon's doorbell. The proximity of knees and vagina, accompanied by the "thundering clap" from the past, evokes in grainy, almost yellowing images one particular scene from the Evergreen High School, when Soo-ah rings her bicycle bell, baring her knees and thighs in the wind. Memory rushing back, Dae-su ascends school staircases to peep at the tryst. A series of jump cuts reconnect the avenger monster with his high school self, both following Woo-jin up the stairs for the rendezvous of sin. As the voyeur peeks through broken glasses, Soo-ah is likewise mesmerized by the suckling she examines at various angles through her mirror. Layers of reflections and narcissistic mirror images problematize demarcations of voyeur and sinners. Ambivalence arises as well in an extra pair of legs, which belongs to the hypnotist, once in Woo-jin's employ, brainwashing Dae-su. Thematically echoing the prison food of Chinese fried dumplings, she wears a revealing Chinese cheongsam, and her legs summon him back to the oneness of incest. This hypnotist is fraught with the duality of the perpetrator and the redeemer. Her bell is initially used to trigger subliminal messages, leading step by step to incest. Moved by Dae-su's plea in the melodramatic finale, the same device of bell ringing expurgates tabooed memory. Dae-su's dubious expression hovering between laughter and tears, however, calls into question the effectiveness of the catharsis.

Chanwook Park's short feature, *Cut*, distills the stylish horror of the latter two films in his revenge trilogy rather than the raw butchery of *Mr. Vengeance*. Park's Gothic comic makes possible his film's idiosyncratic hipness: the gruesome violence is magnified by the comic relief of a clownish perpetrator, his romantic dance number, and his victim's pseudo-striptease and flatulence, an awkward attempt to buy time. The perpetrator's eccentric delivery of lines shuttles likewise between explosive, wrathful rhetoric and explosions of air or aspirated sounds, interspersed with a drawn-out nasal whine. *Cut* revolves around mirror images and doppelgängers, which are tied together by means of sadomasochistic bondage, a symbolic film reel, and the viewers' gaze. The short opens with the filming of a vampiress sucking blood, playing piano into the cell phone for her "darling," and vomiting onto the chessboard floor. A receding shot, seeming to retrace the camera cable, takes the audience from the set to the filmmaker's control room, where he commands "Cut!" to conclude the day's work. Both vampiric and cannibalistic motifs serve to conjoin self and other, inside and outside, and Korea and the West. In addition, thematic refrains counterpoint the have's fantasy world and the have-not's anthropophagic reality. The director's castle-mansion resembles the film set in its chessboard floor as well as his pianist wife or, as he calls her later, the thirty-three-year-old "Botox queen" filled with cosmetic silicon rather than blood. Right above the fireplace in the living room hangs a painting of a room with an identical chessboard floor. The self-referentiality of sets makes the short as much about the deadly game played by a break-in murderer as about the director's own mind.

This murderer turns out to be an extra harboring psychotic rage against the affluent director and his Western lifestyle. The King and Queen in the chess of life are checkmated by a mere pawn, who cuts off the pianist wife's finger every few minutes should the director refuse to follow his command of strangling a girl equally tied up and gagged. The roles are reversed: the extra now orchestrates the corruption of the apparently good Samaritan director. A series of jerky extreme close-ups from a hand-held camera, particularly when the cut-off fingers are smashed in the blender, exteriorize the jolts to the director's mental state, paving the way for his confessions of adulteries and resentment against his wife. Her fingers, sneers the director, are useless anyway and she is a "nothing," a word uttered in English. Harking back to the director's earlier identification of the "extra" in English, "nothing" erupts, once again, in a string of Korean, spewing forth his hate as deep as the extra's. Furthermore, the director's misogynist vitriol is a displacement of ambivalence over the West that lies behind the couples' accomplishment and South Korea's modernization. The director subconsciously duplicates the extra's fury against the social pyramid with the West at the very top. The director is not the only character who undergoes an identity shift to his doppelgänger. The most shocking reversal comes when the pianist bites her tormentor in the neck and hence becomes the vampiress. The multiple, elaborate, and radiating strings with which she is bound to the piano poses her in a precarious yet almost artistic tableau. A prey in the spider's web, she turns into the spider when the extra inadvertently entangles himself in the strings. In the first installment of his revenge trilogy, Chanwook Park already inscribed on the body of the deaf and mute factory worker Karl Marx's classic indictment against capitalism: "Capital is dead labor, which, vampire-like, lives only by sucking living labor, and lives the more, the more labor it sucks" (257). In *Cut*, Park portrays a mutual consuming and bloodletting by the well-off and the dispossessed.

The cannibalistic transfusion accounts for the director's choking of his wife in the final dissolution of his mind. This homicide completes his morphing into the extra, who has earlier murdered his wife and disguised his own son as a girl to be sacrificed. The extra's sadism against the rich coexists with the masochism of bringing about his son's death, aggression targeting others now turned inward. As Freud hypothesizes in *Civilization and Its Discontents*, internalized aggressiveness is imposed by the super-ego against the rest of the ego in the form of guilt, "express[ing] itself as a need for punishment" (70). Hence, the extra punishes himself by what amounts to the suicidal act of having his son strangled. The director manifests an identical psychic process when he, in a nauseatingly quaking extreme close-up, mentally switches the extra's son and his pianist wife. He then proceeds to suffocate his wife, believed to be the boy, while soothing the boy across the room, now taken to be his wife. The director may well be mad, but the killing fulfills his dream for a decade, as he pretends, like the extra, that the son is female. The opportunity seems particularly ripe now that the façade of a happy union is no more. The son's last words, "I will take revenge," foreshadows the perpetuity of violence, as the target of his hate is so ill defined that it could aim at the director and masculinity, survivors of the game, or at femininity, since the pianist does away with the extra, or at society at large, which causes his family tragedy. The amorphousness of the son's revenge promises a repetition of his father's in that it turns inexorably against oneself.

Conceivably, any reflection on Asian horror can go on forever, with each nation contributing its nightmare, followed by a transnational flood of sequels and prequels. Between *Ringu*'s supernatural vengeance and Park's human vengeance, many more filmmakers have tapped into the market of horror and reinscribed captivity within as well as escape from Western modernity. The Hong Kong Peng brothers' *The Eye* deploys the medical science of cornea transplantation as a bridge into the past and the dead, both hailing from Southeast Asia, postindustrial Hong Kong's primitive exotic other. Takashi Shimizu's *Ju-On* locates a cannibalistic female ghost at the heart of a metropolis, eating back at the capitalist patriarchy. Cell phones and various lines of contact carry on with their mission of (dis)connection. *The Eye 2*, for instance, opens with a suicide attempt in the wake of a failed cell phone call and ends with a successful suicide because of that same call. In between, floating spirits manage to wriggle into women's wombs at the moment of delivery. The dead and the newborn reconnect in the cycle of Buddhist reincarnation. Asian cell invariably weds Western technology with "Asianness," be it a traditional Japanese ghost who likes to keep in touch by phone, Korean original sin and repentance, or Buddhist reincarnation via levitation. The terrible beauty or beautiful monstrosity sired by that coupling will chill our spines and warm our hearts for some time to come.

Chapter Two

Asian Diaspora Does Vegas

When Asian diaspora plays, it oftentimes comes to Las Vegas or a casino or venue with gaming devices. Las Vegas and the like provide the culmination of Asian diaspora, which is, in essence, taking risks in casting oneself out of home and into the unfamiliar, a gamble in view of all the variables and pitfalls. The euphoria of possible winning is always haunted by the keen or repressed sense of loss over homeland, identity, or even youthful dream on the other side of the Pacific Ocean. Metaphorically, every facet of diaspora resembles gambling, with the high stakes involved in speculation with one's money and life and the uncertainty of return, pun intended. The wager gets increasingly steep, from one's possession (weekly or monthly wages) to one's body (indentured laborers or illegal aliens) to one's identity and soul (e.g., sham marriage as a Faustian exchange). The parenthetical examples already illustrate that material transactions alchemize into psychological, even spiritual ones. From Marx's *Das Kapital* to Freud's head or capita, the Marxist economy of gamble turns Freudian in that throwing the dice or whatnot come to represent wish-fulfilling dreams. Gamblers are dreamers, whose inhibitions recede in their daydreaming, contextualized by Sin City, giving free rein to the Freudian id, particularly greed and lust for money and sex. Hence, the title alludes to gambling as well as to the slew of adult films, *XXX Does Vegas*. For Asian gamblers, dreaming of gold is never far from wet dreams. Etymologically, Las Vegas is wet: early settlers named it Las Vegas, or "the meadows" in Spanish, after the magical spring and wetland three miles west of the downtown area that have since been depleted by population growth. Once upon a time, though, the spring must have suggested the opening of the earth's life-giving womb in the middle of the Mojave Desert. That association with female anatomy continues unabated today in terms of the highest urban consumption of water in the US and of the city's identity, wryly dubbed by Maia Hansen as the "Skin City" (Fox, *The Desert of Desire* 103; Rothman, *Neon Metropolis* 210; Littlejohn, *The Real Las Vegas* 8; Hausbeck, "Who Puts the 'Sin' in 'Sin City' Stories?" 338; Williams, "Looking into a Dry Lake" 293).

Although human life is routinely divided into work and play, the Asian diaspora at play—particularly those holiday working-class gamblers from metropolitan areas, whether bused into Las Vegas from Los Angeles or into Atlantic City from New York—does not so much play as work with a near-pathological intensity in hope of neutralizing the deficits accrued in a working-class life. The demand on a blue-collar immigrant's life collapses the separation of work and play, absorbing the latter into the former. (The thriving convention business in close proximity to the sex industry and the Las Vegas Strip also combines business and pleasure for white-collar conventioneers, American or international.) Play or obsessive-compulsive betting at the slot machine or the stock market is symptomatic of Asian diasporic dissatisfaction with the other half of life—work—or with life in general. Georges Bataille associates the realm of play in this binarism with transgressions against taboos and imbues it with religio-psychological significance, which quenches the thirst beyond physical and material want (*Death and Sensuality*). It appears ironic that in this mirage of what Hal Rothman calls a "Neon Metropolis" of sensory overload in the middle of a desert, Asian diaspora should be seeking spiritual rejuvenation, as Moses, John the Baptist, and Jesus once did in the wilderness. Nonetheless, the night-blooming city amid total darkness and aridity perfectly exteriorizes the human desire for magical deliverance from the fate of a nobody out of nowhere amounting to nothing. The biblical gamblers who repeatedly won silhouette and ultimately mock the urgency of the gaming motif in trans-Pacific literature and film, ranging from the earliest wave of nineteenth-century Cantonese dreaming of striking it rich at the Gold Mountain (*Gumsan* for San Francisco or the US more broadly), to the wave of wartime and postwar sojourners whose lifelong itinerary revolves around gambling houses, to a classic in the contemporary Korean Wave which opens and ends with Las Vegas, and finally to the reverse flow to the mushrooming, Vegas-affiliated casinos in the Macau Special Administration Region in Southern China, dubbed by journalists "the Vegas of Asia," attracting the nouveau riche from China and all over the world. The global flow of labor and capital across the ocean has now come full circle, fidgeting for the next round, for we are forever driven to and fro by blind forces across a giant pinball machine, some scoring more points than others, all heading for the same exit.

Among others, John M. Findlay maintains that the US, from the time of its earliest European settlers to the present, has been home to a "people of chance," yet arrivals from the time of Jamestown to that of Vegas are secured progressively in their belief that the New World is theirs. With respect to this white assumption of Las Vegas and gambling, the minority pleasure seeker, especially male, differ dramatically. Although both groups share the pursuit for relaxation and sudden fortune, Asian working-class male gamblers carry the burden of what David Eng describes as "racial castration," the feminization imposed by their work conditions and social status. The figurative shriveling-up of the fifth limb—penis—may be less conspicuous than losing one of the four limbs, but it is as psychologically devastating as any other form of disability. The lack of control over one's life, for an illegal alien in the worst case, intensifies the longing to be in control at the poker or mah-jong table. This appears to contradict Sau-ling Cynthia Wong's contention of "necessity" and "extravagance" demarcating the immigrant generation's struggle for survival and the

American-born generation's penchant for luxury. But the two modes are not mutually exclusive: FOBs (Fresh off the Boat) are given to periodic excesses; ABCs (American-born Chinese) to self-doubt and angst plaguing their predecessors. Tony Chan's *Combination Platter* (1993) enacts this generational ambiguity during an immigration officer's raid of illegal aliens at a Chinese restaurant. The ABC receptionist becomes one of the usual suspects when asked for her identification, while kitchen hands scurry and hide. Aside from this precarious moment, one particular waiter, Sam, an inveterate gambler, embodies the immigrant's yearning and disillusionment as he frequents Atlantic City, plays mah-jong, and bets on horse races. To pay off his debts, Sam pockets tips meant for a communal pot to be equally distributed among waiters, hence ripping off his coworkers. Despite Sam's egregious offense and eventual exile from the restaurant, he is not the lone gambler. All the Asian characters teeter on the edge: the restaurant owner worries about slow business and breaks the law by hiring illegal aliens; the employees experience linguistic and cultural problems with American customers and within the kitchen itself, divided by Mandarin and Cantonese speakers; and the protagonist Robert from Hong Kong dates an American woman in hope of a green card through a sham marriage. Slow paced and seemingly uneventful, *Combination Platter* captures the assortment of challenges facing the Chinese working class in New York. More importantly, Chan does this from an insider's perspective, reminiscent of Wayne Wang's early film, *Chan is Missing* (1981), based in San Francisco's Chinatown.

Chan's and Wang's insider, sympathetic filmic portrayal of gambling men contrasts sharply with the Asian American literary tradition of warrior women. Ever since Maxine Hong Kingston's archetype or stereotype of Brave Orchid in *The Woman Warrior* (1976), Asian American female writers—Amy Tan, Gish Jen, Ruth L. Ozeki, and many more—never cease to regale us with pidgin-speaking, stupid and superstitious, yet wisdom-imparting and mystery-bestowing immigrant mothers. In Ozeki's *My Year of Meats* (1998), for instance, the duality of Oriental women is embodied by two Japanese women: the protagonist's Japanese mother, who, in her comical pidgin, advises putting an American coin under the tongue during lovemaking to ensure conception; and the American protagonist's Japanese doppelgänger, Akiko, a submissive family abuse victim who develops a clairvoyant vision of her fetus's growth in the wake of her husband's violent rape. The passive or pitiable and the mystical Oriental woman are two sides to the same Orientalizing stereotype. These Asian and Asian immigrant mothers survive against abusive husbands and Asian patriarchy through perseverance and a certain innate, Asian indigenous magic. That Asia torments these women just as it, inexplicably, heals them suggests the self-Orientalizing impulse of an insider-outsider engaged both in self-representation and in exoticization of the Orient, with immigrant mothers as Orientals. To rephrase the Pledge of Allegiance, such Asian American female writers constitute "one nation under mom," a construct of matrilineage to satisfy the psychological need of empowerment for minority women, doubly disenfranchised by Asian patriarchy and American racism, yet no less a form of self-Orientalizing. This does not decree a simplistic division of representation according to writers' and artists' gender. For instance, Tan's *The Joy Luck Club* (1989), with its proliferation of immigrant mothers, was turned into a film by Wayne Wang in 1993; likewise, some ensuing depictions of male gamblers have been penned by females. Nor are the twin traditions of representation—gambling fathers, warrior mothers—all that different. Both hinge on a transformational desire, realized to various degrees.

The gambling fathers contribute but little to the formation of ethnic identity other than as part of the general backdrop of racism and ethnic pain, from the Chinese Exclusion Act (1882-1943) and bachelor communities to the internment of Japanese Americans and more, against which Asian American writers and artists fashion a panethnic solidarity. As such, these gambling men serve as negative moral lessons for the abyss to which Asian Americans can fall. By contrast, warrior women emerge as positive role models for the height to which Asian Americans can aspire. Once again, the dichotomy is not to be taken at face value. Despite all the attempts to exorcize him, the gambler remains very much the shadow to the "model minority" on the threshold of the twenty-first century, hauntingly evoked in recent "Manchurian candidates," those alleged conniving, duplicitous Asians who are, in effect, scapegoats for American xenophobia—Vincent Chin in Detroit and Wen Ho Lee in Los Alamos. The Asian American championing of justice in the 1980s over the Chin case and from 1999 onward over the Lee case appears to gainsay any separation of Asian Americans and Asian immigrants; both legal maneuvers seem to refute the idea that the Asian American psyche would ever displace onto Asian immigrants in diaspora the role of gambler. However, both Chin and Lee are naturalized Americans, their constitutional rights violated as they are deemed either "Jap" amid Japan bashing or "communist spy" amid fear mongering against China. Strictly speaking, the Asian American defense of Chin and Lee is a self-defense against the American racism that excludes them rather than a defense of the racial other. It is unclear whether this "us versus them" strategy should be diagrammed, from the Asian American perspective, with Asia and America as two circles side by side, barely touching each other, and with Asian America at the heart of the second circle, or as two overlapping circles with Asian America in between. Conceivably, the former diagram dominates in legal defense, whereas both play a role in artistic expression: Asia both empowers and imprisons Asian America. Kingston writes, "even now China wraps double binds around my feet" (57; see chapter 11, "Asian Immigrants with 'Magical' Disabilities," Ma, *East-West Montage*). The irony is that just as the mountain of a patriarchal, oppressive China presses down on Kingston's protagonist, the other matrilineal, mythical China lifts her up. More intriguingly, Kingston's famous dictum whitewashes the other mountain on her shoulder: American racism as a result of her presumed Chineseness. The double bind is knotted by both her Chinese face and her US-American culture.

In texts of male nostalgia, however, gambling men exemplify not so much negative moral lessons as paragons of daredevil courage. Along with boxers and gangsters, such as in Peter Bacho's *Dark Blue Suits and Other Stories* (1997) and

Carlos Bulosan's *America Is in the Heart* (1943), gamblers embody masculinity in the aggressive entering into the unknown tantamount to self-abandoning. In this embrace of danger, gamblers are no different from Kingston's feminist warrior or from Frank Chin's masculinist Guan Gung, Chinese God of War. For example, faced with a Chinaman's chance, the protagonists in Milton Murayama's *All I Asking for Is My Body* (1975) deploy boxing and craps game as means to free themselves from mounting family debts and "inherited" misery in Hawaii's sugar cane plantations (see chapter 2, "Camp Scatology," Ma, *East-West Montage*). But such male nostalgia belongs to a later generation. The first wave of Cantonese workers around the turn of the last century suffered racist laws and racist mobs. As new Chinese workers were barred from entry under the Exclusion Act, many resorted to the "bluff" of "paper sons," purchasing forged identities as blood relations or dependents to those Chinese already in the United States. Granted that such impersonation is a means to survival, the rationale for this bald-faced cheating can be put idiomatically: once reduced to feeding off the crumbs from the master's table, the undesirable spits in the master's soup for revenge and skirts the discriminatory and unjust laws. The duplicity of paper sons stems from a power imbalance similar to those that give rise to the colonized "mimic man" (Bhabha) or to African Americans' "double consciousness" (DuBois). The play *Paper Angels* (1982), written by Genny Lim, illustrates the fate of these paper sons by focusing on detainees on San Francisco Bay's Angel Island, the Ellis Island of the West Coast, where men and women, even husband and wife, are segregated, living in limbo, with the Gold Mountain so tantalizingly close, yet so far. Some inmates gamble; one scholar (soon-to-be coolie) carves poems of sorrow and resentment on the walls of the wooden barracks; one impersonates a woman, thus enacting the castration complex. Ironically, the scholar, who should excel in rote memorization, has not destroyed the coaching papers for his paper son identity for fear of giving wrong answers in the immigration interrogation, consisting of preposterous queries about, for example, the number of steps leading up to one's home in Canton, the number of livestock, and the diseases of alleged relatives. The scholar's coaching papers are nearly found out by the immigration officer, if not for the inmates' concerted effort to sabotage the search. Fearing mistakes during interview and wary of taking chances, the scholar is ill suited for diaspora, that is, a gambler's life. The true cause for the scholar's inability to commit to memory simple facts may be that he subconsciously refuses to take on the new peasant or working-class persona.

Gambling of another sort is inherent in the practice of the "picture bride" in early Asian American history, when lonely laborers in the US arranged marriages with women from their home countries through the assistance of matchmakers and photographs, hence the nomenclature. Similar to the exchange of paper money and male labor, marital transactions depend on exchanges of pictures, money, and female bodies. Quite a few picture brides in Wakako Yamauchi's play, *And the Soul Shall Dance* (1977) and Hisaye Yamamoto's *Seventeen Syllables and Other Stories* (1988) are disgraced women who venture abroad to escape scandal. The New World offers, instead, relentless hardships and often abusive relationships, a total loss for picture brides and all those involved—spouses and children. That the picture brides in Yamauchi's play and Yamamoto's title story "Seventeen Syllables" (1949) exhibit artistic sensibilities in traditional dance and haiku writing deepens the chasm with their farming husbands and surroundings. Although the picture bride in Yamamoto's "Las Vegas Charley" (1961) comes to offer a semblance of family life, Charley slowly drifts into "flower cards" and a familiar trajectory that ends in Las Vegas. Many such disenchanted immigrants seek a total reversal of their fortune in the Nevada desert, only to die ignominiously there, including Chun, the one-time Korean grocer in Kim Ronyoung's *Clay Walls* (1987). Even if the gamblers do not conclude their lives in Sin City, they orbit around gambling dens, such as Yamamoto's compulsive loser in "The Brown House" (1951) and Bulosan's Pinoys, restlessly traversing the American West in *America Is in the Heart* (1943). The frequency of the gambler's demise in Asian American literature appears to validate Freud's reading in "Dostoevsky and Parricide" that betting constitutes a form of subconscious self-punishment where debts equal mounting guilt. The Freudian interpretation attributes Charley's and other gamblers' irrevocable path to self-destruction to guilt rather than to the motive of sudden fortune.

Dwelling on neither paper son nor picture bride, neither migrant worker nor legendary fighter, Louis Chu's *Eat a Bowl of Tea* (1961) portrays the bachelor community in postwar New York's Chinatown. Much of the action is set at Wang Wah Gay's Money Come Club, where "bachelors"—a misnomer, for most of them cannot unite with their wives in China—while away time at the mah-jong table. The only professional gambler, Ah Song, seduces the club owner's daughter-in-law Mei Oi and loses his ear— symbolically, his face and penis—to Wah Gay's razor blade. Despite his transgression and subsequent banishment, the outsider-gambler Ah Song sires a son who is brought up as the bachelor community's own. As Mei Oi and her husband, whose impotence—individual and communal—is healed by a herbalist's "bowl of tea," contemplate inviting their fathers for the son's second haircut party, the gambler's bloodline within Asian diaspora is not only legitimized but it also, like bitter tea or pill, magically cures racial castration.

In Asian American literature, Ah Song belongs to a coterie of professional Asian gamblers vis-à-vis the mass of working-class, amateur gamblers. Well-dressed with "neatly combed black hair" and "a white handkerchief always adorn[ing] the breast pocket" (16), Ah Song never seems to have to work. As such, Ah Song is an embryonic "first-class" gambler, merely glimpsed at in Louis Chu, Ronyoung Kim (the character Gilbert Lyu), and others. Despite these early "sightings," the racial metamorphosis from working- to first-class, from second- to first-rate, from weekend to professional gamblers takes almost a century, the new crop springing full-grown from the millennial Asia, readily apparent in the Korean Wave, films and television serial dramas from South Korea popular in Asia and Asian diasporic communities, which formulaically features Korean stars at such exotic locations as the Eiffel Tower, Big Ben, or Caesar's Palace. The element of crisis is only suppressed, though, under the razzle-dazzle, erupting throughout the length of any TV drama. It is a cliché to mention that the Chinese phrase for "crisis" consists of two words: danger and opportunity, the change of which requires, of course, a gamble. With crisis or gamble in its very makeup, the part of the Korean Wave comprised of television series wins big with the Asian (diasporic) communities, but is virtually unknown to the mainstream American audience. The Asian minority and the Caucasian majority constellate into two parallel universes in leisure activities, if not at work. The main reason for such divergent reception is that notwithstanding its "first-class" glitz of stars and modern cityscape, Korean TV drama has never quite, insofar as distribution and consumption is concerned, taken leave of its working-class gambling roots, which subliminally turns on the diasporic and turns off the mainstream viewer.

Most Korean TV series are distributed as cheaply made VCDs with quality far inferior to DVDs. Negotiating the amorphous copyright laws in Asia and the nascent concept of intellectual property, VCDs, often pirated, allow the Korean Wave to swamp the Asian market in no time. For the Asian diasporic market, Korean TV dramas are unavailable anyway through standard channels of entertainment. Moreover, these VCDs carry the added cachet of subversiveness, circulated underground, so to speak, among fellow diasporic Asians beyond the normal circuit of American companies and movie rentals, a guerrilla tactic that forks into the stars' "first-class" images (self-images really, because of Asian faces and sentiments) on screen and into "working-class" trumping of the authorities in the diskettes' acquisition. Putting a shoddy Asian VCD into a shoddy Asian-manufactured player (it rarely plays smoothly on a high-quality DVD player) to watch at times fuzzy pictures with no chapter or language to choose from satisfies the diasporic Asian's trickster instinct, or the secret desire of beating the system in that this entertainment from home is well-nigh free. A sense of power is perversely derived from the sleight of hand in bypassing the laws and the mainstream tastes that dictate television programming. This ethnic pleasure is no different from the erstwhile practice of paper sons

Rather than a complete switch, the intertwining of working- and first-class gamblers is the central motif in the 20-episode TV series *Hotelier*, broadcast in 2001. The series revolves around a Seoul hotel's struggle to stay afloat, headed by manager Taejun Han (played by Seung-woo Kim) with the assistance of his associate manager and love interest Zhenyin Xu (Yun-ah Song). Repeatedly, the hotel fends off a hostile takeover by a corporate raider, self-professed "hunter" Frank Shin (Yong-jun Bae) in the employ of unscrupulous businessman Kim. An outstanding Harvard Business School graduate, Frank Shin has an exquisite sense of timing for bluffing and deception, which stands him in good stead in the financial battlefield, until he falls in love with Zhenyin at a Las Vegas hotel restaurant. Arriving from Seoul, Zhenyin is entrusted by the hotel staff to find and bring back Taejun, who is in self-exile after an incident three years ago when a nymphomaniac hotel guest accused him of attempted rape. The bulk of *Hotelier* soon turns into a contest between Taejun, erstwhile Vegas dishwasher, and Frank, riding on his winning streak across the US, over the hotel and the girl, the dual prizes for the contestants. Despite their lofty positions as hotel manager and corporate hunter, both Taejun and Frank are similarly flawed. Taejun has never quite shed his humble origin as a hotel bellhop, to the extent that he masochistically gives up Zhenyin to Frank and another admirer, Yunxi Kim (Hye-kyo Song), daughter to Frank's employer, to a younger man. Although winning the bid to salvage the hotel, Taejun loses both women owing to subconscious self-abjection. Providing hotel services, Taejun exhibits the posture of a perpetual stoop, the forward tilt of his upper body suggesting an attitude poised to oblige. The hotel's success spells the hotelier's failure in his private life; making others happy is such a habit that Taejun twice sacrifices his love. Taejun embodies what some describe as the Korean national sentiment of *han*—a pun on his surname—regret or hate akin to the martyr or sacrificial victim mentality.

Opposite to the giving Taejun Han looms Frank Shin, impeccably dressed and groomed, ever so ready to take. Yong-jun Bae, who plays Frank, has a masculine, powerful physique paired with a face of soft, curving, and almost androgynous lines, a yoking of masculinity and vulnerable sensitivity that has won Bae not only the leading role in *Winter Sonata* but also millions of female fans, especially in Japan, where women see in him an alternative to stern-faced patriarchy. In addition, Bae's modern, Western look, including his reddish hair in *Winter Sonata*, seems forever "betrayed" by the stereotypical Korean eyes—smallish, epicanthic, almond-shaped "slant" eyes—veiled behind designer glasses. This mix of Western modernity and traditional Asia appeals to Asian women, who yearn for having and eating the cake, for having a strong man who feels, and for being Western and Asian simultaneously. In the frenzy for cosmetic surgery in East Asia nowadays, Bae's resistance to the relatively simple procedure to acquire round, double-folded, Western-looking eyes further deepens the female fantasy over Bae being the best of both worlds and both sexes. This doubleness of Bae's character Frank includes his working- and first-class entanglement. Frank assumes the façade of a ruthless, "big-game" hunter to mask a painful, "working-class" past: he, along with his sister Jenny, were given up for adoption by an alcoholic widower-father. The post-Korean War history of international adoption has been so disparaged in public opinion that President Dae Jun Kim apologized to Korean adoptees in 1998 for this national shame of trading babies as commodities. Raised by a Christian family in the US, Frank revolts against his Korean ancestry and Christian upbringing, becoming more capitalist than the capitalist America, turning his back on the motherland that abandoned him, and looting corporations across his adoptive land that swallowed up his former identity. Notwithstanding his stylish suit and tie and cold and businesslike demeanor, Frank resembles Asian diasporic tricksters, those working-class gamblers, in his opportunistic angling for a win when both he and fellow blue-collar diasporic Asians have long ago lost themselves in the transoceanic crossing. Jenny, separated from Frank since adoption, also demonstrates the inextricability of the two types of Asian gamblers. While Frank may have made it, sipping champagne high up in a Las Vegas hotel penthouse, Jenny is down on the streets, dogged by debts and thugs. Jenny is rescued from violence by an equally down-and-out Taejun, another of Hisaye Yamamato's dish-washing, floor-scrubbing Las Vegas Charleys. Condensed in Vegas are the riches of the first world Frank indulges in and the low-skilled labor of the third world Taejun signifies. The compulsive gambling for these floating specters thus carries the dream of a rebirth. Dangling between the wooden performance of a pretty face and understated minimalism, Bae exudes a charisma that goes beyond his female fans to symbolize the New Asia in the twenty-first century, shedding the colonial burden, wearing the halo of the miracle of the four mini-dragons and the ascent of the Pacific Rim. Frank Shin rises from a poor Korean childhood to a white-collar adulthood, yet he is no less of a hollow man. All the strategizing and high-stake speculations mask his inner void: passion for money in place of passion for true love; Western capitalism in place of motherland. To sum up, Frank epitomizes the core of the Korean Wave, pivoting on, concurrently, a transformation into Western modernity and a return to Asian "essence," which is where Zhenyin Xu comes in.

Frank and Zhenyin do not engage each other until episode 3, but Frank has quietly observed and grown enamored with her in episode 2. The second episode succinctly introduces Frank the corporate conjurer, who blackmails a jailed American hotel owner through the poker tactic of bluff. With a gambler's instinct, Frank pretends to have secured the cooperation of the owner's chauffeur as a witness to the owner's crime, hence coercing him to sell the hotel. A fine line separates bluffing from cheating. Given that bluffing seeks to deceive, it is usually justified in the context of a game where players are fully cognizant of the possibility of falsehood. Bluffing can also be elevated into an enviable art form, as the universal trickster tradition testifies: Odysseus and Cyclops, the Monkey King in China, the donkey-riding wise man Avanti from Xinjiang, Ananzi the spider in African folktales, the coyote in Navajo and other Native American tribes, and more (see Thompson, *Tales of the North American Indians*; Nazareth, *In the Trickster Tradition*). In each of these tricksters, the power structure is so lopsided that the trickster has no chance of winning except through guile, thus redeeming cheating as a heroic trait. Between Frank and his antagonist in a prison jumpsuit, the power imbalance seems to favor Frank, whose bluff is in danger of lapsing into plain cheating. Seen through Asian eyes, however, Frank, as one of "us," is applauded in subduing one of "them," the raging bull of a white male, his orange jumpsuit hinting at the criminality of Western hegemony. Frank even does this by mastering the master's language: at crucial moments, Bae mumbles some thickly accented English phrases, quite strange for an Asian adoptee, Harvard graduate, and transnational finance wizard. His "speech defect" notwithstanding, Frank strikes a chord with Asian viewers because he personifies both West and East, both first-class carriage and working-class chameleonic audacity. Lapsing perhaps into an Occidentalist outstripping of the Occident, which is no different from Orientalist discourse in the West, the Korean Wave, nevertheless, seeks to (over)compensate for historical traumas and psychological inferiority, which *is* different from Orientalism.

Episode 2 then cuts from the prison scene to what feels like a victory helicopter ride above the night-blooming cereus of Las Vegas. A triumphant Frank Shin busies himself with his palm pilot, totally oblivious to the sea of lights outside the helicopter window. His headphones further detach him from his surroundings. Sauntering from the airport to the waiting limousine, Frank displays the same regal insouciance vis-à-vis some solicitous Caucasian valets. Zhenyin arrives on the heels of Frank, but her exhilaration at the Las Vegas Strip and her awe-struck expression at his white limousine diverges from Frank's indifference. Also at variance with Frank, Zhenyin enjoys the tourist view of the brightly lighted dancing fountain and photographs the night view and the hotel room layout for professional interest. The diasporic audience is doubly pleased as it identifies both with Frank the King descending upon Vegas and with Zhenyin the commoner in its midst. The drama quickly moves to the hotel restaurant, where Zhenyin loudly complains to the hotel manager about the poor food, utensils, and service, while Frank at the adjacent table is enthralled by her charming straightforwardness. Rude by Western standards in raising her voice and making a scene in public, Zhenyin exhibits a forthrightness that draws Frank to her, as the camera pans closer and zooms in on his entranced face, where a knowing smile, as if in recognition of a long-lost friend, gradually blooms. Melodramatic love at first sight, this dining room encounter, nevertheless, sets in motion Frank's return to an essentialized Koreanness, crystallized in Zhenyin's duality—her assertive feistiness as a guest in Vegas and customer-is-always-right submissiveness as a hotelier in Seoul. (This echoes Taejun Han's aggressive managing of the hotel and passivity in his personal life.) Zhenyin's outburst comes, serendipitously, in reaction to Frank's casual remark to his associate Leo that "I love money now and [marriage] will wait till I fancy women." That one woman, whom Leo later surmises to be Korean for her fiery temperament, materializes miraculously. Zhenyin's parting shot at the hotel establishment is a rude awakening to the money-grubbing Frank. She flourishes the credit card to pay for the food and a single cent for the "teep" (tip). A paradox nestles at the heart of the Korean value of hospitality with which Zhenyin judges Vegas service and which the series proceeds to unfold in Seoul: the emulation of Vegas opulence yet the adherence to *cheng* (Korean heart-felt sincerity). That penny pokes fun at the poor service, or the lack of heart, within the urban extravaganza, a fitting metaphor for the dashing yet hollow Frank. Though Zhenyin doesn't know it, she initiates Frank's journey back to Korea to find himself and "Koreanness." By the series' end, when Taejun orchestrates their reunion, Frank whispers to a teary Zhenyin that he would stay forever: an Asian adoptee has not only made it there but also made it home, in fiction if not in reality.

Throughout episode 2, set in Las Vegas, called *ducheng* or the gambling city in Chinese, not a single shot of a casino or gambling is shown, only restaurants, hotel rooms, the Las Vegas Strip, Taejun's shabby trailer, and a street gang. One wonders if the adamant erasure of gambling is due to Korean TV censorship. In view of the business wrangling and high stakes in *Hotelier*, the erasure of actual casinos only accentuates the latency of gamble, even in episode 3, set in the Mojave Desert when

Taejun drives Jenny and Zhenyin to Los Angeles to flee Jenny's creditors. A squabble breaks out between Zhenyin and Taejun, still reluctant to return to Korea to rescue the hotel. A furious Zhenyin forces Taejun to stop and gets off. Taejun drives off in a fury, and he takes a bit too long before turning around his red convertible, for Zhenyin has been picked up meanwhile by Frank's limousine chancing by, where the two begin to know each other. The outcome of the two men's gamble in Seoul has already been decided by happenstance and luck in the Mojave Desert, what William L. Fox calls "the desert of desire" where some loves bloom, and others dry up.

Because the version of *Hotelier* I watched is dubbed in Mandarin, the voice of Yun-ah Song, who plays Zhenyin, is never heard except in such sequences as the English dialogue in the restaurant. Along with Song's genuine voice in English, one also notices more background noise and richer sound quality than the rest of the series when dubbing mutes not only performers' real voices but the soundtrack at large. This auditory trade-off is obviously one non-Korean viewers must decide whether to accept or reject. Yet dubbing is a fact of life in multilingual globalization, as I have just translated into English certain Mandarin-dubbed scenes originally delivered in Korean. Dubbing contributes to the dissemination of the Korean Wave in Asia, long accustomed to dubbing due to the myriad linguistic communities. Western viewers are less inclined to take for granted the divorce of on-screen body and voice (mind), another reason for the sparse attention paid to the Korean Wave. How exactly do the practices of dubbing or subtitling affect *Hotelier* and other TV series? How does the increasingly transnational, at least East Asian regional, production and distribution of Asian cinema with cast, crew, financing, marketing strategy, and remake trends from China, Korea, Japan, Taiwan, Hong Kong, and elsewhere shape the product and the culture? What role does the reception of a multilingual, transnational audience play in the conceptualization and execution of Asian cinema? While physically removed from Asia, I compose under similar market constraints. Have I not selected episodes from *Hotelier* most accessible to English-speaking readers, such as scenes set in Las Vegas and in English? Is any given moment throughout the twenty episodes on the tug-of-war over the Seoul hotel less revealing than Las Vegas? Forever beachcombing for bottled messages from home, I choose to share with English speakers those passages they tend to connect fairly easily, whereas the detritus left on the beach, like the Korean voices silenced, tell stories that escape me.

I have herein concentrated on Asian gamblers in Asian American literature and Asian cinema, crossing the boundaries between genres and geography. Beyond these specific representations of gamblers, Asian diaspora as a voluntary scattering of oneself runs the risk that the dispersed seed may or may not put down roots and blossom. The next question to ask is whether there is something in Asian culture that predetermines Asian diaspora's proclivity to gamble; the spotlight thus turns from American conditions back to Asia, especially to Macau boasting of the highest revenue from gambling in the world since 2006 (Rivlin, "Las Vegas Caters to Asia's High Rollers"). Rather than a racialist, genetic interpretation of Asian compulsiveness, my argument from working- to first-class gamblers has suggested a cultural viewpoint hinging on the ambivalent desire of the Asian mimic man trying to catch up with Western modernity. Gaming and gaming tropes, including the Korean Wave's emplotment of gambling, enable the underdog of Asia and Asian diaspora to envisage triumph and to release tension, at least for a while, until the next wave arrives from somewhere called home.

Chapter Three

Diasporic Authors of Children's and Young Adult Books

The concept of childhood, according to Phillippe Aries, "first appeared in the 1600s and gradually developed as children began to be distinguished from adults" (qtd. in Griswold, "The Disappearance" 35). Lillian Smith contends in *The Unreluctant Years* (1991) that "the first modern picture books . . . appeared in the last quarter of the last century. With them are indissolubly associated the names of Walter Crane, Kate Greenaway and Randolph Caldecott" (108). Such attempts at genealogy are, needless to say, always West-centric. As a result, shadowed by early giants such as the Brothers Grimm, Hans Christian Andersen, Charles Dickens, Frances Hodgson Burnett, and Rudyard Kipling, Euro-American children's and young adult literature have contributed in no small measure to the interpellation of young readers with mainstream culture values (Inglis, *The Promise of Happiness* 3). Within this context, the agendas of multiculturalism and racial diversity have been at the forefront of the US public school system (Hade, "Reading Children's Literature" 113-22). With the gradual thawing of the imperialist heritage and hegemonic interpellation, many groundbreaking publications have begun to approach children's literature from psychological, reader-response, feminist, ecocritical, and other perspectives. Amid this revisioning energy, I intend to analyze Allen Say and Kyoko Mori based on Asian diaspora and Asian American studies.

Before focusing on the pair, however, I consider the term "Asian American" children's and young adult literature. Situated in a Western context where Euro-American whiteness is a given or, in George Lipsitz's term, "invisible," texts for children and young adults must bear certain racial markers in order to be defined and, hence, marketed as Asian American ("The Possessive Investment"). How is this identification as Asian American accomplished, especially in view of the collaborative nature of much of children's and young adult literature? In certain cases, Asian American artists both write and illustrate the text; they join forces with nonethnic illustrators; they pictorialize nonethnic writers' texts; or nonethnics provide both text and illustration. To suggest the four scenarios come in descending order of ethnic authenticity risks essentialism, whereby the ethnic identity of creators is privileged. It is conceivable, in fact, that ethnic subject matter can be handled with as much verity and subtlety by "yellowface" artists as by Asian Americans. In reverse, Asian Americans are free to produce mainstream American texts just as any other Americans of various ancestries. While ties between an artist's ethnicity and ethnic text are in dispute, the logocentric nature of children's and young adult literature surfaces in the fact that the written text generally dictates whether the product is to be ethnic or not; the illustration, although perhaps the selling point, exists to primarily accompany the story.

In contrast to the view that creators' ethnic backgrounds lead to ethnic texts, a far better way to define ethnicity is to interrogate the Asian American identity within the text—how that identity is constructed by characters and by textual references, both verbal and pictorial; and how that identity is perceived by readers and by a society apparently bent upon a democratic, egalitarian multiculturalism. To fashion an Asian American identity, a trio of building blocks are often conjoined in a multitude of ways: the setting of Asia (including exotic Chinatowns and other ethnic ghettos) and Asian characters; Asian immigrants in the process of assimilation; and Asian Americans coming to a rude awakening about their perpetual stranger status. Whatever the combination of the three strategies, Asia and Asian immigrants never fail to register themselves as the mortar in building a politically and culturally informed ethnic consciousness. Specifically, in children's picture books with limited words, Asia is often the setting where the totality of uncanny scenery, characters, and plot piques children's curiosity. In the worst case scenario, the consciousness this reading process creates perpetuates Orientalist rather than Asian American ideology. In comparison to children's books, young adult literature regularly revolves around new Asian immigrants struggling to adjust to the US. Asian immigrants' difficulties echo the sense of unease shared by most adolescents, Asian American or otherwise; the aliens on the pages are the psychological transference of young adults' alienation. Immigrant families with troubled adolescents recur with amazing frequency in Laurence Yep, Marie G. Lee, and the Yang siblings series by Lensey Namioka. Certain artists, Marie G. Lee among them, exhibit growing sensitivity to identity politics, featuring American characters of Asian descent fighting racism and fashioning self-worth via the twin discoveries of a lost origin or culture and the trope of immigrants. Against this literary motif, a number of Asian American scholars, spearheaded by Lisa Lowe, have long urged replacing the vertical paradigm of loss and nostalgia, namely, Asian American culture being a deviation from the originary, imaginary roots, with the horizontal paradigm, namely, Asian American community engaged in a strategic essentializing among disparate constituent groups for the sake of political unity (see Lowe, *Immigrant Acts*; Espiritu, *Asian American Panethnicity*; Wong, "Denationalization"; Cheng, *The Melancholy of Race*). With respect to Say and Mori, there is no denying that both vertical and horizontal paradigms are intricately intertwined. Their texts are both immigrant and ethnic, reaching across the Pacific Ocean in time as well as across US-American racial divides. Arriving at these shores from Japan as a sixteen- and a twenty-year-old, these two artists-writers anchor immigrant experiences at the heart of their quasi-autobiographical works in various genres. Intriguingly, Say and Mori express their experiences in the US-American context by writing in English and by remaining sensitive to the needs of a young mainstream, rather than just Asian American, audience in the US market.

Allen Say

Since one seeks an identity only when there is a felt absence, the absence of Asian American identity is the a priori condition for any children's and young adult literature that calls itself Asian American. To forge this identity out of nothingness, Asian Americans construct or find a lost Asia. Freud's 1917 "Mourning and Melancholia" theorizes precisely this paradox of lost and found. While loss has occasioned, in Allen Say's picture books and Kyoko Mori's young adult fiction and essays, a revisualization of Japan and their family members, this repetition compulsion points to, as Freud postulates, the ego's devouring of, and thus the becoming of, the lost object. The union is, of course, psychological rather than literal. By the same token, that Asian Americans keep telling the same story suggests that that story remains ultimately untold and untellable. In the refrain of the master narrative, Asian America attempts to retrieve and, problematically, to become Asia. The knotty identification with Asia stems from the fact that unlike our joy when the missing mate to a glove, key, or document miraculously materializes from a lost and found box, any given moment at a given place can never be relived. Asia that was part of the lived experience is to be recreated in one's mind and writing, which is certainly the case for Say and Mori. Whether nostalgic or grieving for their formative years in Japan, Say and Mori write with moving poignancy. By contrast, Asian Americans born and raised on American soil reach back to Asia in a feat of imagination. To be part of the multiethnic America, Asian America fetishizes Asianness, which is disavowed—for Asian Americans are not Asians—yet simultaneously acknowledged as the heritage and source of empowerment. Rather than an irredeemably negative concept, emptiness is the photographic negative to life's color photograph, with the potential of reanimation, except diasporic Asians hold in their mind's eye filmic negatives of their earlier selves and their loved ones, whereas Asian Americans hold negatives of fictitious Asian characters—double negatives, if you will (see Burgin, Donald, and Kaplan 1). Such double negatives promise an intriguing investigation of self-reflexiveness, but have oftentimes lapsed into single negatives in Asian American children's literature and literature in general. In mathematical terms, given that both share the history of subtraction that leads to the present standing of zero, Asian diaspora starts out with actual numbers—age when one took leave of Asia; length of time away from "home"; family members left behind (Kaplan, *The Nothing That Is* 1). Asian America, on the other hand, plays with virtual numbers. The difference is one between actual and virtual reality, actual and virtual Asians. In the Asian American imaginary, those virtual Asians may feel virtually Asian, but to confuse constructs with reality, such mental images with the Asian other is not a virtue. Nothingness entails, in Asian diaspora, visualizing what one has lost and, in Asian America, visualizing what one imagines what one has lost.

In his 1994 foreword to *The Ink-Keeper's Apprentice* (1979), Say characterizes his works as "essentially autobiographical," and says that this book "set[s] the tone." Say goes on to confide that his father anglicized the family name of Seii. The name change heralds a lifelong reconstruction of autobiographical materials: the lost self is repeatedly transferred onto *The Lost Lake* (1989), *Stranger in the Mirror* (1995), and many other children's books since the publication of *The Feast of Lanterns* (1976). Born in Japan to Korean father and Californian-born Japanese mother, emigrated to the US at the age of sixteen, Allen Say revisits the motif of loss and hybridity throughout his corpus. Conceptually, words and illustrations in Say's picture books always represent something missing, and they are, by definition, parts that cohere as much as contradict. *El Chino* (1990), for example, dwells on an empty room with open windows and doors, left behind by the dead, the protagonist Bill Wong's father, whose image remains with his portrait on the wall. At a summer camp amid Indian ruins of the American Southwest, the Japanese American protagonist of *Home of the Brave* (2002) chances upon, in a subterranean as well as subconscious search, a Japanese internment camp. Two kinds of camps—the internment camp and the summer camp where identification tags are required—overlap; the emptying from the land suffered by Native Americans segues into that by Japanese Americans. Because what is found is unlikely to be the exact object or experience that was originally lost, new cultural elements integrate with the old. Accordingly, cultural hybridity—incongruity in extreme cases—permeates Say's works: Bill Wong is only accepted as a Spanish matador after he dons traditional Tang dress, enacting racial and ethnic performativity for survival; the Japanese mother in *Tree of Cranes* (1991) so misses her native land on the other side of the Pacific that she decorates the Christmas tree with origami, Japan's paper cranes. Western customs merge with Japanese art. Arguably, these and many more examples of cultural fusion derive from a keen sense of emptiness. Like a vessel that is full, a person who is full of himself rejects others. Say is neither full of himself nor at ease where he is. In interviews with Stephanie Loer, Say uncannily echoes the thesis of lost and found when he describes ideas for his books in the analogy of "found objects." In addition, Say casts himself as an "eternal outsider." Such alienation motivates the process of rediscovery and search for compatible soul mates in other ethnic experiences.

This drive is informed as much by individual as by familial history, as Say's family saga is the history of twentieth-century Asian migration. Say's watercolors and texts in dozens of children's books share this wistfulness over not only personal loss but familial and generational ones, for both his parents and grandparents on the mother's side have undertaken transoceanic exodus. Pictorially in *Grandfather's Journey* (1993), Say turns his family members into look-alikes, all with a small, bud mouth and a pointed jaw. They all have a *guazi lian*, or an oval, melon-seed face in the shape of an inverse teardrop. Such facial traits run not only in the family—Say's grandparents, their daughter (Say's mother), and the child Allen Say—but also in Say's father, who is genetically unrelated. Characters become the allegorical Everyman in this bittersweet drama, with similar longing and homesickness for California or for Japan. Say's stylization of facial physiognomy extends from 1993 to almost all the following picture books, manifesting both the repetition compulsion and the impossibility of repeating what has been lost.

To anatomize emptiness and consequent hybridity in Say, I take up in particular two picture books, *Tea with Milk* (1999) and *The Sign Painter* (2000). The former revolves around the diasporic legacy of Say's mother, who has migrated from California to Japan and then back, a convoluted journey now sedimented in what appears to be the narrator-author's habit of tea with milk and sugar. The latter work pushes the genre of children's books to young adult and even adult spheres, balancing a young Asian American's road story with Norman Rockwell's idyllic commercialism, Edward Hopper's urban alienation and despair, and the myth of the American West in Ansel Adams's landscape photographs. The title of *Tea with Milk* juxtaposes two cultures: Asians drink tea straight, without adding anything, whereas Westerners add milk and sugar. This style of montaging dissonance extends throughout, such as in the title page's dark-haired girl with her blond doll in almost identical white dress and ribbon, except the girl's black sash around the waist and black shoes. The blackness complements her straight "rice-bowl" haircut, in contrast to the doll's curly blond hair. The Caucasian doll becomes the Asian-looking girl's doppelgänger. *Tea with Milk* illustrates how this girl, Masako or May, searches for her own niche in the middle ground between Asianness and whiteness. The book opens with a young Asian girl standing at the front door under the glaring sun. The sunlight is so bright that she turns her head slightly from the sun. The lines of shadow cast by the roof dissect the front door into two, with an adult peeping from behind the drape of the front door glass panel, as if Asianness is lurking, despite the US flag waving in the wind and a typical welcome mat. The composition stresses a split between light and shadow, Americanness and Asianness. Masako then returns to Japan along with her parents and is next seen in a series of portraits, in Japanese kimono in front of a Japanese house with hardwood vestibule, sliding paper doors, bamboo roll-up shades, and other Japanese architectural features, all in somewhat slumping or rigid pose, betraying an unhappy adolescence trapped in an unfamiliar, stifling environment. Alone on the high school grounds, accompanied by her shadow, her alienation is palpable, a blank stare at the ground a short distance away. Masako can neither look up into the sky to appeal for help nor into the distant future; casting her gaze down implies a withdrawal into herself. This sequence of stiff composition is finally disrupted when she ventures out in a red Western-style jumper, beret, purple tie, and handbag. The red Western dress contrasts sharply against the surrounding hues of gray; her tie hints at masculinity, and her body's curve situated to one side of the frame breaks the straight, symmetrical lines thus far.

Arriving in Osaka, Masako continues her muted rebellion against traditional Japan, working for the metropolitan and Westernized Japan. She climbs up the corporate ladder from an elevator operator to a tour guide for English-speaking guests.

While gently poking fun at the male-dominated Japanese society where female employees work as pleasant, hardly noticeable automatons, Say manages a happy ending when Masako's English proficiency lands her the job of a tour guide, who, ironically, must wear kimono in the name of Japanese authenticity for Western eyes. Moreover, her job leads her to Joseph, another lonely soul with a similar background, an Asian adoptee with a British upbringing. Accepting Joseph's invitation for tea, May replies "in her very best English, and bowed as a proper Japanese lady should" (24). The potential discord between language and body language is neutralized and naturalized by Masako, who is also May. An illustration of them having tea continues this harmony: a Japanese-dressed couple (doubles?) in the foreground serve to counterpoint Joseph and May in Western dress in the background, the woman in kimono so demurely Japanese that she covers her smile with her hand. The wistful ending of the young couple determined to "adopt this country [Japan]" and to create a new family is Say's wish fulfillment in the sense that the couple eventually divorces and their child adopts another country—the US. As autobiographical as *Tea with Milk* is, Say has exorcized unpleasant details of his family history, such as its breakup, in view of the tender age of his readers. Such details surface only in his early autobiographical fiction, *The Ink-Keeper's Apprentice*. All his picture books in the 1980s and 1990s hold up the illusion of a happy Japanese family.

The Sign Painter (2000) is named, wryly, after a line in *Tea with Milk*. Just as Masako questions the purpose of Japanese calligraphy lessons because she does not plan to become "a sign painter," the protagonist in *The Sign Painter* is loath to mechanically churn out roadside billboards. The story opens with an Asian-looking young man passing by a small-town main street one early morning. The text throughout the book never refers to the Asian's race, whereas the Asian face and physique in illustrations highlight his race that is otherwise suppressed. Words fail to define race, yet it is indubitably "written" on the face and body. Set on the same street lined with shops and a second story painted in red, the small town of early morning in the first panel turns into an urban night scene in the last panel, which is modeled on the all-night diner of Edward Hopper's *Nighthawk* (1942). Yet Say strips Hopper of his aura of film noir by denuding the diner of any customer or server. The lone character in Say stands outside an empty diner. Sociologist George Ritzer, borrowing from Ray Oldendburg, categorizes diners as one of the "great good places," where individualized service provides customers a sense of bonding and community, as opposed to McDonaldized nonplaces of centralized, mechanized, impersonal chain stores (*The Globalization of Nothing* 42). While diners help anchor nostalgia for baby boomers, such as those in indie filmmaker Quentin Tarantino's *Reservoir Dogs* (1992) and *Pulp Fiction* (1994), Jim Jarmusch's *Coffee and Cigarettes* (2003), and even the Canadian mixed-race writer Fred Wah's *The Diamond Grill* (1996) and Wong Kar-wai's *In the Mood for Love* (2000), it is questionable whether an Asian customer like Say's character would be welcome (or promptly served) at a pre-civil rights diner in America. In view of the book's subtext on race, Say's outsider may well be literally barred from the diner. Any emphasis on diner-era racism jars against the lyrical tenor of this picture book; therefore, the Asian protagonist's isolation, particularly from American mercantilism, as the reader soon finds out, is made to resonate with wistfulness for the passing of pre-McDonald's diners. Between the two street scenes, Say's Asian protagonist is recruited to paint mysterious billboards along a highway leading into an arid desert. The billboard consists of a blonde whose hair flies in the wind beside one single word, "ArrowStar."

When a middle-aged painter asks the Asian, "Are you lost, son?," it illustrates the patronage that people of Asian descent are generally subjected to in the US. Admittedly a sympathetic, benevolent, and fatherly white male reminiscent of Norman Rockwell's small-town professionals—medical doctor, dentist, optometrist, baseball umpire, and the like—the painter who later turns into the Asian's boss remains, nevertheless, ignorant of the irony that Asian diaspora is adrift due to, in part, the history of white hegemony. Rockwellian patriarchal, capitalist order joins hands with the Warholian duplication of seductive pinups. However, the cooptation into US-American advertising and pop art is tinged with the Asian's discontent; his irrepressible artistic instinct leads him to fantasize adding mountains and clouds to the billboard design. This Say accomplishes in the middle of the book when the completed billboard is set in the larger frame of mountains and forests in the vein of Ansel Adams's landscape photograph, *Winter Sunrise from Lone Pine, California* (1944), except Adams's lit foreground, where a single horse grazes, is now replaced by the billboard. Commercialism stakes a claim in the wilderness, consistent with the business enterprise, ArrowStar, imposing its will on the land. Human ambition notwithstanding, the awesome, forbidding landscape unfolds through the snow-capped mountains, the endless highway vanishing into the horizon, and the desert sand storm. The myth of the US-American West also infuses the boss's cowboy hat, jeans, red bandanna, brass belt buckle, boots, coffee mugs, and beans cooked over the campfire. At the end of their journey, they arrive at the site of ArrowStar, a mammoth complex of roller coasters and an amusement park perched on a mesa, a flat-topped mountain in the Southwest. Like Las Vegas, the barren wasteland metamorphoses into a dream factory manufacturing thrills amid fears. The highs and lows of a roller coaster ride crystallize the vertical ascent of ArrowStar out of the desolate landscape.

Outside the adobe arch doorway to the ArrowStar office, the boss and his Asian assistant overhear a bald entrepreneur, who has apparently financed ArrowStar, talking on the telephone about the disappearance of his muse for the project, the blonde on the billboard. She has lost her patience over the protracted undertaking and driven off, true to character, with her hair flying in the wind. Close to detective stories, the protagonist and his employer come to find out about ArrowStar at the precise moment of its collapse, the company logo of Golden Fleece shorn, so to speak. The duality of the barren yet mirage-filled dreamscape desert (in David Jasper's term, the "sacred" desert) emanates from a cow's skull mounted above the office door, reminiscent of Georgia O'Keefe's paintings of skulls yoking mortality and nature's immortality. The Asian appears not to be the sole passer-by; even the financier and his idol inhabit their dream only for a while. The progression of American icons from Rockwell to Hopper, from the early morning to the chilly night, bodes ill for the perennial alien "just passing by" deserted city streets and the desert. Likewise, while demonstrating his virtuosity in the allusions to American masters, Allen Say continues to work under the auspices of the children's book market, profitable indeed but an outsider to the pantheon of great American works. Nonetheless, emptiness—empty street, diner, desert, even self—enriches Say's art to the extent that children would be utterly lost reading this book as a litany of absent presence; adults, on the other hand, who have lost their childhood, among a few other things, would be better positioned to appreciate the full range of meaning of, for lack of a better term, Say's "Zero Aesthetics." A children's book intended perhaps for adults, *The Sign Painter* complicates Karin Lesnik-Oberstein's thought-provoking reflection that "if it is a book written 'for' children, is it then still a children's book if it is (only) read by adults? What of 'adult' books read also by children—are they 'children's literature'?" ("Essentials" 15). Who is Say's intended audience anyway—the child who reads the book, the adult who buys and sometimes reads it for the child, the adult in the child reader, or the child in the adult reader? Will the child's or the adult's eyes be filled with tears when the book is closed? If the eyes are dry, empty of tears, do they indicate an empty heart yet to experience loss, or a heart too full, "too deep for tears"? (Wordsworth, "Ode: Intimations of Immortality"). Whichever the case, we may do well to remember that the cultural and psychological divide between adulthood and childhood is, like any boundary, arbitrary and meant to be judiciously redrawn. While we legislate on the biological age when one transitions into adult responsibility, we may never fathom the mystery of an adult-child or a child-adult. A related lesson Say teaches us through his art across the Pacific is the embeddedness of East in West and vice versa.

Kyoko Mori

Kyoko Mori's *Shizuko's Daughter* (1993) also bears out the blurring between adult and children's culture in that a novel promoted as young adult fiction on the basis of a precocious, melancholic teenage protagonist Yuki was, originally, published as separate short stories in such academic journals and ethnic literature collections as *The Kenyon Review* and *The Forbidden Stitch: An Asian American Women's Anthology*. The stitching together of short stories results in a variety of points of view: while privileging Yuki's third-person perspective, the book features several chapters told from other perspectives: the first chapter from the suicide Shizuko; chapter 8 from the stepmother Hanae; chapter 13 from the father Hideki; chapters 14 and 16, which is also the epilogue, from the maternal grandmother Masa. The weighty subject matter of a mother's suicide, a father's callousness, a stepmother's cruelty and physical violence, and a teenager's alienation may pose emotional challenges to young readers. The motif of emptiness, which opens the book with Shizuko's preparation for suicide, paves the way for this book of deaths (her maternal grandfather dies toward the end, too), filled with refrains of loss and grief, perhaps a bit beyond the depth of young adults.

At variance with Say's pensive nostalgia over a romanticized Japanese family, Mori's fiction stems from the harsh, unmitigated trauma of her mother's suicide. Betrayed by a promiscuous husband, oppressed by the patriarchal Japanese culture, Mori's mother gassed herself when Mori was twelve years old. The subsequent eight years witnessed a deeply scarred teenager preparing herself for self-exile and freedom. This emancipation was accompanied by nightmarish revisitations of trauma. The mother character's gassing of herself in the closed kitchen in *Shizuko's Daughter* becomes in Mori's memoir, *The Dream of Water* (1995), the more ghastly picture of the mother, who taped all the window crevices, holding the gas pipe in her mouth, with a plastic bag over her head to ensure, as it were, the outcome. Mori's *Polite Lies* (1997) somehow leaves out the detail of the plastic bag. The decade-long revisioning of the suicide's specificities demonstrates how much Mori remains in its throes.

Contrary to the confession of Fyodor Dostoyevsky's delirious, suicidal, and terminally ill character Hippolite, "A person who is dead has no age" (*The Idiot* 308), the dead person is born at the very moment of expiration, immediately beginning to age and decompose. The life span of a ghost is thus exactly that of the bereaved, who is haunted by memories that only dissolve when does the mind, a haunted house of brain cells and nerves. Such is the paradox of memory, which constitutes individual identity by virtue of a series of absences recalled: one's being here and now pivots on nonbeings there and then, always already lost. Hence, Mori's corpus—novels, collections of essays, memoirs—over the past decades dwell, to various degrees, on her mother's suicide, resembling postmortem narratives that reanimate the dead through memories. Imagining Shizuko's last moments, the opening pages of *Shizuko's Daughter* cast the suicide as a gesture of love, of unburdening the survivors, where emptiness acquires a positive value. Awakening from her depressed slumber, Shizuko wonders where Yuki is and remembers that "She is not here because I am. She can't come until I am gone" (1). Hence, the emptying of self makes the space available for the loved one, triggering a proliferation of allusions to the void. Yuki's aunt Aya writes, "my house seems empty without you [Yuki]" (28). Yuki flashes back to "the empty doorway" when her mother left amid a conversation, foreshadowing the tragic end. To fill the void in her life, Yuki busies herself with her school's track meets, which, nonetheless, sharpen her loneliness, as other athletes are accompanied by their families. Nearing the finish line in one competition, an exhausted Yuki gasps for air, suddenly realizing that this sensation must have resembled Shizuko's before she had drifted into unconsciousness: "To keep going where there's no air . . . Is this how it was, Mama?" (48). Yuki's question doubles the absence: no air and no answer. Looking for a surrogate female companion, Yuki develops a burgeoning homoerotic longing toward a female runner, Sachiko, which also hints at a regressive movement back to a lost womb. Full of nervous excitement, as if in love, Yuki memorizes the phone number of Sachiko, who has just promised to practice with her. Yuki shifts abruptly to azaleas she picked with Shizuko: "When the petals came together and narrowed like the mouth of the trumpet, there were spots of intense sweetness—so intense that her tongue tingled. Sometimes, the pale flowers were spotted bright red inside. These were the sweetest of them all. Suddenly faint, Yuki sat down on the stone bench. Still repeating the number Sachiko had given her, rapidly, fervently, she remained for a long time gazing at the azaleas. She wishes she could eat the flowers, thousands of pink trumpets, and suffocate with their sweetness" (55-56). The graphic depiction of the sweet trumpets of azaleas with their "bright red inside" suggests lesbian oral sex. The faint or swoon comes in the wake of an orgasmic muscular tenseness. Yet the concluding desire to "suffocate with their sweetness" evokes Shizuko's end, when "the gas smelled almost sweet" and the flowers near the house of Shizuko's parents "smelled foul and sweet" (7). Yuki's wish fulfillment of a homoerotic ecstasy returns to her mother's final sensation and memory. The void inside a womb moves from a lack to a potential fulfillment, the absence given positive value.

Accordingly, emptiness becomes far subtler than an inadequacy. Yuki's last telephone conversation with Shizuko, for instance, illustrates an emptiness that is no longer one but somehow bifurcated: "Yuki pulled her hand slowly out of the water. 'I remember her voice without her body and her body without her voice. Sometimes, I dream that her voice has been trapped in the telephone line somewhere'" (86). Both water and dream signal alternate states of mind, evoking the searing loss that splits asunder not only her memory of Shizuko's body and voice but also her own self, which shuttles between wakefulness and trance, reality and watery dream. Even more positively, the independent-thinking Yuki turns the three minutes allotted for her analysis of Monet's *Gladioli* in art class into a silent tribute to a painting whose beauty eludes words. In the same vein, Yuki "releases" all the dead frogs for anatomy from the school laboratory. Most significantly, on the eve of Yuki's departure for college, she refrains from bringing any particular memento of her mother, for the memory of Shizuko cannot be reduced to mere objects. Taking nothing means Yuki takes the whole of Shizuko with her to college and beyond. What Yuki leaves behind is doomed for conflagration by the stepmother Hanae, bent upon exorcizing "the dead woman" (91). As Hideki is enlisted by Hanae to burn boxes of mementos, he subconsciously salvages a sketchbook, where the happy days of his first marriage are preserved in Shizuko's sketches of him, the last of which finds him among hydrangea blossoms "shaped like round-edged crosses" (192). Despite the Christian symbolism of the crucifix, Hideki is beyond redemption, as he fails to recall even the circumstances surrounding the sketch. Emptiness turns out to plague Hideki as well in the form of amnesia and callousness. As if compensating for his sin against Shizuko and Yuki, Hideki mails this sketchbook, anonymously, to Yuki in college. A lost object finds its way back to the rightful owner. The novel concludes with the aging grandmother Masa longing to be released from life in order to rejoin her loved ones, yet the sadness of impending death is attenuated not only by her illusion of "all her children and grandchildren going down the slide" that her late husband had built but also by the newborn cicada, buried seven years underground before taking to the air (207). The cicada embodies, like children running around the slide, the circle of death and rebirth, of emptiness and being. In addition to the hydrangea, all the losses in *Shizuko's Daughter* are superimposed with flowers and plants. Shizuko's opening dream prior to suicide has "white cherry blossom petals" (1). Hydrangea blossoms trigger the memory of bygone happy days in the marriage of Shizuko and Hideki. The incipient lesbian amour is accompanied by the azalea's dizzying sweetness. Before the maternal grandfather Takeo dies of a heart attack, he silently thanks his wife for bringing in zinnias. While befitting the novel's feminine motif, flowers contain in their blossom the element of fading—death is implicit in the most glorious moments in nature.

Having developed in recent years into an essayist on cross-cultural communications and a feminist with an international perspective, Mori remains a unique voice in the singleness of vision and the unrelenting mourning of her mother. *The Dream of Water* (1995) chronicles Mori's 1990 "home-coming" after thirteen years, continuing to work out psychological complexes over her mother Takako's suicide, her father and stepmother's heartlessness, and the loss of her maternal relatives and her own youth. Although in the form of a memoir, Mori adopts such narrative strategies as juxtaposing thoughts on her religious fanatic aunt Keiko while lap swimming, punctuating breathing and strokes with meditations on Keiko. Whereas the New World and the English language prove to be liberating against the patriarchal, misogynist Japanese culture, the return to Japan amplifies her sense of loss, which arises, among other things, by way of a ghost story, traditionally associated with female suicides in East Asia. On passing the Mansion of the Plates near the Himeji castle in her trip, Mori reminisces that her mother used to tell of "the ghost story that made this mansion famous. Okiku, a maidservant here in feudal times, broke one of her master's twenty heirloom plates and was beheaded by him. Rather than giving her a proper burial, he threw her body into a well. From then on, her ghost crawled up from the well on rainy nights. Amid the gusts of wind and rain, her master heard her counting the plates and weeping because no matter how many times she counted, one was always missing" (153). Heirloom plates symbolize paternal lineage, for which women are temporary, even replaceable, custodians, to be beheaded or to be driven to suicide like Mori's mother. Mori's repetition compulsion over the decades likens her as well to Okiku, recounting in book after book the missing mother.

In this homecoming, her English language begins to fail. Compelled to use her rusty, teenage-level Japanese, Mori finds it difficult to explain herself, fearful that she might embarrass and offend her relatives. The forthrightness inherent in English and US-Americanization evaporates, only to return in the finale of the memoir when Mori, ironically, resorts to a wedding of Japanese and English rather than English alone for a heart-wrenching confession. Whereas the whole book is written in English, with conversations and memories translated into English seamlessly, Mori chooses to bid a bilingual farewell to her beloved cousin Kazumi, still trapped with their mean-spirited paternal grandfather: "'Kai-chan daisuki.' *I love you*" (260). For words from the bottom of her heart, she elects to retain the Japanese expression and then render it into English, now italicized as foreign words and, deliberately, for emphasis. Although a memoir in English, "*I love you*" in italics looks almost strange, defamiliarized not only by its font but also by its non-Japanese straightforwardness. Had she used "I love you" and not "daisuki," it would sound corny and melodramatic. The Japanese words, inexplicable momentarily to English speakers, are spontaneous and nearly transgressive, since readers know by the end of the memoir how indirect and roundabout the Japanese language is and how veiled emotions are. The inversion of English, italicized, and Japanese, in regular print, points to a conceptual reshuffling whereby a bold Western-style admission of love is naturalized as a Japanese gesture. Mori's parting confession is so shocking that it elicits the sudden outburst of tears from the reserved Kazumi—also a deviation from Japanese etiquette. Such teary smiles characterize both Allen Say and Kyoko Mori's revisits to the real or imagined Asia, emptiness and pain slowly transformed into joy.

Chapter Four

A Child's Passing into Asian Diaspora

When Hakyung Kang, my daughter's twelve-year-old classmate in East Lansing, Michigan for four years, prepared to return to Seoul, Korea, with her family in the summer of 2006 at the completion of her dad's doctorate, she, quiet and reserved, never voiced her feelings about the imminent departure. On the eve of their flight, when she carpooled with my daughter and I asked her what she herself would have chosen, she whispered in the backseat: "Stay." "How about your mom?" I pursued. "Go," she answered. Somewhat atypical in her family's circular itinerary, Hakyung is, nevertheless, one of many Asian children in diaspora: having left her home country at the age of five, she now leaves her adopted country for "home," where language, schools, customs, and lifestyle pose daunting challenges. Perhaps Hakyung's return is not all that unusual; it just comes sooner than expected, in view of the root searching, "home-coming"—real or imaginary, touristic or fictitious—so favored among Asians in diaspora, such as Asian Americans, in this global era. I am haunted, however, by Hakyung's monosyllabic replies, which remind me of the game of "*fort/da*" ("gone/there" or "lost/found") played by Freud's one-and-half-year-old grandson in *Beyond the Pleasure Principle* (1920), a personal experience deployed by the psychoanalyst to demonstrate repetition compulsion. Surely Hakyung, mature beyond her age, was not a toddler who failed to distinguish make-believe and reality. She knew that her family would not return to East Lansing for a long while, but she most likely would rejoin her American friends, my daughter included, in her Seoul dreams. More revealingly, her faint "stay" hints at the wish to freeze the present. Like a freezer that keeps fresh packaged meat, the meat is, alas, dead meat. Once "stay" escapes Hakyung's lips, it is already gone. Nothing stays, except the human longing to stay.

Many an Asian child since the latter half of the twentieth century has crossed the ocean for the West and been given a new life in England, the United States, and elsewhere, leaving behind a self barely recalled. The ocean crossing is tantamount to the passing or demise of the child's old self. Eerily resembling the traditional Asian ghost with long black hair weeping by the well over the drowned, which is herself, the bereaved adult mourns the deceased child (drowned in the crossing?) within her (or his) own person, as in the works of Kazuo Ishiguro and Chang-rae Lee, novelists who have undergone the trauma of transplantation when they were five and three years old, respectively. The novelists' early trauma was considerably alleviated by the support of their families. The two families relocated in 1960 and 1968 to England and to the United States as a consequence of the fathers' expertise in oceanography and psychiatry, respectively. Loss and homecoming, however, recur in their corpuses to the extent that they resemble repetition compulsion. Their novels are cathartic in that the dead or rather dormant child is re-awakened again and again; they are a "stay" of the child's vanishing, a deferral of time. Yet a child's passing may point as much to a child's end as to an adult's beginning. Passing means not only death but also a passage into, or an adoption of, self-identity. The child's passing becomes the adult's rite of passage into membership of the Asian diaspora, most vociferously exemplified by Asian American identity politics. The Asian American (as well as Anglo-Asian) ethnic identity championed since the 1960s is a volitioned enactment of selfhood, the rise of which signals, on the face of it at least, the fall of an imposed Orientalized image. Rise and fall are rarely so clear-cut, birth and death perennially intertwined. To borrow conceptually from transnational and transracial adoption, Asian America adopts a minority identity to contest the double orphanhood inflicted by home countries of the West and by ancestral countries of the East. Asian America, feeling like an adoptee forsaken by Asia and foreclosed in the US until the civil rights movement, chooses to turn adoptive: it—the invisible, stereotyped "perennial alien"—turns "he" or "she" by adopting itself (see Kim, *Reading Asian American Literature*; Witt, "Family Resemblances" 142). As Asian America opts for a self-identity, that is, as it adopts itself, it echoes the adoptee-philosopher Kimberly Leighton's contention that "identities are neither born nor made but are *adopted*" ("Beng Adopted" 148)

While Asian American self-adoption "claims America," in Maxine Hong Kingston's words, it does so by the sleight of hand of claiming Asia. Each of Kingston's works stems from a phantasmagoric Asia that is paradoxically repudiated and recuperated, her woman warrior empowered by Fa Mu Lan, who materializes against a stereotypically racist, sexist, backward China. This self-empowerment presupposes a splitting of the other into stock images in extremis, either the heroine and the surging red masses or the barbarian horde and the corrupt feudal China. From Kingston to Chang-rae Lee, Asian American identity writes itself into existence by writing off Asia, an apparition retired from human agency and even humanity. Asian American literature is thus replete with ghost stories, subconscious mea culpas of endocannibalism, the primitive practice of eating members of one's own tribe. Given that adoption is used metaphorically and politically in the preceding paragraphs, it turns literal among one particular group of Asian Americans—Asian adoptees. Transnational adoption ceases to be a figure of speech; it is lived experiences for adoptees. In comparison to Ishiguro and Lee, internationally adopted children in the latter half of the twentieth century make the voyage alone, as in cases of Korean adoptees, or accompanied by strangers who are adoptive parents, as in cases of Chinese adoptees (Foster, "Once Upon a Time in America" 156). Adoption narratives in recent years by adoptive parents and adoptees themselves share the paradigm of "born-again," the alleged orphanhood in home countries coming to an end once the children reach the other shore. Just as the child adoptee is reborn upon touching American soil, the adult adoptee feels reborn yet again upon touching Asian soil in the root-searching reverse flow. The search for birth culture in place of an absent origin, particularly a mother, motivates not only adoptees and adoptive parents but also Asian Americans who feel disinherited. Alienation as a minority in the West lies ultimately behind Amy Tan's wish fulfillment that the protagonist's Chinese genes be "reactivated" in China, an exotic romanticism striking the chord of "Sugar Sisterhood," as Tan's white female fans are diagnosed by Sau-ling Cynthia Wong in *Reading Asian American Literature: From Necessity to Extravagance* (1993). The fantasy of rebirth is universal, shared by Asian adoptees seeking birth culture in place of birth parents, by Asian Americans playacting homecoming, and by mainstream Americans empathizing and identifying with the exotic other. Born-again presumes, of course, that one dies first, at least one's old self.

Ishiguro's loss, Lee's guilt, and Asian American endocannibalism

That the novelists Kazuo Ishiguro and Chang-rae Lee share a sensibility uncannily similar does not prove that the younger Lee's work is derivative. Rather, the "primal wound," to use Nancy Newton Verrier's coinage for adoption, of childhood passing imprints the psyche so paradigmatically that it recurs in various manifestations. As a consequence, Ishiguro's whiteface protagonists, all of them de facto orphans—the butler Stevens in *The Remains of the Day* (1989), the pianist Ryder in *The Unconsoled* (1995), the detective Banks in *When We Were Orphans* (2000), and the Hailsham clones in *Never Let Me Go* (2005)—relentlessly yet futilely search for their lost origin. For Lee, who left Korea at three years old, two pivotal years younger than Ishiguro, it is not so much a vaguely remembered home that his narratives try to return to as a repressed yet irreconcilable schism that continues to plague his characters, story after story. While Ishiguro gives vent to an elegiac mourning of a traumatic past, Lee plays with politically charged racial identities, attended with a tinge of self-blame over exploitation. Passing acquires yet another dimension in view of Lee's characters who pass themselves off as white. Lee's protagonist Henry Park in *Native Speaker*, for instance, has so internalized the stereotype of Oriental abjection and duplicity that he retains copies rather than the original of his wife's note, as if the real has no place with a two-faced Korean American.

The title of Ishiguro's *When We Were Orphans* suggests, of course, that "we" still *are* orphans and that orphanhood is but the human condition, existentially. Ishiguro concludes the novel on this note: "But for those like us, our fate is to face the world as orphans, chasing through long years the shadows of vanished parents" (335). Doomed from the start, this "shadow play" is necessitated by the void within

Christopher Banks, driving him to become a private detective in the literary tradition of Sherlock Holmes. Banks's mission for parentage is compounded by a sense of guilt over his hostage mother, who has sacrificed herself for his well-being. Banks's existence hinges on his mother's nonexistence, a sex slave at the hands of a Chinese opium warlord. Furthermore, the child Banks was betrayed by Uncle Philip, a family friend working for the drug king.

Evoked by Uncle Philip's betrayal is Ishiguro's own ambiguity over the poetic license of Orientalism, namely, Ishiguro may be betraying "his own kind." Not only are his later novels wearing, in Frantz Fanon's terms, white masks, but he also draws from Orientalist stereotypes, albeit self-consciously. Banks's search for the past leads him back to a Japan-occupied Shanghai as surrealist as any of Dali's or Escher's dreamscapes (See Ma, *The Deathly Embrace*, ch. 8, "Kazuo Ishiguro's Persistent Dream for Postethnicity"). Indeed, for Western sensibility in search of the quintessential metaphor of disorientation, Shanghai provides fertile soil with its combination of Oriental exoticism and Western colonial familiarity. This merger lurks behind Banks' discovery of his made-over childhood home in Shanghai:

> The ceiling was high and beamed. Beyond the diners, right at the back, was a kind of minstrels' gallery, from the rail of which hung a brace of paper lanterns. It was this section of the room that had drawn my gaze, and I now continued to stare past the table towards it, hardly hearing my host's words of welcome. For what was dawning upon me was that the entire rear half of the room in which I was now standing was in fact what used to be the entrance hall of our old Shanghai house. (198)

Despite renovations over a period of two or three decades and Chinese decorations such as paper lanterns, Banks is transported back to his early days, oblivious to the social etiquette of heeding his host. In lieu of the mother's womb, Banks settles for a regression into the old home, the vessel containing his lost childhood. The childhood trauma was so searing that Banks subconsciously tries to restore the past: a wounded Japanese soldier, hence, is absurdly taken to be his childhood playmate Akira. His disorientation culminates in an arduous trek across Shanghai's warren, a war-ravaged rubble of maze-like alleys and slums, an expressionistic projection of Banks' mental collapse as well as the Orientalist crystallization of the abject East. That such expressionistic and Orientalist visualization should be "dubbed" by a single voice (voice-over?) with an apparently crisp British accent from characters as diverse as a Chinese patriarch inhabiting Banks's old mansion and a Japanese Colonel escorting him out of the warren debunks, by way of incompatibility, both Chineseness and Englishness. The duality implodes, accentuating the inextricability of the Orientalist set of concentric circles of the warren, the foreign concession, Shanghai, and China as well as those of the Anglo-Japanese novelist and his alter ego of a whiteface Sherlock wannabe.

Banks's orphanhood is shared by the clones bred for organ transplants in the sci-fi novel, *Never Let Me Go.* These human guinea pigs are sequestered away from the human society at Hailsham, an orphanage disguised as a boarding school, whose strange name insinuates "Hey, you fake!" All Hailsham graduates, all sham hailed or called upon for their body parts, the clones engage in a subconscious mimicking of the outside world. Hailsham activities are either named with a capital letter or shrouded in quotation marks to give them more prestige than they deserve. "Exchange," "Sale," "Gallery," and "collection" offer a sense of private ownership in a simulated market economy, which subliminally denies that the students themselves are commodities. The protagonist Kath's cassette tape with the song that is the novel's namesake signals, of course, personal possession in the form of a tape. More importantly, Kath's slow dance hugging a make-believe baby to the tune is a wish fulfillment by a human replica conceived to be barren. Kath and the clones own nothing, not even their bodies; they are disposable, the attrition coming one organ at a time. Given their destiny, they nevertheless search for meaning and self-definition, even after they join the "work force" post-Hailsham, which spells their doom in a few short years. Their drive for love, camaraderie, and community makes them, ironically, more human than human. As a coping strategy, they indulge in the fantasy of looking for "Possibles," from whose DNA they allegedly derive. They inhabit a web of euphemisms and rituals to mask their tragic fate—"donations" for scheduled transplants, "completion" for death caused by multiple donations. They flock to see a beached boat, the embodiment of their lives, with no past, no future, and not much of a present. They mourn the close of Hailsham, the only home they could claim. Most disturbingly, they never entertain any thought of revolt against or fleeing from this unjust world. The most they fantasize is to defer donations by demonstrating that a particular couple differs from others in that they are truly in love. Of course, no deferral is granted, as love makes absolutely no difference. The sci-fi genre leads one to suspect mind control, a genetic programming to preempt the stirring of unbecoming, seditious thoughts. That speculation aside, Hailsham graduates follow the long genealogy of Ishiguro orphans contesting their parentless destiny—all in vain.

That Ishiguro's later novels are routinely two stories bundled in one—orphans' bildungsroman spliced into crime and detection or into science fiction—suggests a narrative rift mirroring minority schizophrenia, one that negotiates between ethnic differences and the mainstream marketplace. Having never seriously taken the point of view of an Anglo-Japanese in his fiction, Ishiguro shuttles between the extremes of his early Japanese stage and his British, or white, stage. While both stages feature equally alienated protagonists, Japanese as opposed to English, the shift echoes the duality of passing; leaving behind one's race and ethnicity only intensifies the sense of loss. With his most recent novel, *Aloft* (2004), Chang-rae Lee follows the same flight from ethnic identity. In his debut *Native Speaker* (1995) and, subsequently, in *A Gesture Life* (1999), the Korean American novelist casts ethnic characters squarely, yet does so problematically in that he betokens the ambivalence of childhood passing, both to self-identity and to, in Lee's own words, "self-betrayal," both to birth and decease. The latter involves conforming to the majority culture to the extent that one passes oneself off as white.

"In every betrayal dwells a self-betrayal," confesses Henry Park in *Native Speaker* (314). Park's conscience is pricked by the conflicts between his private and professional lives. Park inhabits multiple families, all at odds with one another: his Korean immigrant parents and, subsequently, surrogate mother Ahjuhma; his "lengthy Anglican goddess" wife Lelia and their preschool son Mitt, the mixed-race future for humanity crushed to death like a mutt at the bottom of the neighborhood kids' "dog pile"; his profession at a spy agency under the father figure of Dennis Hoagland, conning and informing on other Asians; his assignment to sabotage the Korean American politician John Kwang and his family-like staff. Park comes to Kwang to redeem himself from his debacle with a Filipino psychiatrist. Instead of collecting materials from the psychiatrist, Park exposes his own fantasy of an "invisible brother with no name" (205), nameless because Park cannot grasp the subtleties of Korean names while fashioning a doppelgänger armed with the best of both worlds—Asian martial arts and American science and pop culture. The irony lies in the fact that while anonymous and amorphous, the dream-self so invigorates the dreamer that the grip on reality is jeopardized. The dream-self is hence deeply buried; Park is, literally, his brother's keeper and gravedigger. On the psychiatrist's lounge chair, on the verge of betraying his fellow Asian from the Philippines, the specter of the exorcized brother arises to indict Park of repeated offenses of, not to mince words, endocannibalism, living off the death of his own kind.

Park manifests the proverbial minority self-loathing, punctuated by mea culpas of guilt. This explosive cocktail bordering on racist representations comes through most conspicuously in immigrant schizophrenia (see Ma, *Immigrant Subjectivities*, part 1 on immigrant schizophrenic). Formulaically, Chang-rae Lee's immigrants exhibit behavioral and conceptual gaps that essentialize them into dissociated facets rather than an integral whole, in practice rendering them the inexplicable other. Park's father, a graduate from "the best college in Korea," with a master's degree, is a stereotypical, vitriolic Korean grocer, cursing in his ghetto pidgin: "my hot mama shit ass tight cock sucka," "slant-eye spic-and-span motha-fucka" (63). Even Park's fond memory of a water battle somewhat dehumanizes his father, who protrudes his "rump" to be sprayed. This animal imagery concludes when the father dies of multiple strokes, clinging onto life like a "gritty mule" (48). Lee leaves unresolved the fissure between a highly educated Korean and a bitter immigrant. Even with all her maternal affection, Park's mother fares no better, as she is said to wear the "smoothest mask," duplicitous and mysterious (62). When she dies, Ahjuhma joins the family as maid, replacement mother to Henry Park, and mistress to the father. Ahjuhma assumes various guises, ranging from a "zombie . . . only partly possessed her own body" (65) to a poor dresser resembling a "huge trout," and to a late-night consolation, with "almost smooth" skin and "pretty shape[d] . . . face," to the father (79). Ahjuhma's metamorphoses from alien to clown to femininity are motivated by a self-conscious, guilt-ridden revision of racial stereotypes, each unsavory stock image followed in its heels either by a confession of the sin of Orientalism or by an aesthetic, merely cosmetic, gesture.

Such a pattern is reversed in John Kwang, who debuts with as much charisma as befits a political celebrity, whose oratory on ethnic self-hate sways a multiracial crowd, whose aura is "seemingly resistan[t] to dilution" (138)—seemingly, though. Signs of fraudulence destabilize Kwang's performance. Kwang's trousers are tailored "to flatter his short Korean legs," the unseemly lower half of his body undercutting his upper half "in something silken and double-breasted, the lines rakishly cut down to hug his youthful waist" (137); an eerie feeling of "mysterious dubbing" plagues Kwang's speeches; Kwang's rise in New York is attributed to his business on "high-end dry-cleaning equipment," (179) akin to one of early immigrants' professions—the laundry business; Kwang's Asian patriarchal background (the penis hidden in the tailored trousers?) is glimpsed in his abusive attitude toward his wife and womanizing with the campaign manager; Kwang's campaign finances come from *ggeh*, the Korean money club, deemed illegal contributions that eventually cause his downfall. As Kwang unravels, his speech and mannerism revert back to Korean. His disintegration appears to unmask a Korean essence lurking beneath the suave surface, much like jars of kimchee with its pungent smell secreted in Kwang's basement. In the final pages of the novel, Park attempts to shield from a mob the disgraced Kwang, brought down by Park's betrayal of *ggeh*. The fact that the secret is a foreign word taps into the Oriental myth: the double-faced Korean immigrant politician is exposed by a double agent of Korean ancestry.

By way of Henry Park's confession of guilt, Lee gives a dubious acknowledgment of his own implication in racist representation, an acknowledgment in Park's narrative voice that lends itself to further authorial exploitation: "my ugly immigrant's truth, as was his [Park's grocer father] is that I have exploited my own, and those others who can be exploited. This forever is my burden to bear. But I and my kind possess another dimension, we will dismantle every last pretense and practice you hold, noble as well as ruinous. You can keep nothing safe from our eyes and ears. This is your own history" (319-20). Park is no immigrant from whom he has distanced himself in order to create a US-American self and family. His marriage to Lelia and the birth of Mitt, who inherits Lelia's physical traits, can be argued as a culmination of minority self-erasure. Such self-annihilation is troubled, nonetheless, by guilt. In a moment of expiation, Park recants his life-long preference and self-identifies as an immigrant. Should Park be a disingenuous or deluded character, then this final act of self-deception can be chalked up as part of his consistent folly. However, Park has exhibited throughout a mind so torturously bent upon self-scrutiny that it belies his alleged "immigrant's truth" in the finale. In fact, "immigrant" is a front for Park to launch a critique of mainstream US-Americans, a nod in concluding paragraphs to even out the preponderance of minority neurosis. As though occupying a fluid positionality, Park's parting shot against an American readership adheres yet again to Oriental mystique, since the narrator and "[his] kind" are said to be so prescient as to see through mainstream culture. Such Eastern transcendence is but the opposite to Eastern degeneration, polarities of Orientalism imagined by Westerners situated squarely in the middle ground of humanity.

Lee's confessions of (self-)betrayal and overtures toward Eastern spirituality are psychological and aesthetic compensation, the mea culpa of transgressions against his brothers and sisters. Confessions gradually turn into indulgences in Lee's oeuvre because the sin of Orientalism is perpetrated again and again. The zombie Ahjuhma is indeed excised from Lee's subsequent novels, yet the mysterious and alien Oriental woman, as opposed to the transparent and expressive Lelia, materializes in the doppelgängers of K and Sunny in *A Gesture Life* and in the Korean suicide Daisy in *Aloft*. The dead mourned by the bereaved protagonists include not only these female ghosts but also Mitt and the phantom, nameless brother. Instead of chasing after parents' shadows, as Ishiguro is doomed to repeat, Lee transfers the lost Koreanness onto ghostlike characters, particularly the comfort woman K. Invariably, the Asian female is missing, a fetish for repressed trauma. Koreanness is subconsciously banished, only to return to haunt, with a vengeance, the assimilationist Korean American Henry Park, Doc Hata in *A Gesture Life*, and the whiteface protagonist Jerry Battle in *Aloft*. Lee and Asian America, part of the West with ancestral ties to Asia, Orientalize Asia as an exotic other, while cuddling it as their own. This paradoxical dissociation from and identification with Asia, as in Park's claim of his "ugly immigrant's truth" after hundreds of pages on immigrant aliens, merges America and Asia. In this psychological double move, the repressed Asian half of his self is othered first, turned into an Oriental spectacle and specter. Such problematic representation smacks of self-exploitation to the extent that a minority capitalizes on ethnic differences for survival and success, the so-called "food pornography," decried by Frank Chin and analyzed by Sau-ling Cynthia Wong, of Asian American catering to mainstream taste in the name of authentic Asian food or Asianness. In Freudian terms, the ghosting of the Asian half circumvents the taboo of endocannibalism, that is, a metaphorical gorging of the self or self-consumption. Seemingly thriving on identity politics, Asian American literature is, however, fraught with guilt and self-incrimination, ridden by doubts of feasting on Asian bodies and haunted by Asia's ghosts.

The Asian American problematics finds a rationale in Freud: "the 'uncanny' . . . is that class of the terrifying which leads back to something long known to us, once very familiar" (369-70). Employing conjugations in the German language, Freud explains that "the *unheimlich* [the uncanny] is what was once *heimlich*, homelike, familiar; the prefix 'un' is the token of repression" (399). Asian ancestors are repressed as ghosts, but their repeated returns foreshadow Asian Americans' longing to embrace their ancestry. In the West, the genre of the Gothic is characterized by such dark shadows of the self, pointing to repression and taboo. Horace Walpole's *The Castle of Otranto* (1764), which initiated Gothic novels, bases the horror of the haunted castle partly on repugnance over incest. Walpole's protagonist, Manfred, is not only committing potential incest by proposing to marry his dead son's fiancée, but has also already committed incest by having married Hippolita, "for [they] are related within the forbidden degree" (66). Incest represents an urge to return to the infantile oneness where self and other are not yet separated. Bent upon possessing everything and everyone, Manfred reunites first with his cousin and then his daughter-in-law to mend any splintering within himself. Manfred later becomes the Byronic hero in the 1817 dramatic poem. This attempt to cannnibalize the nonself lies at the heart of Emily Brontë's *Wuthering Heights* (1847) as well. Heathcliff, the "dark skinned gypsy" (47), is the adopted, perhaps illegitimate, son, the other by race who may share the Earnshaw family blood. His love, Catherine Earnshaw, confides in Nelly, the loyal family servant: "I *am* Heathcliff—he's always, always in my mind—not as a pleasure, any more than I am always a pleasure to myself—but as my own being" (122). What the lovers desire is a total immersion in each other, a possibly incestuous union. Tormented by unrequited love, both Catherine and Heathcliff starve themselves to death. The twin suicide suggests that when they fail to be/eat each other, they cease to be/eat at all.

Gothic longing for a pseudo-incestuous oneness may not run through Asian American literature, which, nevertheless, reveals a similar psychic process of projecting repression as a shadow or ghost. Asian America remains rueful over such splintering, an externalization that diminishes the self, pragmatically and spiritually. Put another way, by discursively producing the other, which is but the self, Asian America in effect guts or consumes itself, a practice also known as endocannibalism. The pioneer Maxine Hong Kingston has penned perhaps the classic Asian American ghost story in *The Woman Warrior: Memoirs of a Girlhood among Ghosts* (1976), fraught with the mutual devouring of Asian Americans and their Asian ancestors' ghosts. Kingston transfers this cannibalized or cannibalistic impulse onto certain legendary figures: "Another big eater was Chou Yi-han of Changchow, who fried a ghost. It was a meaty stick when he cut it up and cooked it. But before that it had been a woman out at night" (104). On the surface, Kingston attacks the misogynist, patriarchal culture, which not only labels women as ghosts but executes them, hence turning them into ghosts. Yet Kingston also gnaws through Chinese tradition in search of materials for a Chinese American identity. This consumption of the other for self-fashioning brings about a sense of guilt: "and there were adventurous people inside my head to whom I talked. With them I was frivolous and violent, orphaned. . . . I had vampire nightmares; every night the fangs grew longer, and my angel wings turned pointed and black. I hunted humans down in the long woods and shadowed them with my blackness. Tears dripped from my eyes, but blood dripped from my fangs, blood of the people I was supposed to love" (220-21). The imaginary China Kingston constructs as the basis of Chinese American identity requires, paradoxically, a self-orphaning, the elimination of the other evidenced in the sucking of their blood. Their life story becomes Kingston's source of life, in the course of which, confesses Kingston, the ones "I was supposed to love" are decimated. Unwittingly, Kingston taps into the lore of Dracula in the Western tradition to illustrate a cannibalistic feasting of the loved ones, which elicits "tears" and guilt. Choosing Dracula, Kingston ignores the countermyth of bat, which symbolizes blessing in the Chinese tradition, "bat" and "blessing" being homophones (*fu*). Even on the level of symbolism, Kingston's merger with the Western archetype of evil betrays a subconscious remorse over what she has perpetrated against Chineseness.

Such ghost stories as Kingston's vampire nightmare are almost always anchored in dreams or visions, insubstantial borderlands between drowsiness and consciousness, in order to evade taboos over (endo)cannibalism. As a consequence, both Kingston and Tan situate their narratives in such fissures: "Night after night my mother would talk-story until we fell asleep. I couldn't tell where the stories left off and the dreams began, her voice the voice of the heroines in my sleep" (Kingston 24). Likewise, Tan locates the genesis of *The Hundred Secret Senses* (1995) in bedtime stories about China: "eventually I would fall asleep, at which point in her story I always forgot. So which part was her dream, which part was mine? Where did they intersect? Every night, she'd tell me these stories. And I would lie there silently, wishing she'd shut up" (29). Despite Tan's derivativeness, the recurring motif two decades apart suggests an urge to break through the American reality in search of an ethnic alternative to mainstream culture. Thus, many Asian American protagonists are endowed with what Tan describes as "the yin eye," an extrasensory perception that makes possible the sightings of ghosts, an embodiment of an ethnic past and identity distinct from the majority-dominated discourse. For example, Tan's Libby and Kwan revisit China and their previous incarnation, Miss Banner and Miss Moo; Cynthia Kadohata's protagonist in *The Floating World* (1989) encounters the ghost of her father; Fae Myenne Ng's *Bone* (1993) depicts a San Francisco Chinatown family haunted by memories of ancestors and the daughter who committed suicide; the mixed race Heinz Insu Fenkl features numerous phantoms in *Memories of My Ghost Brother* (1996); across the border in Canada, Hiromi Goto locates magic in the apparitional kappa child (*The Kappa Child* 2001); Goto's fellow Japanese Canadian novelist Kerri Sakamoto orchestrates, in *One Hundred Million Hearts* (2003), her protagonist's return to Japan in search of her deceased father's wartime kamikaze pilot past. Asian American hauntings are not restricted to literature. D. Roberts' radio play *Mei Mei: A Daughter's Song* (1989) includes the Taiwanese folk goddess Kuan-yin Pu-sa ("Lady Buddha") and her opposites—female ghosts at a cemetery. Rea Tajiri's film *Strawberry Fields* (1997) describes a search for the internment past of the protagonist's family, a search guided in part by a dead sister. All the ghosts in these and many other texts are conjured up by the intense longings of the Asian American protagonists.

In nonfiction, such a genuine pursuit for ethnic roots brings forth a large number of Asian American memoirs and even travelogues on the return to Asia. This genre of root searching smacks of ghost stories as well, with dead ancestors summoning Asian Americans to cross the ocean. This journey back, literally or metaphorically, has been undertaken by many, including Frank Ching's *Ancestors: 900 Years in the Life of a Chinese Family* (1988), June Chang's *Wild Swans: Three Daughters of China* (1991), Leslie Li's *Bittersweet* (1992), Lisa See's *On Gold Mountain* (1995), and Pang-mei Natasha Chang's *Bound Feet and Western Dress* (1997). Frequently, family history interweaves with China's history, with a pedigree shining through certain powerful figures, such as Ching's ancestor, Qin Guan, a Sung dynasty poet of nearly a millennium ago; Leslie Li's grandmother, wife of the acting president of China in the late forties; and Pang-mei Natasha Chang's grand-aunt, once married to the romantic poet, Hsu Chih-mo. These personal memoirs involving dead ancestors resemble the fictions of Kingston and Tan in that family ghosts need to be reconstructed, oftentimes from stories told by the immigrant parents' generation and rarely from personal experiences with the deceased. In other words, Kingston has never lived with No Name Woman or Fa Mu Lan in *The Woman Warrior*, nor has Tan with Miss Banner and Miss Moo in *The Hundred Secret Senses*. Before the yarns, such as Kingston's self-described "talk-stories," are spun from Asian American lips, Asianness must be processed somewhat in the digestive system. Even talk-stories derive as much from Chinese legends as from the Chinese term for the predecessor to the novel, *shuoshu*. Yet when the ghost is truly a ghost, when there is absolutely no information on Asia, the root searching is all but impossible and hence most intense, as in the case of Asian adoptees and their adoptive parents.

Asian adoptees

Transnational adoption narratives in recent years reinscribe the double or even triple entendre of "passing." Asian adoptees are reborn, passing into or passing off as American, their Asian selves buried. Recent adoption narratives seek to reanimate the past, with varying results. First of all, the born-again refrain runs through all these stories, by adoptees and adoptive parents alike. Katy Robinson in *A Single Square Picture* (2002) writes: "Instead of emerging out of my mother's womb naked, I picture my arrival at age seven fully dressed, traveling down the escalator and being delivered to my adoptive parents. Upon delivery, I cried, received a slap from the Korean escort, and was thus awakened to the reality of my new life" (61). Using metaphors of birth, Robinson adroitly documents a shared affect concerning the moment of deplaning or delivery. This deliverance supposedly lifts orphans out of abandonment and a life at the bottom of Asian hierarchical societies. Karin Evans's *The Lost Daughters of China* (2000) agrees from the perspective of an adoptive parent. To avoid the appearance of presumptuousness in designating the return flight as rebirth, Evans projects her feelings of rejuvenation onto the point of view of Max the "stork," the Chinese adoption agent: "To watch the moment, not of birth but of something so close to it" (134). Despite the fact that the qualifying tone of voice is once or twice removed from the "newborn," it does not lessen the impression of a fresh start.

In adoption narratives, that authors invariably attempt to link with the past suggests a keen sense of loss, but the void is often filled in such a way as to reaffirm adoption. Karin Evans strikes a melodramatic pose when she empathizes with her daughter's Chinese birth mother: "I had a Chinese soul mate, a mother who had by her own unfathomably sad loss allowed me to realize an almost impossible dream" (135). One hesitates to be cynical in such circumstances, yet this "soul mate" remains a figment of imagination, the emotional bonding a rhetorical one. In view of the saga of adoption and a keen interest in things Asian shared by Evans and others, Toby Alice Volkman sees adoptive parents' "fascination with the imagined 'birth culture' of their adopted children" as representing "displaced longings for origins and absent birth mothers" (82). "In the absence of the [birth] mother's body," Volkman continues, "the longing for origins may be displaced onto the body of the nation and its imagined culture" ("Embodying Chinese Culture" 96-97). Commenting on the motif in adoption narratives over the baby's origin, Margaret Homans echoes Volkman's thesis: "adoptive origins and origin stories are not discovered in the past so much as they are created in the present and for the present" ("Adoption Narratives" 5).

From her more historical perspective in retracing the history of Korean adoption, Eleana Kim finds that since Harry and Bertha Holts's Christian rescue mission in 1954, over 200,000 children have been adopted from South Korea to foreign countries, mostly to the US, a circuitous solution to social welfare problems after the devastation of the Korean War ("Wedding Citizenship" 57). The 1988 Olympic Games in Seoul raised awareness of this issue, prompting President Kim Dae Jun to apologize to Korean adoptees in 1998. Eleana Kim bemoans that "the diasporic imaginary or cultural identity of Korean adoptees is based less on memories of a mythic homeland and more on a shared experience of violence and loss" (69). Faced with such collective trauma, popular culture in South Korea contributes tales of national healing. One of the best in Korean television serial dramas, brilliantly scripted and innovative in cinematography and lighting, *Hotelier* casts Yung-joon Bae as a corporate raider, whose ruthlessness originates from his adoptee identity, steeled by Christian adoptive parents, Harvard Business School, and Las Vegas casino mergers. Bae's rehabilitation comes about when he symbolically returns to the Korean family of the hotel staff. His initial hostile takeover of the hotel is replaced by the promise of love and marriage with a hotel manager. Less happily reconciled than Bae's character, certain Korean adoptee groups have reacted to such violent disruptions to children's psyches by working against transnational adoption, calling themselves, provocatively, Transracial Abductees and Bastard Nation, as testified by Sara K. Dorow (*Transnational Adoption* 278). Katy Robinson gives an inkling of that which so tears apart adoptees that some may elect to play the role of agent provocateur against adoption. Failing to locate her birth mother, Robinson settles for her father: "I despised my father and loved him with equal strength, as I did Korea itself, for the strong hold it had on me, while at the same time rejecting me as one of its own" (153) This anguish-ridden relationship with Asia reenacts Lee's fictional ambivalence of self-hate and guilt.

The majority of adoptees prefer a personal approach in chronicling the pang of childhood passing to the policy revamp advocated by Transracial Abductees and Bastard Nation. Deann Borshay Liem's hour-long documentary *First Person Plural* (2000) deploys interviews, dramatization, and footage to recount her experiences of being adopted at ten years old. For nearly a decade, Liem had relegated vague memories of her Korean family to the realm of dreams, imitated her American sibling and peers, joined the cheerleading team, and even undergone plastic surgery. Adoptees' denial of Asianness in favor of the facade of Americanness follows the Asian American ritual of endocannibalism, one part of self consuming the other part. The documentary brings alive Korean ghosts, culminating in the bittersweet meeting between her adoptive parents and her Korean biological family, separated, as they are, by language and culture. The most poignant segments of *First Person Plural* involve Liem's self-reflection while looking straight into the camera, tears filling her eyes at times. Liem's agonizing soul searching and ghost hunting remain open-ended at the hour's end, but she negotiates a truce with herself in that "the only way to be close to my Korean [biological] mother is to admit she's *not* my mother." Liem's pained demeanor in delivering this conclusion makes it, despite the brusqueness of rejection, almost a gesture of love. Liem relinquishes part of herself—her mother as well as the desire for reunion—in order to be close. Deann Borshay Liem has come to accept first-person plural and dual mothers and families, each side a phantom to the other.

As Liem's story demonstrates, the ten-year-old passes, simultaneously, into this world and beyond, coming into herself by leaving it. Her heart-rending decision as she drives away from the Korean mother and Korea in the finale highlights the paradox of any dichotomized relationship: self and other, life and death, human and ghost. Jacques Derrida urges in *Specters of Marx* (1994) a deconstructive intimacy between opposites: "Learning to live . . . can happen only between life and death. Neither in life nor in death *alone*. What happens between two, and between all the 'two's' one likes, such as between life and death, can only *maintain itself* with some ghost, can only *talk with or about* some ghost" ("Exordium" xviii). Writing during the war in 1944, Horkheimer and Adorno put it more bleakly: "only the conscious horror of destruction creates the correct relationship with the dead: unity with them because we, like them, are the victims of the same condition and the same disappointed hope" (*The Dialectics of Enlightenment* 215). Accordingly, Liem symbolically terminates a blood relationship in order to resurrect emotional bonding. In view of all the phantoms in Asian American literature, let us heed such advice, exemplified in Derrida's ethical imperative "to learn to live *with* ghosts, in the upkeep, the conversation, the company, or the companionship, in the commerce without commerce of ghosts" ("Exordium" xviii). Asian diaspora, by definition, traverses the ocean of oblivion. Instead of severing the living from the dead, those who are losing from those already lost, each diasporic ferry—Charon's, Liem's car, or mine—should string together the two. Hakyung is gone, yet her faint answers stay to this day.

Chapter Five

yEast for Modern Cannibals

Much ink (computer printers' blood) has been spilled by Western critics on Dracula and his dark horde, by Asianists on Lu Xun's "Diary of a Madman" and the Korean Wave's cannibalistic motif, and by Asian Americanists on food pornography. My argument herein, however, proposes a dinner table of three, each guest drawn to the host of yEast, the construct of East or Orient, including self-Orientalizing, as the agent for selfhood. The gathering of blood-sucking and flesh-eating cannibals reveals a communal interest in modernity, which is but a veiled, sublimated form of monstrosity, a projection of one's own neuroses, a self-amputation and -consumption to conceive and satiate the modern self (see Kristeva, *Powers of Horror*; Wang, *The Monster That Is History*). Freudian anthropophagic metaphors betoken the liminality inherent in all three, dwelling as they do in the limbo between self and other, which segues into tensions between West and East, man and woman, and life and death.

The East has always been the yeast for the West's psychodrama of hegemony since imperialism. The yEast serves, as does any fungus agent or any seasoning in food preparation, the paradoxical functions of transforming qualitatively the taste, smell, color, and size of food while remaining invisible, unnoticeable. As trivial as a pinch of salt or a tablespoon of soy sauce, the yEast is vital to Western culture in concocting its identity, a chain reaction that brings to mind Paul's warning against "the old leaven . . . of [sexual] depravity and wickedness," for "a little leaven leavens all the dough" ("The First Letter of Paul to the Corinthians" 5: 6-8). Indeed, the "y" in yEast suggests the subordinate yet indispensable "yin," or femininity, to the dominant West's "yang." In this Orientalization, not only the Orient but Asian America suffers a "racial castration," as David Eng argues in *Racial Castration* (2001) when he points out that *Oxford English Dictionary* defines "Oriental" as "submission," "weakness," and "woman" (1). By making possible the autoerotic, masturbatory fantasy of the masculinist West, the feminized yEast becomes the West's wet dream, an assemblage of mental constructs, albeit illusory, essential to orgasm, or fulfillment of desires. Yet sexual and dietary desires satiate biological as much as psychological need. Eating, lovemaking, and other forms of interpenetration erase boundaries between subject and object, allowing a blur of self and other. As Freud notes in "The Direction of the Psychical Personality," psychic "identification has been not unsuitably compared with the oral, cannibalistic incorporation of the other person" (56), both in terms of food intake and intercourse. This theory of "cannibalistic incorporation" lies at the heart of the Oedipus complex. In *Totem and Taboo,* Freud links the complex with "cannibal savages," whose incestuous transgression remains implicit: "one day the brothers who had been driven out came together, killed and devoured their father . . . Cannibal savages as they were, it goes without saying that they devoured their victim as well as killing him. The violent primal father had doubtless been the feared and envied model of each one of the company of brothers: and in the act of devouring him they accomplished their identification with him, and each one of them acquired a portion of his strength" (141-42). If one accepts, in symbolic terms, Freud's daring reconstruction of prehistoric evolution, then the Oedipus complex entails not only the slaughtering of the victim but the partaking of and substituting for it. The feasting of flesh allows one to literally become the other.

Not only in Freud but in myth, folktale, and children's stories can we find human-eating ghouls: Hansel and Gretel, Jack and the Beanstalk, Little Red Riding Hood, and Cyclops, just to name a few from the Euro-American tradition. In Greek mythology, cannibalism of the Olympians, especially of an oedipal strain, taints the very origin of civilization. Cronus devours all his offspring, until Zeus escapes to usurp the power of the father. Euripides's *The Bacchae* dramatizes the revenge of a scorned Dionysus, who tricks Agave, in a frenzied state, to dismember her own son Pentheus. Centuries later, Shakespeare articulates anti-Semitism in the character of Shylock in *The Merchant of Venice*, the Jewish usurer who demands a pound of flesh close to the heart if the debt is unpaid. Characterizing Jews with the twin sins of usury and cannibalism, Shakespeare masks Christian resentment against Jews, whom George Steiner calls the "bad conscience" of the Western world. In addition to the politically incorrect Shakespeare, Jonathan Swift's "A Modest Proposal" (1728) proposes, tongue-in-cheek, solving the Irish problem by selling Irish one-year-olds as meat to the English landlords, "who, as they have already devoured most of the parents, seem to have the best title to the children." Of course, cannibalism is not pure academic, theoretical parlance, for even in our modern, "civilized" times, news or rumors of cannibalism continue to reach us. A few examples of such news include the 1846 Donner Party in the Sierra Nevada, the 1972 crash of an Uruguayan Air Force plane in the Andes, the 1970s dictatorship of Idi Amin in Uganda, and Jeffrey Dahmer in Milwaukee in the early 1990s. The last one unwittingly promotes Anthony Hopkins's *Silence of the Lambs* (1991), based on Thomas Harris's 1988 novel. But, of course, the literal or symbolic eating of fellow human beings is found in any civilization at any given time.

The twentieth century and modern literature invariably silhouette themselves against the primitive other, for instance, the Dark Continent and cannibalistic practice in Joseph Conrad's *Heart of Darkness* (1903). Africa comes to infect the sanity of the white man Kurtz in this narrative. The protagonist Marlow is greeted by a grotesque sight upon entry into Kurtz's territory: "and there it was, black, dried, sunken, with closed eyelids—a head that seemed to sleep at the top of that pole, and with the shrunken dry lips showing a narrow white line of the teeth, was smiling, too, smiling continuously at some endless and jocose dream of that eternal slumber" (85). Although only the head is visible in *Heart of Darkness* and there is no direct evidence of the body having been consumed, Reay Tannahill's *Flesh and Blood: A History of the Cannibal Complex* (1975), a light, humorous exegesis of cannibalism in human history, yokes together "rituals of cannibalism, blood drinking, and headhunting" (2). Tannahill links headhunting with cannibalism by suggesting that "headhunting was almost invariably accompanied by a cannibalism" (169), with no more evidence than the presumed level of barbarity required by both endeavors. Conrad's description of Kurtz, nonetheless, conflates the colonialist with the colonized. Kurtz appropriates African resources and lays waste the jungle, and is in turn wasting away. A capitalist perversion of the mythic uroboros chewing its own tail in a circle, the dying Kurtz "open[ed] his mouth wide—it gave him a weirdly voracious aspect, as though he had wanted to swallow all the air, all the earth, all the men before him" (87).

While anthropophagism has remained a monstrosity that symbolizes the ultimate horror of the unknown other, Conrad illustrates that an ideological, postcolonial dimension lodges squarely in the heart of cannibalism, which propels one to read Freud's myth against Edward W. Said's politics in *Orientalism* (1978). Juxtaposing the two thinkers, one is immediately struck by the commensurability of Freudian cannibalism and postcolonialism, specifically the dynamics between the West and the Orient. "Orientalism is a style of thought," proposes Said in his groundbreaking book, "based upon an ontological and epistemological distinction made between 'the Orient' and (most of the time) 'the Occident'" (2). Repeatedly he claims that the Orient does not exist other than in Western discourse, nor does the Orient equate with the geographical non-West. Orientalist texts, to Said, are representations rather than "'natural' depictions of the Orient" (21); they are concerned with the "exteriority" of the Orient. But when Said adds that Europe sets itself off "against the Orient as a sort of surrogate and even underground self" (3), he points away from an oppositional, adversarial, or mutually exclusive relationship between the West and the Orient. Rather, he identifies a symbiosis, with a sense of self-reflexivity shot through the manifest and hegemonic as well as the subterranean and repressed half. On the one hand, the imperialist instinct drives the West to study and hence gain control of the Orient. On the other, the contrapuntal instinct leads the West to absorb, to identify with, and to *be* the Orient. Granted, the two complementary instincts result in disastrous consequences: colonizers' "civilizing mission" projects their own paranoia and savagery onto the colonized; present-day multiculturalism and globalism are subtle ways to "manage" US minorities and to forge or fabricate a New World Order. But the antipathy as well as the sympathy between West and East seems readily apparent.

Nourished by Freud's theory on psychic identification and "recent studies of imperialism and 'colonial discourse'" on cannibalism, Maggie Kilgour explores this paradox of the eater and the eaten within the context of canonical writers and the

Christian symbol of Communion (*From Communion* 5). Kilgour contends that the ambivalence embodied in the Eucharist when "both God and man play 'host'" (15) actually denotes human beings' "attempt to eliminate any remaining external remnant, to turn . . . the outside inside, [and it] suggests that at the basis of the dualism is a nostalgia for total unity and oneness. . . . I [Kilgour] hope to explore the ways in which antitheses support totalizing systems by showing how the inside/outside division presupposes a lost state of total inwardness . . . a nostalgia for a state of total incorporation that underlies many of the major trends of Western thought: idealism, scientific rationalism, traditional psychoanalysis, as well as imperialism, and theories in general which try to construct a transcendental system or imagine a single body that could contain all meaning" (5). Kilgour goes on to point out that "like the doctrine of the Trinity and the incarnation, the Eucharist is a paradoxical relation involving the simultaneous identification and differentiation of opposites. It is a banquet at which host and guest can come together without one subsuming the other, as both eat and are eaten" (79). Despite the metaphysical tenor of her argument, Kilgour also sounds a cautionary note in terms of "physical" reality, that is, power differentials. Although eating suggests "total identity between eater and eaten," it also entails, as Kilgour writes, "total control—the literal consumption—of the latter by the former" (7).

Parallel to the Western tradition, China has developed its own history of food metaphors. Indeed, so integral a role does food play in Chinese culture that the daily greeting is "Have you eaten yet?," a preoccupation the author of "The Biography of Li Shi-qi" in *The Book of Han* of the fifth century A.D. must have shared when he wrote, "The emperor depends on the people; the people depend on food," or, literally translated, "The emperor sees the people as the Heaven; the people see food as the Heaven." The latter phrase, *minyishi weitian* ("The people see food as the Heaven"), is found on the lips of any Chinese. Even earlier, in the first century B.C., Sima Qian in "The Biography of Xian Yu" from *Shi Ji* (*Selections from Records of the Historian*) writes the memorable "Others are the meat cleaver and the chopping board, I am the fish and meat," an adage any average Chinese would use. Gang Yue in *The Mouth that Begs: Hunger, Cannibalism, and the Politics of Eating in Modern China* (1999) dissects "*chi*, the Chinese word for 'eating,'" as "the mouth that begs" and one that "encompasses a far broader semantic and discursive field and possesses more generative and transformative capacities than its English counterpart" (11). Referring to the long tradition of the grotesque from *The Book of Hills and Seas* to the sixteenth-century *The Journey to the West*, Yue asserts that "a central feature of this genre is the fantastic image of the human-eating monsters and demons that at once stands for the insatiable hunger of the outside world and stimulates artistic imagination" (26). Throughout the history of Chinese literature, the literati's poetry tradition erases cannibalism, whereas the mass, popular genre of fiction unequivocally features it. *The Journey to the West* follows the journey of Tripitaka from China to India, protected by the half-human, half-beast Monkey, Pigsy, and Sandy against an army of monsters, which all clamor for a piece of Tripitaka's flesh, said to bring longevity. The nefarious innkeepers in the sixteenth-century *All Men Are Brothers* by Shi Nai'an and Luo Guanzhong are said to peddle human-flesh buns to their guests. (*All Men Are Brothers* 107; see also John and Alex Dent-Young's 1994 translation *The Tiger Killers: Part Two of The Marshes of Mount Liang*). With regard to colonialism and the collapse of traditional society, a common phrase to describe the dividing up of the late Qing dynasty by foreign powers is "silkworm nibbles; whale swallows."

Cannibalistic metaphors provide a bridge between Asian and Asian American studies, transferring the Asian colonial condition to the US-American neocolonial domination of Orientals. Ethnic scholarship often analyzes the relationship of consumption, specifically, the discrepancies between the multicultural fallacy of the white eater to incorporate the other and the pang of the Asian American morsel. The Chinese American playwright Frank Chin has long championed the provocative view of "food pornography," minority survival—even prosperity—by means of capitalizing on majority expectations. Sau-ling Cynthia Wong, in *Reading Asian American Literature: From Necessity to Extravagance* (1993), defines "food pornography" culturally as "reifying perceived cultural differences and exaggerating one's otherness in order to gain a foothold in a white-dominated social system." Wong likens it to prostitution, but with a key change: "superficially, food pornography appears to be a promotion, rather than a vitiation or devaluation, of one's ethnic identity" (55). Examples of food pornography are, alas, too numerous to catalogue, from the host of the TV show *Yan Can Cook* to many other Oriental celebrities. Martin Yan, for instance, is the host who sports the persona of a perennial alien, or a house guest in white hegemony, entertaining with his antics and embarrassing pidgin, serving up for the duration of the show his clownish self and "Orientalness." These performers' personal success perpetuates stereotypes more effectively than any yellowface Charlie Chan or Fu Manchu could as a result of their presumed authenticity.

Wong turns food into her overarching thesis in *Reading Asian American Literature*. Wong's subtitle stems from Kingston's *The Woman Warrior* (1976), where immigrant parents are "big eaters" out of necessity and American-born children extravagant "treat lovers." Casting a wide net over Asian American literature, Wong conducts an exhaustive study on symbols of food: Joy Kogawa's *Obasan* (1982), where "stone bread" suppresses the Japanese Canadians' World War II sufferings; Lonny Kaneko's "The Shoyu Kid" (1976), where a boy prostitutes himself for sweets at an internment camp; the donut making woman in Toshio Mori's prelapsarian or pre-internment *Yokohama, California* (1949); the pigeon bone-savoring parents in Fae Myenne Ng's "A Red Sweater" (1986); and many more. Possibly due to her avowed objective to shun "de-Americaniz[ing]" Asian American literature and to stress its "grounding in American historical experiences" ("Denationalization Reconsidered" 9), Wong does not investigate Asian influences on the recurring theme of what she calls "quasi-cannibalism." It is perhaps presumptuous to subsume in *Reading Asian American Literature* Joy Kogawa from north of the border, hence folding the whole array of issues within Canadian ethnic writings into the term "America," which stands for the United States. In fact, much has been done in theorizing the Canadian ethnic condition that merits a closer look. Steven Tötösy de Zepetnek, Asma Sayed, and Domenic A. Beneventi's "Selected Bibliography of Work on Canadian Ethnic Minority Writing" is an exhaustive collection of publications in the field (for relevant work, see, in particular, Aponiuk; Blodgett; Chao; Dimić; Gunew; Mukherjee; Tötösy de Zepetnek, "Literary Theory," "The Importance"). Further, Lien Chao's *Beyond Silence: Chinese Canadian Literature in English* (1998) has indeed broken the silence on ethnic and minority cultures and literatures. Tseen-ling Khoo's *Banana Bending: Asian-Australian and Asian-Canadian Literatures* (2003) moves toward an approach in linking two English-speaking countries with problematics at variance with the hegemony of US scholarship with regard to multicultural literature.

Whereas each of the three modern cannibals has developed eating habits somewhat independently, such habits entail partaking and, subconsciously, being partaken by the other. Cannibalism is abominable and titillating exactly because of this horror of indeterminacy: modernity turns into monstrosity; batmen drink blood yet the count (cunt) suckles Lucy Westenra in Bram Stoker; Lu Xun's madman is perhaps the sanest Chinese; chow mein is made of Asian (American) flesh. This duality characterizes Anglo-American batmen, such as Dracula and the young Hannibal Lecter, both hailing from Central and Eastern Europe, with the latter accompanied by Gong Li in *Hannibal Rising* (2007). The two Asian (American) guests inhabit similar borderlands. On the Asian shore of the Pacific Ocean, Lu Xun's and Chanwook Park's madmen arise at the juncture of East meets West, or tradition meets modernity, leaving males symbolically castrated and females demonized, even vampirized in Park's short film *Cut*. On the American shore, caught within the mainstream culture, Cathy Song, Wayne Wang, and David Wong Louie fashion an Asian American identity by way of culinary tropes, challenging and reinscribing Orientalist representations, prostituting themselves in the manner of "food pornography." To combat disenfranchisement, Asian American writers mummify, that is, desiccate and immortalize, their purported Asianness.

Batmen

The unease over indeterminacy hinges on transgressiveness against boundaries, most familiar to Western readers in terms of the Dracula folklore. Bram Stoker's 1897 *Dracula* pinpoints this belief: "He may not enter anywhere at the first, unless there be someone of the household who bid him to come; though afterwards he can come as he please" (240). Count Dracula's arrival in England is prepared by his first victim Jonathan Harker, a solicitor who locates for Dracula the estate of Carfax (*Quatre Face*, four cardinal points of a compass that points to one direction only, like a homing pigeon). Another of Dracula's victims, Lucy Westenra, may resist, but someone close to Lucy subconsciously extends the invitation. Lucy's mother, Mrs. Westenra, removes garlic on the windows to let a "whole myriad of little specks . . . come blowing in" (143), the dust and ashes that is Dracula's true form. Mrs. Westenra's final gesture in life consists of tearing off Lucy's garlic wreath to give the opening to Dracula's kiss of death. Following Stoker, many critics note that Dracula's victim must make some inviting move. James B. Twitchell elaborates: "she must unhasp the window, open the door, do anything that shows she is acceding, even slightly . . . for the vampire cannot cross a threshold without this invitation" (*The Living Dead* 10). This impulse for transgression motivates both victimizer and victim, on-screen and off. That generations of moviegoers continue to enjoy the blood ritual proves that Dracula embodies our own wish fulfillment.

A case in point: near the finale to the 1931 classic *Dracula* starring Béla Lugosi, viewers gaze, voyeuristically, at Castle Dracula with its vaguely Turkish, vagina- or sesame-shaped pointed arches and catenary curve of the grand staircase. The set is reminiscent of the palace in the 1924 silent film *The Thief of Bagdad*, an early Orientalist production. On the curving stairs at Castle Dracula, the audience witnesses the alien master command his female victim Mina to descend as well as strangle his servant Renfield. On the one hand, victims on-screen lose themselves in a trance of heterosexual control and homosexual, in Georges Bataille's term for orgasmic ecstasy, "little death" (see *Death and Sensuality*). On the other, the audience off-screen is mesmerized by cinematographic eroticism, the treasures inside the vagina revealed through a double "Open sesame!" of the camera aperture and the vaginal arches and stairs. Within the Orientalist architectural void are Dracula and Mina, the West's nightmare of and attraction to the East. Hence, masculinity and femininity, heterosexuality and homosexuality, living and undead, Orientalism and Englishness are hybridized. Drawing from Julia Kristeva, Jerrold Hogle likens Dracula to "the most primal, and thus the most abject-ed, state in *Powers of Horror*: the moment of birth where the emerging infant is half-inside and half-outside the mother, partly dead and partly alive (arguably, 'un-dead'), in a liminal 'either/or' of which we retain dim somatic memories" ("Stoker's" 206-07).

The in-between designation of "undead" or *nosferatu* merely tinkers with the ultimate unknown, for Dracula is death, coming and going in the shape of biblical ashes and dust. Dracula enters window and door crevices as flecks of dust. Once he is killed, he crumbles to dust. The strongest evidence to identify him as death is the absence of image in the reflection. Death means the voiding of life or the becoming of what we know as nothing; therefore, Dracula fails to show himself, which is nonexistent anyway, on a blank mirror. By definition, nothing is beyond words and, finding total emptiness unendurable, Stoker makes something out of nothing, or the undead Dracula out of death. Even a messenger of death, as ghastly as he may be, is more imaginable than death itself. Nevertheless, whenever Dracula appears, Stoker's language is obfuscated, through layers of rhetorical veils. Mina witnesses the sleep-walking Lucy close to an unidentifiable being, a "something": "it seems to be as though something dark stood behind the seat where the white figure shone, and bent over it. What it was, whether man or beast, I could not tell," reiterated soon as "there was undoubtedly something, long and black, bending over the half-reclining white figure" (90). Yet a second sighting of Dracula comes in equally fuzzy terms: "seated on [Lucy's] window-sill, was something that looked like a good-sized bird" (94). Lucy's own diary testifies to the same equivocation: "the boughs or bats or something flapped almost angrily against the window-panes" (135). Lucy's last memorandum in effect tells Dracula for what it is, which is nothing: "I went to the window and looked out, but could see nothing, except a big bat" (142).

Casting Dracula as the undead "something" rather than the incomprehensible death or nothing nudges him toward a positionality between life and death, West and East, culminating in his role as an alien. Stoker does encourage a reading of alien invasion: Dracula sees himself in England as a "stranger in a strange land, he is no one" (20). "No one" alludes as much to the nullification of selfhood in death as to a fall in social status. Throughout his career, Dracula cannot cross bodies of water by himself; therefore, he is loath to emigrate. In fact, he never does. Once in England, he turns the isle into Castle Dracula as he sleeps in an "earth-box" covered with home soil, like a corpse, which is the quintessential homebody, never venturing away from the domicile—even in exile. Dracula also turns Britons into vampires, hence assimilating the English instead of being assimilated. What Dracula demands is to remake others in his image, no less than an anti-Genesis. Rather than the absolutism of death, Dracula is modified to embody a struggle between East and West, death and life. To set the stage for the clash, Stoker opens *Dracula* (1897) with Jonathan Harker's journal: "The impression I had was that we were leaving the West and entering the East; the most Western of splendid bridges over the Danube, which is here of noble width and depth, took us among the traditions of Turkish rule" (1). Harker believes that he is going among descendants of "Attila and the Huns" (2). Through this bridge across Strauss's *The Blue Danube*, Harker steps beyond, of his own will, the threshold, heralding the coming of the anti-Christ (Garber, *Vice Versa* 102). The threshold experience repeats itself immediately at the Borgo Pass, where Harker boards Dracula's carriage and, throughout the novel, in the trances between wakefulness and dream, life and death, when victims fall prey to Dracula. These trances proliferate in episodes revolving around somnambulism and hypnotism. Sleep-walking brings Lucy Westenra, whose surname contains the West, into Dracula's fold. To combat this, Mina Harker is hypnotized to gain information on Dracula's whereabouts. Both women serve as the battlefield for seemingly antagonistic males. Just as the maiden's neck to be bitten is the portal between head and body, reason and passion, her body provides the bridge for homoerotic men to reach one another, exchanging bodily fluids suggested by blood transfusion from the Crew of Light of four gentlemen—Van Helsing, Seward, Arthur Holwood, and Quincey Morris—to the damsel in distress, Lucy. Toward the end of the novel, when the Crew of Light is in hot pursuit of Dracula back into the Orient, four suitors in disguise as vengeance, Mina's mind hypnotized—rather than Lucy's body—functions as the conduit for the wooers and the wooed to rendezvous.

All such borderlands nominally highlight the fierce combat between the army of darkness led by Dracula from the East and the Crew of Light led by Dr. Van Helsing of Amsterdam, apparently from the West. But even the name Helsing can be construed as Hell sings. The arsenal Van Helsing imports from his native Netherlands to fight Dracula is a combination of Christian iconography such as the Sacrament and Transylvanian lore such as garlic flowers. Moreover, Van Helsing's awkward English and quirky personality turn the fearsome vampire slayer into a clown discoursing on "King Laugh," the allegorical figure for laughter or the comic spirit (175). Much of *Dracula*'s power derives from such narrative ambivalence, as Stoker deploys rhetorical devices of oxymorons and paradoxes to underscore the doubleness whenever Dracula meets his victims. Dracula descends upon his victims amid a trance, the equivalent of the narcotic-induced drowsiness Van Helsing produces in his patient. A trance is a mental state marked by both heightened and deadened senses, whereby one perceives with perspicuity or is deluded. As such, Dracula and his horde always appear in an oblique, suggestive way. When Jonathan Harker is aroused by the three voluptuous vampiresses, he "l[ies] quiet, looking out under [his] eyelashes in an agony of delightful anticipation . . . [he] was afraid to raise [his] eyelids, but looked out and saw perfectly under the lashes" (38). The extrasensory perception to penetrate eyelashes and even eyelids is shared by Mina Harker, Jonathan's wife, who, as Dracula approaches, "could see through [her] eyelids . . . The mist grew thicker and thicker . . . a sort of pillar of cloud . . . through it all came the scriptural words 'a pillar of cloud by day and of fire by night'" (258-59). The earlier obfuscation of Jonathan's seeing through eyelashes gives way to seeing through eyelids, as the pretension of realistic portrayal is replaced by the reality of psychosomatic discernment. In Mina's "pillar of cloud" and consistently throughout the novel, Stoker resorts to biblical references to underline the parodic yet symmetrical nature of Dracula's realm.

In reference to Dracula, the heavy biblical ring serves to demonize him, turning him into the opposite of Christ. Such rhetoric yokes together the sacred and sacrilegious. At first blush, Stoker appears to valorize Christianity, which triumphs in the end. Yet the narrative disavows neither party, with the evil intensified tenfold due to its kinship to the virtuous. The zoophagous madman Renfield is none other than the anti-John the Baptist paving the way for the anti-Christ. Renfield's refrain, "for the blood is the life" draws from the admonition against unclean blood in Deuteronomy 12: 23, but rituals of blood sucking reverse the interdiction by consuming the blood—the life or the spirit—and leaving untouched the flesh, which becomes an automaton under Dracula's spell. Even the central set of the novel forms a Blakean "fearful symmetry" between dark religion and enlightening science. Dracula's lair in London, Carfax with its old chapel, is adjacent to Dr. Seward's (in charge of the sewer of the human mind?) mental institution from which Renfield flees in search of his "Lord and Master" next door (279). Dr. Seward, one of the Crew of Light, beseeches his own mentor and master Van Helsing to attend to Lucy's strange anemia. In addition to the Christian overlay to demonize and paradoxically glorify Dracula, the Count situates himself in a limbo of modern capitalist economy and of sexual orientation. The Count not only figuratively counts money but also puns with "cunt," the vulgar slang for femininity. At least twice in the novel is Dracula explicitly coupled with money. In Dracula's room lies a heap of gold (47). When Jonathan slashes

Dracula's coat, gold and bank-notes fall out. Making his getaway, Dracula manages to grasp "a handful of the money from the floor." Hurling himself through the window, Dracula's fall is accompanied by "the 'ting' of the gold, as some of the sovereigns fell on the flagging" (306). The sovereignty or monarchy from Transylvania indeed flags or wanes as his gold scatters.

Just as Dracula superimposes feudal aristocracy with capitalist commodity, he blurs heterosexuality and homosexuality, sadism and tender love. Ken Gelder likens Dracula's nightly visits to "nocturnal emissions," a theory developed by Ernest Jones's *On the Nightmare* (1929), where blood substitutes for semen (67). Drawing from Jones, Gelder writes: "The vampire's 'exhausting love embrace' is complicated by forms of sexual perversity which return to the primitive world of infantilism. The chief form is oral sadism—where sucking (love) turns into biting (hate)" (*Reading the Vampire* 67). Gelder proceeds to analyze Dr. Seward's two diverging witness accounts of the "primal scene" between Dracula and Mina, the first account sadistic and the second affectionate. Echoing the Freudian primal scene of parents' intercourse witnessed by the child, the father is both hurting and loving the mother (72). Gelder also sees the Crew of Light creating an "erotic triangle," "where men can touch each other only through the woman" (76), referring to the blood suckings and subsequent blood transfusions. Needless to say, this triangle is founded by Dracula. Yet in Van Helsing's comic rendition, a heterosexual front is kept up in that the blood transfusions make Lucy a "polygamist" (59) or "polyandrist" (176), ignoring the polygamist community of men.

To elucidate the Dracula mystery, Marie Mulvey-Roberts sees female menstruation where Jones sees male ejaculation: "A conflation between menarche and sexual knowledge is made in a Victorian euphemism for the menses, as when a mother asks her daughter if she has received a visitor in the middle of the night" ("*Dracula*" 82). Positing homoeroticism, Mulvey-Roberts is not bound by Stoker's apparent gender, as she cites Stoker's letter to Whitman: "How sweet a thing it is for a strong healthy man with a woman's eyes and a child's wishes to feel that he can speak so to a man who can be . . . wife to his soul." Stoker further thanks Whitman for the love and sympathy he has given him "in common with my kind" (80). Mulvey-Roberts concludes that "Dracula is a hybrid of both male and female characteristics. Breeding and bleeding are functions of both women and vampires" (83). Maggie Kilgour seconds that "vampirism is a perverse form of reproduction; like the other forms of 'unnatural' sexuality the text flirts with—various vampiric forms of oral sex and homosexuality—it is a substitute for 'natural' procreation" ("Vampiric Arts" 58).

Stoker's enthrallingly ambiguous story has led to a legion of literary and filmic retellings, many of which discuss Dracula as an Orientalized monster. Laurence A. Rickels writes in *The Vampire Lectures* that "the history (the hysteria!) of Europe has always covered for the West making a move on the East. What is Back East, however, comes into focus as a potential total threat to the West . . . Vlad the Impaler: monstrous Eastern European subhuman" (11). Matthew Gibson, in *Dracula and the Eastern Question,* maintains that Transylvania "represent[s] the fear of 'reverse colonisation'" (69), where Dracula poses as an "unidentified . . . racial Other," "an abstracted conflict of Orient against Occident," and the "Ottomanised European" (70). Priscilla L. Walton, in *Our Cannibals, Ourselves,* identifies the protagonist in Francis Ford Coppola's 1992 film as an "Orientalist Dracula" without bothering to detail his specific Orientalist traits (79-80). Some critics, such as William Hughes and Andrew Smith, inspired by Jules Zanger, assert that Count Dracula, with his "hook nose" and "pointed beard," resembles the stereotype of the Jew (Introduction 4). Ken Gelder agrees in linking Dracula with anti-Semitism, the influx of Jews into London from Eastern Europe, and their alleged hording of money and gold (13-17). Of these interpretations, artistic and critical, one art-house film stands out not only in its cannibalizing multiple genres, much as the novel itself omnivorizes narrative strategies of all kinds, but also in its deliberate casting of an "Oriental" for Dracula—Guy Maddin's *Dracula: Pages from a Virgin's Diary* (2003). In "Fire and Ice," Steven Shaviro characterizes Maddin's filmic style as melodramatic, one that deploys "the backlighting, the shadows, the frontal close-ups, the figures in silhouette, the arbitrary jump-cuts." All these techniques lead to, Shaviro muses, Maddin's "entirely non-functional" images and "a cinema of spectacle" (216). Furthermore, Shaviro finds "anachronism" in Maddin, who often goes back to silent films with title cards, a stagey set, "exaggerated gestures," and "gratuitous details" (218). All these traits stand Maddin in good stead in his production of the ballet *Dracula*, since ballet is a stylized performance art, like silent film, without dialogue and sound, except an accompanying orchestra. *Dracula* is a filmic rendition of the ballet by Mark Godden, performed by the Royal Winnipeg Ballet, including Zhang Wei-qiang for the lead role. According to Lyndon W. Joslin in *Count Dracula Goes to the Movies* (2006), the first intertitle in this retro silent film heralds the imminent arrival of Dracula, played by the Chinese-looking Zhang, hence the coming of the yellow peril. In Gothic-lettered tabloid headlines, the screen screams "IMMIGRANTS!!" "OTHERS!" "FROM OTHER LANDS!" "From the East!" What Joslin misses is that "From the Sea!" follows the preceding headlines, further underscoring the otherworldly, alien quality of the newcomer. It also implies an ambiguous longing for the origin of life in the ocean or the womb. While these intertitles are montaged with the psychotic Renfield's raving and the ballerina Lucy's erotic moves, one particular close-up of Zhang the Dracula reposing inside a wooden box en route to England is presented, provocatively, between the first two intertitles "IMMIGRANTS!!" and "OTHERS!" Dracula is on a ship that brings rats and plague, as in F.W. Murnau's 1922 *Nosferatu*, or an Oriental, as in Maddin. The opening credit rolls with Renfield howling behind bars: "Master is coming," which echoes Stoker's "I shall be patient, Master. It is coming—coming—coming!" (103), as if master and slave unite in an orgasm. In his tongue-in-cheek style, the idiosyncratic Canadian auteur also satirizes white paranoia over Asian immigrants throughout Canadian history, especially during the Hong Kong exodus of 1997 and the spread of SARS around the millennium (Joslin 148).

Joslin finds the film saturated with a "sexual aura," which peaks at the castle, or the final crypt scene, where "doors are shaped inescapably like vaginas" (150). These doors are the pointed, sesame-shaped arches we see in *The Thief of Bagdad*, the 1931 *Dracula,* and, earlier in the film, at the convent dance. Likening a Catholic convent to Dracula's crypt is consistent with Maddin's overall strategy of equating light and darkness, or the vampire and Van Helsing, the vampire slayer. Even the choice of filming the ballet in black and white brings out the contrapuntal, doppelgänger nature of the psychodrama. In a film that is otherwise a swath of gray, only three colors stand out: blood red, money green, and gold coins. Red exudes as much from the bite marks on the virgin's neck as from Dracula when he "breastfeeds" Mina from an opened vein and when he is impaled with a phallic stake. The blood transfusion prosecuted by the Crew of Light to save a damsel in distress comes across like a gang rape; one wonders whether it is blood or semen being pumped into her. On the other hand, gold coins seep out of Dracula's body and green paper notes flutter out of his coffin when they are ripped open. The Marxist identification of vampire capitalism is heavy-handedly advanced in a Brechtian move of epic theater. Seemingly a gratuitous detail incompatible with the melodramatic, erotic tenor of the film, the green and gold are so shocking and blatantly "ideological" that it achieves the alienation effect of compelling viewers to think beyond the vampire myth, to bridge blood sucking with money grubbing, and red with green and gold. Despite being the namesake for the film, Zhang Wei-qiang makes few appearances, in part to cultivate his lurking, mysterious persona. The two *pas de deux* with Lucy and with Mina and the concluding death scene in the hands of Van Helsing the Impaler and his henchmen, including a rehabilitated Mina, are the extent of his performance. After *Dracula*, Zhang seems to have vanished into the dark night behind the constellation of ballerinas and male leads, landing no other major roles. For performers of Asian ancestry in the West, they may be as pivotal as yeast in food preparation in shaping the art in which they are cast, and as negligible.

Madmen

Deemed the beginning of modern Chinese literature, Lu Xun's "Diary of a Madman" (1918) has turned the literary lineage of anthropophagic tropes into a critique against four thousand years of Chinese tradition, which cannibalizes the Chinese as the catchphrase *lijiao chiren* (traditional rituals and moral tenets eating people) accuses around the turn of the last century (Lee, *Voices from the Iron House* 54). Lu Xun is far from the only writer who draws from this cannibalistic metaphor in depicting the Chinese tradition. Ba Jin's *Family* (1931) likewise depicts "Cannibal Confucian Morality" (7). While the West makes no explicit appearance in this tale, the protagonist's paranoia is caused by the collapse of China in the face of Western modernity. Indeed, that the West remains invisible and omnipresent can be construed as proof of its supremacy. The ultimate irony of Lu Xun and nearly all the ensuing Asian madmen, including those from the Korean Wave and Ha Jin's *The Crazed*

(2002), lies in the reversal: the handful of madmen are symptomatic of Asia's pathology under the duress and in the frenzy of Westernization and modernization. Indeed, the metaphor of disease preoccupies not only "Diary" but the entire collection of short stories *Na Han* (*Call to Arms* 1923) in which "Diary" is included, from the preface's reminiscences of the illness and death of Lu Xun's father to China's disintegration, from the individual to the collective, from the physical to the psychological. Stylistically, Lu Xun's "Diary" reflects this personal and national malady as a yawning schism. Whereas the preface to "Diary" is in classical Chinese, the diary entries themselves are in vernacular Chinese, advocated by the May Fourth Movement of 1919 to promote literary modernization, which is literature's attempt to keep up with the promulgation of Western science and technology in other spheres. The madman's persecution complex begins when he suspects a conspiracy against him after inadvertently treading on "Ku Chiu (Ancient Times) account sheets" two decades before (8). The symptoms deteriorate as he discovers that not only the villagers but his own family members have acquired the physiognomy of typical Chinese demons, looking "Green-faced, long-toothed" and eating "heart and liver" (9). Far from delusion, the protagonist is struck by visions of a mad prophet, as the title "*kuangren*" suggests. Instead of calling him "*fengren*," a common way to refer to mental instability, Lu Xun chooses "*kuang*," which, as Xiaobing Tang analyzes in *Chinese Modern* (2000), implies "the ecstatic" (58), and, one might add, the visionary.

Likewise, "Medicine" (1919) revolves around an alleged magic cure for consumptives, which turns out to be the blood from a recent beheading. Considering the tumultuous late Qing and early Republic setting, the beheaded happens to be a revolutionary. The blood of a martyr fails to save a China gradually wasting away; likewise, the tuberculous patient dies and is buried alongside the revolutionary. Leo Ou-fan Lee, in *Voices from the Iron House,* probes into the significance of surnames in "Medicine." The consumptive is Hua, and the revolutionary Xia. Jointly, their names constitute Hua-Xia, the ancient name for China. Consistent with the thrust of "yEast for Modern Cannibals," the characters unwittingly perpetrate endocannibalism, one part of China eating the other part and both dying together. The most comical of Lu Xun's Asian madmen is depicted in "The True Story of Ah Q" (1921). The protagonist is stripped of subjectivity to the extent that he goes around as an English alphabet in the shape of a blank, featureless face with a hair queue epitomizing the national shame of the late Qing dynasty (Lee, *Voices from the Iron House* 76). Such disgrace presupposes surrogates, if not the presence, of the West, such as a village "imitation foreign devil" who had studied "in a foreign school in the city" and "gone to Japan." Upon his return, he walked with his legs "straight and his pigtail had disappeared" (77). (The illustration to Peking's Foreign Languages Press edition of *Selected Stories of Lu Hsun* [1960], translated by Yang Hsien-yi and Gladys Yang, further Westernizes this imitation foreign devil's image. He is drawn in a Western suit, a top hat, and a cane. Only the last item is mentioned, obliquely, in Lu Xun's text. In Norton's reissue of the Foreign Languages Press edition in 2003, all five illustrations are deleted. "Mr. Foreigner" is blamed for Ah Q's dilemma of not having been allowed to join the revolutionaries (103). Toward the end of the story, Ah Q is shocked by the village spectators lining the road as he is paraded to the execution ground for a crime he did not commit. Recalling a hungry wolf in the mountains years ago, Ah Q finds the villagers' "eyes more terrible than the wolf's: dull yet penetrating eyes that, having devoured his words, still seemed eager to devour something beyond his flesh and blood. . . . These eyes seemed to have merged into one, biting into his soul" (111-12). An asinine coward all his life, either Ah Q acquires exceptional insights in the eleventh hour tantamount to a deathbed conversion or the author finally breaks his ironic detachment to rail against China's cannibal collective.

Likewise, "The New Year's Sacrifice" (1924) depicts a maid sacrificed by the Chinese patriarchy—sold, abused, humiliated, rendered "unclean" to service the Chinese New Year ancestral worship. This maid is so taken in by other women's—not men's—tales of horror in afterlife that she follows their advice and purchases "a threshold [at the Tutelary God's Temple] to be your substitute, so that thousands of people can walk over it and trample on it, in order to atone for your sins" (141). Individual ignorance is indicted along with communal superstition, both appalling to modern readers. The ironic tone in which these tales are narrated derives from Lu Xun's modern sensibility, closely allied with the absent yet ubiquitous West, one allegedly marked by reason and individual agency, qualities missing in old China's madmen and madwomen. Lu Xun's Western modernity comes mediated by way of Japan, where he studied from 1902 to 1909 and where he decided to take up the pen to awaken what Sun Yat-sen labeled as the subcolony of China.

Almost a century later, emanating from the postindustrial South Korea to global cinema, the Korean Wave is so fraught with anthropophagism that there is an uncanny resonance with Lu Xun. The serendipitous kinship between two nations and generations springs from the unresolved tension of modernity and tradition. The Korean sentiment of *han* (remorse and hate) is shaped by a history of colonization, a feeling of being devoured by foreign powers that harks back to Lu Xun's story on the subcolonial China in the 1910s and 1920s. Adrift in modernization and plagued by *han*, a self-torturing, self-gnawing emotion, the Korea Wave oftentimes features violence—self-abjection, self-mutilation, even incest—directed against the self and against others. Chul-Soo Park's film *301/302* (1996) explores the ambivalence of violence as manifestations of love and hate in the two female characters living in adjacent apartments, 301 and 302. Both feel so oppressed by the Korean patriarchy that they turn hate inward, the anorexic neighbor sacrificing herself as cooking materials for the chef to create her magnum opus. As the chef savors her neighbor, the montaging of the two creates the illusion that both are the eater, inherent in the title's merging of their apartment numbers. Wedded as one, the two females exhibit repressed, displaced lesbianism, which becomes violence against women due to the inability to dislodge patriarchy.

Unequivocally, the Korean master of cannibalism is Chanwook Park, whose revenge trilogy is laced with consumption of the human body, literally. *Sympathy for Mr. Vengeance* (2002) follows the botched abduction and ransom committed by a laid-off laborer, Ryu. Ryu first tries to sell his kidney, only to wake up from anesthesia stripped naked, minus his kidney, with no monetary payment. Executing his retaliation against society, he ends up disposing of not only his abducted victim but also himself. Ryu is dismembered by the victim's father, who, in turn, is stabbed to death. The cycle of violence ensures that exocannibalism is endocannibalism. The second installment of the revenge trilogy, *Oldboy* (2003), deals with a protagonist who is imprisoned for fifteen years for some unknown offense. Desire for vengeance prompts him to reiterate that he is to eat his perpetrator alive. As a warm-up, the first thing he does upon his release is to devour a large live squid, with tentacles squirming from his mouth. The finale to the trilogy, *Sympathy for Lady Vengeance* (2005), is set in part in a female prison, where a predatory inmate bullies newcomers. This inmate had earlier committed the crime of killing her husband and lover and cooking them on the backyard barbecue grill. The protagonist, Lady Vengeance, exhibiting a halo at night like the Virgin Mary's, however, restores prison justice when she pretends to attend to the cannibal, spoon feeding her bleach to eat her up from inside out.

The cannibalistic theme culminates in Chanwook Park's short feature *Cut* (2004), where the Eastern European, Orientalized monster makes its way to Korea as a Western import. What allegedly originated in the East returns to the East in the image of the West. The Orientalist Castle Dracula metamorphoses into Park's doubling of Western-style movie sets, mock-ups of a medieval castle with a chessboard floor, furnished with modern amenities. The protagonist, a film director, not only shoots his film in such a castle setting but goes home to the identical interior design. Self-referentially, the architectural detail of a chessboard floor is even repeated in the paintings hanging over the mantelpiece in the movie studio and at his castle home. The Western milieus of the castle, piano, and vampire myth at work and at home symbolize not so much the "givenness" of Western modernity in the East as the extent of entrapment and self-alienation of Asian subjects, hollow and hypocritical, whose ugly secrets are to be extracted by an intruding madman, a negligible "extra" who has appeared in the director's numerous films.

The incongruity exists as much in the film's content as in its form. The split between characters' exteriors and their inner worlds correspond to Park's style. Park's hip Gothic comic conjoins horror and comedy, their incompatibilities accentuating each other. When the vampiress in the director's film complains to her "darling" on the cell phone of an upset stomach from eating expired food, she refers wryly to the blood of a frozen, wax statue of a middle-aged man she was just sucking. As she plays piano in response to her darling's request, one suspects that it is Dracula himself, the connoisseur of refined, aristocratic tastes, that she entertains. The grotesquerie is made even more so because of its juxtaposition with art and beauty. Before she vomits what one assumes to be rancid blood onto the chessboard floor, her last few words into the cell phone and her gagging acquire the quality of a doubletalk: her sweet, fragile voice cracks and is spliced with a hoarse growl so low and menacing that it evokes male beasts in rage. Of course, Park merely follows the convention of the horror film soundtrack when the monster always seems to speak with a forked tongue. The matriarch ghoul in Tsui Hark's *The Chinese Ghost Story* (1987) switches between a coquettish female voice and an animalistic masculine roar. Jonathan Demme's *The Silence of the Lambs* (1991) features, likewise, a transvestite serial killer, whose lines prior to flaying of his victim shuttle rapidly between male vulgarity and female sentimentality. Gender indeterminacy and monstrosity surface in the layering of female and male vocal registers

Similar to Stoker's plot of blood transfusion to allow homosexual intercourse via Lucy Westenra's body, the figure of vampire yokes together Westernized, elite Koreans and the indigenous poor, both parties stained by the same blood thirst. Should the former suck dry, as Marx's famous metaphor of vampire capitalism suggests, the labor of the latter, the latter, the deranged "extra," now cuts back, symbolically castrating (binding and manipulating) the filmmaker husband and literally chopping off his pianist wife's fingers. But revenge in Park is so universal that it is infectious. Like Dracula's kiss-bite, the extra's madness spreads to the pianist, a vampiress biting the extra in the neck when he slips and falls near the piano, and to the filmmaker, equally insane as he slowly chokes his wife to death. The director's descent into lunacy is foreshadowed by his confession of hate toward his wife, whom he dismisses as "nothing," spoken in English. The fact that this is one of only three words delivered in English by the director—"cut," "extra," and "nothing"—points to a Freudian-Marxist interpretation of Dracula as fetishistic capitalism. Like the Freudian fetish, Dracula is absent yet looms large psychically. Like capital or currency, Dracula is empty yet self-proliferating and self-circulating, a nothing that is synonymous with globalization (Ritzer, *The Globalization of Nothing*). This accords well with the lore that Dracula has no reflection in the mirror: although nothing is duly reflected (or not reflected) in a physical mirror, it multiplies into every conceivable fear in everyman's mental mirror. Not only the words but the concepts they relate are foreign in origin; the resulting marriage of the West and Korea is far from a model of domestic bliss. The estranged couple feed on and are consumed by the seductive vampiric modernity.

Chow Mein

Mirroring the struggle between East and West within Asian madmen, Asian Americans exhibit identity conflicts between Asianness and Americanness, simultaneously refuting and resorting to Orientalism in the metaphors of ethnic (as) food in such works as Cathy Song's poem, Wayne Wang's film, and David Wong Louie's novel. When McGraw-Hill's *American Tradition in Literature* (1999) needs to include Asian American writers since the sixties, the editors choose Amy Tan and Cathy Song, a Korean American poet from Hawaii. The second edition of *The Norton Anthology of Modern Poetry* (1988) also includes Cathy Song as a representative Asian American poet. Let us consider Cathy Song as a representative Asian American poet in relation to the theme of cannibalism. One of the poems in her debut, *Picture Bride*

(1983), combines ethnic and anthropophagic motifs. Song opens "Chinatown" with the self-conscious stereotype: "Chinatowns: they all look alike." Although the opening points to the place rather than the people, what follows is a collage of racist clichés. Aesthetically, this poem is stunningly imagistic, each bare-bone stanza superimposing descriptive with prescriptive images: descriptive of the socioeconomic deprivation and the human conflicts in Chinatown; prescriptive of age-old Orientalist stereotypes: "Dead / center: fish eyes," "A network of yellow tumors," "bamboo chopstick tenements," "hoarding sunlight / from the neighbors / as if it were rice." Song's strategy is to seize with her poet's eyes the essence of her subject—the stifling Chinatown street scene—and fold it into Western preconceptions, whether fish eye, yellow peril, chopsticks, or rice consumption. Granted that the portrayal of old Chinatown's decay across the US is largely accurate, the poet's tone remains chillingly detached, with no apparent compassion for and identification with the urban underclass. While Song's poem amounts to a gagging, a vomiting, in order to expel the part of her Asian American self—"fish eye" and "yellow tumors"—that is undesirable, that intense self-loathing gives away how intimately she identifies with "Chinatown."

The nauseating street scenes of an "oily joint" with "roach eggs" intensify as Chinese residents merge into the general ruin. The cook Father of part 3 of the poem is in danger of chopping off his own fingers, thus graduating from preparing food to being food himself. The pregnant Mother of part 4 is swollen in the manner of "Sour plums / fermenting in dark cellars." Food imageries abound, escalating from the Father feeding guests to the Mother feeding the family and the fetus—both nearly with their own bodies, culminating in part 5 and the finale when their children are eaten: "The children are the dumplings / set afloat. . . . bobbing up to surface / in the steamy cauldron . . . Wrap the children / in wonton skins" (61-63). Reserved for special occasions, the making of dumplings and wontons are labor intensive, requiring concerted efforts of a group of people. When the family are preparing food for, say, the Chinese New Year, small coins the size of US pennies are secretly wrapped into a couple of dumplings. Whoever eats those dumplings with coins is supposed to have a lucky year. Dumplings, in other words, carry memories of childhood fun and family togetherness; in Song's poem, nonetheless, they turn into symbols of torment. Dumpling and wonton eating represent how Asian America is ruthlessly consumed by tradition. Even their escape in the concluding stanza as "incense to a strong wind" returns them to the ritual of ancestral worship.

Consistent with Song's dubious cannibalist imagism, Wayne Wang features ethnic (as) food in *Dim Sum: A Little Bit of Heart* (1985), shot in the same grainy, experimental style of *Chan Is Missing* (1981). Wang plays on the paradox of the subtitle. The literal translation of the celebrated Cantonese cuisine brings out the dilemma of the Chinese American mother-daughter relationship in the film. The subtitle suggests that food is prepared with great care and affection from the heart, but it also suggests that the human heart *is* the food. Dim Sum means not only the food they share daily but the burnt offerings of their lives for each other. The plot revolves around three characters: an unnamed, thus archetypal, immigrant mother who has been widowed for fifteen years; her daughter, Geraldine, who postpones her marriage to Richard in order to live with her mother; and Uncle Tan, a close family friend and the mother's admirer. To depict how the family members are checkmated by love for one another, Wang employs many long shots of still life, particularly the dinner table and the caged bird. Slow movement of the camera and dim lighting in the apartment similarly contribute to the atmosphere of stagnation.

The mother figure seems to be the cause of the predicament, but she declines a second marriage because of tradition and love for her dead husband. Free to criticize her decision as old-fashioned, one is made to be aware of the sacrifices the mother has made in having single-handedly raised her daughter. She rarely appears without either the sewing machine or food, implying the domestic duties that have consumed her life. Indeed, Wang's quiet, gentle style refrains from any harsh condemnation. To console a depressed Uncle Tan over the wasted years, Geraldine says: "Don't be upset. We're similar casualties." Yet her tone is not accusatory; instead, it is full of tenderness and love. The only explicit criticism of the mother comes from the man who cares for her most deeply. As the daughter moves out of the apartment, at the urging of the mother, in the middle of the film, the confused and almost pouting mother does not answer Geraldine's goodbyes. The mother gives away her longing when she, under the pretense of straightening the curtain, peeps out the window to see if Geraldine has left. Uncle Tan then points out her inconsistency of hoping Geraldine will marry and yet stay by her side. As for Geraldine, Uncle Tan jokes that "you can take the girl out of Chinatown, you can't take Chinatown out of the girl," a bodily metaphor that suggests how human lives are inextricably meshed. True enough, Geraldine returns once her mother is hospitalized—out of loneliness more than any actual illness. Uncle Tan worries about the mother so much that he drinks himself to sleep, comforted by the litany of the mother's best dishes. Just as the mother expresses her love through her cuisine, Uncle Tan reciprocates by an inventory of her dishes. The trio's mutual affection consumes one another, much as the food they partake.

The mother recovers and decides to take a last trip back to China. She intends to prepare for her own death based on a Hong Kong fortune teller's prediction that she will not live beyond the age of sixty-two. The mother returns from China happily, even boisterously. As the mother unpacks, Geraldine braces herself to tell her mother of her decision to marry Richard reached during, or because of, the mother's extended absence. But Geraldine is stopped short by the mother, who informs her that the fortune teller believes that since sixty years constitute a full cycle in Chinese lunar calendar, her life has just been renewed, and the sixty-two-year-old mother is a mere baby. Consequently, this self-serving logic goes, Geraldine does not have to consider marriage "at least until [the mother] become[s] an adult." For the first time in the film, the mother appears to be lively, almost ecstatic in her childish behavior of squeezing an ear-splitting toy and laughing in a shrill voice. Her joy juxtaposes with Geraldine's teary smile. Pleased to see that her mother has regained the will to live, Geraldine will once again put on hold her own prospect of happiness. A reversal of roles has taken place in that the daughter is now the mother, caring for the elderly woman who claims to be a two-year-old. The old China—the mother, the Hong Kong fortune teller, the lunar calendar, and the concept of filial piety—that used to nourish Geraldine turns to feed on her youth. The film concludes with shots of the bird in the cage, of the neat and tidy living room, of shoes well lined up.

Through metaphors of food as well, but in an obsessively ironic and self-reflexive voice, David Wong Louie's *The Barbarians Are Coming* (2000) probes into the minority complex of self-loathing and heightened ethnic consciousness. Louie's protagonist is Sterling Lung, the pathologically abject, hypersensitive resident chef at Richfield Ladies' Club in Connecticut, serving rich white women not only his specialty of French cuisine but also himself: "My greatest desire, the one that inspires the others, is to please my diners, that they love my food and love to take me into their bodies, into their hearts" (88-89). The urge to "make a new dish of myself" (99) stems from an escape from his background, having grown up in his parents' laundry, resenting his parents' "immigrant oddness, the square-peg-in-a-round-hole quality of their life in America" (59). To remake himself in the fashion of Western fine dining, he calls the master chef A. Auguste Escoffier "my French father." Sterling recalls Stephen in Kogawa's *Obasan* (1982), one of the interned Japanese Canadians who immerses himself in classical European music. One chooses masters' cooking, the other music, to demonstrate how thoroughly assimilated they are. The success of assimilation rests in their professional ambitions in alignment with the leisurely and, in Sau-ling Wong's terms, "extravagant" taste of the upper-middle class, a denial of the life of "necessity" of their immigrant parents: "an immigrant has no business even contemplating such a luxury as happiness . . . it was an American affectation, slipperier than Chinese luck or money lust" (Louie 289). While Stephen is a minor character marked only by his coldness toward his family, Sterling proves to be far more complex. His abjection is so irremediable as to be fetishistic: he imagines himself having intercourse with club ladies while masturbating against club house objects they use, much like the young Sterling's "crush on" the white customers of his parents' laundry (32).

His flimsy attempt to appear US-American or un-Chinese is repeatedly dashed. Club ladies insist on Chinese food, a trendier, more health-conscious form of Chinatown chow mein, despite his pedigree from the prestigious CIA, the Culinary Institute of America. When a party at the club develops into a racist discussion over the contemporary politics of the opening of China in the wake of President Nixon's visit, Sterling suddenly becomes the representative Chinese, a Long Islander believed to mangle English. Even Sterling's long hair queue, a legacy of the "Beatles, Jerry Garcia" (40), is taken to descend from the Qing dynasty. Indeed, if America symbolizes power, Sterling's pitiful life continues the history of castration of Asian males in America. Like the capon, a castrated rooster, he prepares, Sterling is the virtual houseboy at the club. Part 3 of the novel offers a point of view from Sterling's father, Genius, who reminisces about his infatuation with Lucy, a white woman with loose morals, before Zsa Zsa, his wife, joins him in New York. Although in the stereotypical image of immigrant clowns, Genius also perceives that Sterling's career is not much of an improvement over his own at the laundry. Herein lies the ambiguity of Louie's representations: his characters are a mixture of stilted stereotype and politically correct self-awareness. For instance, his Genius is stereotype incarnate but has a voice in part 3; his Sterling requires a decolonization of the mind, while growing to a stronger ethnic consciousness. By contrast, the Jewish usurer Morton Sass, Sterling's father-in-law, is as unscrupulous as Shakespeare's Shylock.

Increasingly in this novel, Sterling comes to realize that he "embraced . . . European cuisine because Escoffier wasn't home, Bliss because she wasn't home" (323), a deathly embrace of white culture, especially of white women. Sterling is compelled by circumstances to marry Bliss, a Jewish woman with an inexplicable crush on Sterling, especially in view of her "Frenchify[ing]" (300) "Lung" to "Lunge" and her sudden extramarital affair. Louie parallels Sterling's and Bliss's motives for marriage as revolts against the patriarchs in the racist stereotypes of Genius the Chinese coolie and Morton Sass the Jewish usurer. Having internalized majority views of themselves, the young couple chart a gradual return to their ethnicity with their growing roles as parents. Soon after the birth of Moses, Bliss moves back to the Sass mansion and takes up Jewish ways. Sterling's "journey home" is more torturous and protracted. Deploying Freudian metaphors, Louie implies that Sterling is married as much to Bliss as to Bliss's father. In the gentleman's room at the wedding ceremony, Morton Sass challenges the bridegroom's masculinity, resulting in an injured ring finger imagined to be covered with (bridal?) blood, onto which Morton gingerly slides the wedding band, as if it were an uxorilocal arrangement. Through his cable television, the father-in-law also puts Sterling's cooking show on the air, but *Enter the Dragon French Kitchen,* plus *The Peeking Duck* following that, cashes in on the stereotypes of Oriental food and fools, with a dash of Bruce Lee. Fleeing into the Sasses, Sterling finds himself ensnared by an essentialized notion of US-Americans of Chinese ancestry.

This improbable union between two social classes, between Jewish business mogul and Chinese laundryman, is a narcissistic fantasy, the Siamese twin to self-hate. Bliss's persistent wooing of Sterling in the face of his fancies for other women can, I suppose, be interpreted as the blindness of love, yet when Bliss meets Sterling's odd parents and when the two families finally meet at the wedding and at the funeral of their second son Ira, the Sasses are genuinely drawn to the Lungs, totally oblivious to Genius's quaint and servile mannerisms. Class and race differences are completely suppressed in order for the cannibalistic scenario to unfold; that is, by marrying into the Sasses, Sterling seeks a culmination of his self-loathing: to be eaten whole, to submerge into a non-Chinese genetic line, which is why he takes to Ira, a Morton Sass look-alike, and secretly rejects his first-born, Moses, practically a child Genius with black hair. What Sterling strives for is no less than a "genealogical suicide" (323).

The novel concludes with the deaths of Ira and Genius, the killings of one's future and one's past, of the US-Americanizing drive and the Chinese heritage. The trauma of the twin deaths opens Sterling's eyes to his self-loathing and heralds a return to Chineseness. "Decay finally has outpaced regeneration. The ongoing violence in our cells," reflects the chef on the deaths and on his profession: "I have made a career out of this violence" (354). A chef, after all, works with dead meat. The last meal the chef makes in this fiction is "Chinese" food for Moses, crackers soaked in milk and hot water, comfort food Genius used to prepare for Sterling when he was a child. The "Chinese" food consists of Western ingredients (crackers and milk) and Chinese habits (use of hot water from a pump thermos). The heirloom of Asian America is that one can turn things Western into the basis of ethnic identity by way of love and fond memories associated with the objects: a bowl of Chineseness to replenish one's ethnicity.

While Stephen in *Obasan* resembles Sterling, Joy Kogawa's Aunt Emily, politically active in seeking compensation for Japanese Canadian internees, also manifests Sterling's dubious simplification of identity, except it is the Canadian rather than the Asian half that she emphasizes. In response to her niece's claim that they are raised on the "culture clash" of "milk and Momotaro"—the latter a Japanese fairy tale of peach boy, Emily admonishes: "Not at all . . . Momotaro is a Canadian story. We're Canadian, aren't we? Everything a Canadian does is Canadian" (57). Aunt Emily chooses, in Werner Sollors's terms, consent over descent out of political exigency, whereas Sterling ends his story on a reconciliation with his family and heritage due to a sense of guilt. The ethnic (re)discovery in the form of fabricated Chinese food should be contextualized in the ever-present power relationships. The kitschy names of Genius and Zsa Zsa—à la Zsa Zsa Gabor—are given to them by Lucy, who christens not only the immigrants but their child: Lucy is the name of Genius's eldest daughter. Yet embedded in this power of naming, Louie continues to register the irony of the minority psyche: Sterling immolates and resurrects his Chineseness at once in Moses, a Hebrew prophet with a Chinese face, siring a new line of interracial "Americans."

But that new line is considered less than American, since Jews are implicitly excluded from the membership of Richfield Ladies' Club. Jewishness becomes a stand-in for whiteness only insofar as Asian Americans are concerned. A hierarchy of race can be constructed in this novel—Euro-American whites on top, followed by Jewish nouveau riche, with Chinese Americans trailing far behind. Chinese Americans, part of the model minority and dubbed the "New Jews" in the media, somehow affiliate themselves with Jews in recent literary imagination, as if Jews were more accessible than Euro-Americans. Jeffrey Paul Chan's "A Chinese in Haifa," collected in *Aiiieeeee!: An Anthology of Asian American Writers* (1974), teeters on the brink of racial strife between two Chinese American and Jewish American families, once the affair of the Chinese man and the Jewish neighbor's wife is found out. The apparent middle-class cordiality shrouds the seventies sexual liberation, whereby a Chinese can be so American as to find himself not necessarily in Haifa but inside a Jewish woman. Also set in the sixties and seventies, Gish Jen's *Mona in the Promised Land* (1996) is a retro look backwards, creating a multiethnic "summer camp" of sorts where young people of different races and social classes come together in an era of social activism and idealism. Jen's Chinese American protagonist falls in love with a Jewish young man. Chinese and Jews join hands once again in Louie's *The Barbarians Are Coming*. While the three cannibals consume yEast to fashion their respective modern identity, each favors what it sees as the choicest part on the carcass—most out of reach and, therefore, most coveted. Batmen love Transylvania, the eastern reaches of Europe; madmen desire the West on the other side of the world; food pornographers court the Asianness that, in turn, caters to White clientele.

Chapter Six

Bugman in Modernity

According to the *Animal Encyclopedia* published by the popular Dorling Kindersley book publisher, the animal kingdom "divides into two types: those animals without backbones, called invertebrates; and those with backbones, called vertebrates. . . . Most invertebrates are insects—with more than one million described and catalogued" (16). The counterparts to insects, or the most populous species among vertebrates, are, of course, humans. Yet it appears that the two ends of the animal kingdom are often forgotten—the top tier occupied by *Homo sapiens* and the bottom occupied by insects within the Anthropoid phylum; both seem to have taken leave of animality by virtue of human intelligence and bug insignificance. In addition to science that brings the two strays back into the fold, literature and art intuit the totality of living things in the image of "bugman," the epistemological fusion of the lowest and the highest in the animal kingdom, such as in William Blake's "The Fly": "Am not I / A fly like thee? / Or are not thou / A man like me?" (Deeney, Yen, and Chi 61). In deceivingly innocent rhyme and tone, Blake not only infers human mortality from the fly, the traditional metaphor of decay and death in the West, but projects human subjectivity onto the fly. Blake's romantic sensibility embraces subject and object as one. On the cusp of modernity in 1793, Blake's aesthetic vision of bugman bears an eerie resemblance to Eastern cultural representations in its archaic ("thee," "thou") melancholia (indeterminacy of questions). More importantly, Blake's poem enlightens us to the oft-ignored fact by critics and readers alike that insects are everywhere in literature, gracing nearly every book, like bugs in all corners of the world. Wherever humans dwell, bugs crawl in their shadows, and, as Blake suggests, the other way around as well.

In the mid- and late twentieth century, Blake's romantic identification of human and fly turns literal and abhorrent in Western horror genres, exemplified by the fantastic sci-fi imaginary as well as by crime thrillers on serial killers. Across the ocean in the East, Blake's vision echoes the traditional aesthetic of *wuwo* or no self and the contemporary nostalgia for a premodern, pre-Westernization ethos. Interpellated by the Age of Machine, the West and the East come to see their self-image in bugman, yet in a diametrically opposed fashion, as synecdochic affixing versus symbolic transference. On the one hand, the West finds in bugman futuristic and sociopathological horror, a metonymic grafting of human and insect, resulting in sickening dehumanization and existential angst in Kafka's *Metamorphosis*, sci-fi horror films (the 1958 *The Fly* and its spawns in 1959, 1986, and 1989), the collector of butterflies and of Mother figures in John Fowles's *The Collector* (1963), and the serial killer with the "calling card" of a moth in the Hollywood blockbuster *The Silence of the Lambs* (1991). With the exception of characters of children's culture, such as Eric Carle's hungry caterpillar, Jiminy cricket in *Pinocchio* (1940), George Selden's slightly racist *The Cricket in Times Square* (1960), and Eddie Murphy's loquacious cricket in *Mulan* (1998), bugman—"it"—signals to the West a sinking to repulsive insects like flies, a fall as a consequence of playing God. The overreaching for infinity is dashed into infinitesimal pieces of self. On the other hand, modernity means, to East Asians since the latter half of the nineteenth century, Westernization. Instead of the West's self-inflation to the transgressive point of subhuman adulteration, the East views modernity as an infiltration from the West. Hence, the East escapes the grip of modernity into a nostalgic unity of human and nature, or a metaphoric substitution of human by insect, the latter symbolized by nurturing, maternal silkworm (Mothra in Godzilla films), by crickets (*Shi Jing*, *Shower* [*Xizao*]), by butterfly (*Zhuangzi*, *Butterfly Lovers* [*Liang Shanbo yu Zhu Yingtai*]), and fireflies (*Sasameyuki*, *Grave of the Fireflies*). Insects also grace East Asian literati painting, material culture, and nostalgic sixth-generation Chinese films. Bugman signals to the East the idealized state of wuwo (no self), a soaring to the aesthetic, a return to the indivisible Tao.

Whereas the condition of being a "bugman" constitutes existential abyss to the West, the East finds in it a blissful lack of ego. The West dreads the "fall" to a bugman, for human beings inhabit the apex of the animal kingdom in Christianity and science; however, reincarnation and the literati culture in the East reconfigure the verticality of life as a circle. Julia Kristeva, following theorizations on the taboo by Freud, Claude Lévi-Strauss, and Bataille, describes in *Powers of Horror* (1982) the repulsion over such a fall as the abject or the crossing of boundaries into the forbidden from cleanliness and humanness. Modern technology has enabled a venturing beyond heretofore-prescribed human limitations, but interior affect lags far behind exterior exploration, manifested through gnawing self-doubt over potential violation. Whether Freud's psychological or Mary Douglas's anthropological account, they serve to map out the fear over the nonself, or over the "bug" in bugman in the modern West. Roman Jakobson's structuralist distinction between metonymy and metaphor illustrates the difference in responses from the West and the East. By examining aphasia, Jakobson advances the metaphoric and metonymic poles in speech delivery. The former is the ability a speaker has in connecting words through similarity, the latter through contiguity. As opposed to Donna Haraway's celebration of cyborg, "a cybernetic organism, a hybrid of machine and organism" ("A Manifesto" 7), sci-fi films in the West are alarmed by synecdochic splicing in futuristic, urban, (post)modern dystopias, evincing unease over the truncating of the self by technology in the trope of prosthesis fastened contiguously to the human body. The modern West hence cherry-picks the undesirables from the multitude of insects: flies for decomposition and mortality; ants for robotic collective; bees for mindless division of labor and species propagation. By contrast, the horrifying possibility of one's insignificance when likened to a bug is exactly what endears it to the classical Eastern litany of life's ethereality. The literati tradition has long perfected the stylized and aestheticized representation of the most desirable bugs: butterfly, cricket, fireflies, and more. The modern East, in denial of its irreversible Westernization, resorts to escapism of the vanquished by substituting insect for self. The sixth-generation film-making hence enacts a return to the old, rural, pre-industrial, even anachronistic China, which is a poetic, utopian transformation of present crisis, one reminiscent of the butterfly's metamorphosis.

Shared by both Western and Eastern bugman is gender politics. Since science and technology are traditionally viewed as male provinces, uncertainty over progress in Western horror or withdrawal to nature in Asian aesthetic is symptomatic of masculine angst over the loss of power. Indeed, bugmen are usually male; a female, such as Richard Corman's *The Wasp Woman* (1959), can enter such distinguished company only when she aspires to be a man or the head of a corporate. Not only does bugman in the West transgress against boundaries between God and human, but between man and woman, resulting in perverse sexuality. By contrast, sexuality is largely downplayed in bug-cum-man in the Eastern literati and aesthetic tradition. This essay investigates how bugman is represented as an "injurious pest" in the West and a "beneficial pet" in the East, concluding with "aberrations," namely, how certain texts take on the other culture's perspective on bugman. In addition to Carle, Selden, and other children's literature authors, Westerners such as Lafcadio Hearn, Gary Snyder, and Bertolucci in *The Last Emperor* anthropomorphize and idealize insects. Kobo Abe's *The Woman in the Dunes*, by contrast, metamorphoses humans to sand-boring insects in the spirit of Kafka and existentialism.

Injurious

To be sure, the premodern West has not always viewed insects as injurious pests or corruptions of the self. David Spooner explains, for example, that "psyche is a key word in Greek since it evolves from Homer to signify not only 'breath of life,' but also mind and soul, and is ultimately imaged as a butterfly" (*The Insect-Populated Mind* 45). Christopher Hollingworth, in *Poetics of the Hive* (2001), analyzes insects as a metaphor for collective humanity since Homer. But whenever the collective atomizes into an individual, especially in an existential sense, the insect metaphor instantly turns negative. Beginning with Giotto di Bondone (1266-1337), who painted flies that looked so real that his master Cimabue shooed them off, European *trompe l'oeil* painters in the fifteenth and sixteenth century often included flies in the composition to demonstrate "the painter's skill at realistic depiction, or as a talisman, protecting against disease, or as a kind of *memento mori*, a reminder of the nearness of death, which can be transcended through religious death" (Ebert-Schifferer 164). This interest continues, for instance, in Jan van Kessel I (Flemish, 1626-1679), known for his insects and flowers, reflecting "the seventeenth-century's fascination with the natural world" (178).

Areas where insects are favorably or magically depicted are children's literature and nature writing. Lewis Carroll's *Alice in Wonderland* (1897) features a caterpillar smoking a hookah and parts with the riddle-like advice to Alice: "One side will make you grow taller, and the other side will make you grow shorter" (41). Not until Alice follows up with "One side of *what*?" does the caterpillar reply: "Of the mushroom." By way of the other—a talking, smoking bug—Carroll evokes the other's drug, be it the consciousness-altering Mexican hallucinogenic mushroom or the hashish-laced Arab hookah, as the means to reach the other side beyond logocentrism. The caterpillar's parting shot of a riddle points to the possibility of shape shifting, magic inherent in the metamorphosis into chrysalis and butterfly. This process, of course, reflects Alice's experiences in wonderland. Despite its key role as her doppelgänger, Alice cavalierly dismisses the insect when asked by a gnat: "What sort of insects do you rejoice in, where *you* come from?" To which, Alice answers: "I don't *rejoice* in insects at all" (*Through the Looking-Glass* 132). David Henry Thoreau does not share Carroll's flippant attitude toward insects. Thoreau first quotes Kirby and Spence's *An Introduction to Entomology* (1846), followed by his own commentary "'that some insects in their perfect state, though furnished with organs of feeding, make no use of them . . . that almost all insects in this state eat much less than in that of larvae. The voracious caterpillar when transformed into a butterfly . . . and the gluttonous maggot when become a fly' content themselves with a drop or two of honey or some other sweet liquid. The abdomen under the wings of the butterfly still represents the larva. This is the tid-bit which tempts his insectivorous fate. The gross feeder is a man in the larvae state; and there are whole nations in that condition" (*Walden* 262). The transcendentalist unduly romanticizes because insects, rather than elevating themselves into celestial beings, graduate from the consuming passion for food and growth to the consuming passion for sex, the species' procreation coming as an afterthought. The hunger for food merely turns into the hunger for sex. Instead of transcending biological instincts, the insect follows a different kind of physical want.

Presaged by Stoker's *The Lair of the White Worm* (1911), with its combination of ancient myth of worm-cum-serpent and modern industrialization, aided by Orientalist xenophobia, the modern West's bugman nightmare begins when Gregor Samsa wakes up in Kafka's *Metamorphosis* (1915) and finds himself changed into a vermin. That the Samsas readily accept the monstrosity as Gregor, never suspecting that the family breadwinner could have been devoured in sleep, suggests that they subconsciously equate Gregor with the vermin. Dependency on Gregor engenders subconscious resentment to the extent that it turns the family into unloving, despicable insects themselves. Indeed, the end of the story circles back to the opening as Gregor's sister Grete "got up first and stretched her young body," a morning ritual shared by perhaps every human being and every "dung beetle." In a deliberate caricature of the Trinity—three surviving family members, three boarders, three repulses of Gregor, three letters the family compose, and three family prospects after Gregor's death, *Metamorphosis* alchemizes Christ's apotheosis into Gregor's ignominious end. Kafka's existentialist protagonist, the lone bugman awakened to his true state, is an apocalyptic break from what Christopher Hollingworth describes as the Western tradition of "hive," which is "living emblems of the human social order" (*Poetics of the Hive* xiii). This sharp break is facilitated by the fact that Hollingworth concentrates on written texts, rarely venturing into films. By turning attention to films, particularly the genre of sci-fi where bugman proliferates, one is instantly struck by the bleakness of vision.

Since its rise in the 1950s, sci-fi film embodies the anxiety of the Cold War and of the atomic age. Spinning out of works of the Gothic genre, such as Mary Shelley's *Frankenstein* (1818), sci-fi revolves routinely around "mad scientist" characters to initiate horror and catastrophe. Within sci-fi, there exists a subgenre of, for lack of a better term, bugman, illustrated by Richard Corman's string of B-films. *The Wasp Woman*, for instance, maladroitly employs a wasp mask for the aging, "venomous" female entrepreneur, which epitomizes male paranoia over the postwar instability of gender roles. But the films that define bugman are the swarm over the 1958 film, *The Fly*, by Kurt Neuman. Inspired by George Langelaan's story published in *Playboy* in 1957, the 1958 production comes to sire *Return of the Fly* (1959; which turns the spotlight on the son of the human fly), *The Fly* (the 1986 David Cronenberg remake), and *The Fly II* (1989; Walas). All these films reprise the motif of patriarchal legacy from the mad scientist to his son as well as the fall of a godlike scientist to a bug. The genesis of these films lies in a botched scientific experiment moving individuals over space. It results in the disastrous merging of human and fly, which happen to inhabit the same vehicle of transport. Scientific advances are reflected in the films not only in terms of the 1950s atomic versus the 1980s genetic splicing with a fly but also in terms of the technical and special effects of the films. The Neuman fly wears a mask with compound eyes, veiled under a hood until the climax, and a left hand that is a claw, concealed in the pocket. The Cronenberg fly, by contrast, is Jeff Goldblum in elaborate make-up; the special effects create a monstrosity vomiting slimy glop. Whether the atomic or the genetic Frankenstein, the fly horde capitalizes on Kristeva's hypothesis on horror over the nonhuman, particularly the basest in the animal kingdom.

Cronenberg's film is designed to shock, to jolt the audience into awareness of unpleasant reality. *The Fly* offers vintage Cronenberg moments of the macabre and the sickening: the failure of teleporting or transporting a baboon turns the baboon inside out; the maniac scientist Seth Brundle, with a fly's physical strength, snaps his opponent's bone during an arm-wrestling match; Brundle vomits stomach acid to break down food and removes his fingernails, teeth, ears, and other accessories nonessential to the life of a fly; Brundle corrodes human arm and foot into stumps. All these images inverse what is considered the natural, exposing the interior—human bones or vomit—

as well as the fly inside the human body. Here, Cronenberg exploits two distinct insect characteristics: metamorphosis and exoskeleton. Brundle's gradual dehumanization coincides with his maturing as a fly crawling across ceiling and leaping over walls. With the exteriorization of bone structure and digestive secretion, Brundle's physical changes deform the human yet liberate the fly in him. Despite Brundle's fleeting ecstasy over the emancipation from humanity à la Zhuangzi's butterfly dream, Cronenberg presents the metamorphosis in a decidedly dubious manner.

Equally doomed are a man playing God and a machine giving birth to life forms. Originally, the telepod succeeds in transporting only inanimate things. Learning of love and the flesh from Veronica Quaife ("Ronnie," played by Geena Davis), the cerebral Brundle tries to teach the computer to recognize emotions and living things, a project that involves male hubris and female sexuality right from the start. Like another twisted Gothic figure, the first thing Brundle does upon entering his back-alley laboratory is to play a piano tune with such fanfare that it is reminiscent of *The Phantom of the Opera*. Surely meant to impress his lady caller, the practiced hand suggests, nonetheless, a routine to satisfy some inner impulse. Scientific breakthrough and human darkness are simultaneously evoked by the snatch of piano; Brundle is at once a scientist and a magician, slim and tall, eyes glaring, hand gestures expansive in his debut of the telepod. Ronnie, true to typecasting, mistakes the telepod for a phone booth or a microwave, both guesses partially correct since it transmits and transubstantiates. The oven reference is particularly apt: as a Freudian metaphor, the seed-like telepod comes to engender new life forms. From the outset, female sexuality permeates not just the venue of *Playboy* for the original 1957 story but Ronnie's offering of her stocking for the experiment. The telepod arises as the new womb to replace woman, fusing Brundle and the fly. Ronnie serves subsequently as a surrogate mother to give birth to the telepod's egg of a "Brundle Fly."

Designed to transmit human bodies on the molecular-genetic level, the telepod comes to erase not only spatial boundaries but physical, indeed epistemological, boundaries between self and nonself. In addition, the telepod cancels out gender differences in that it takes over the womb in the propagation of species, an area it excels in, adding third parties other than sperm and egg. Seth Brundle the male scientist joins forces with an apparently male fly, financed by Bartok Science Industries, to render femininity obsolete in the age of machines. Bartok's namesake Béla Bartók, of course, composed the opera, *Bluebeard's Castle* (1918), on the ultimate subjugation and elimination of women. Despite her role as an enterprising journalist for the science magazine, *The Particle*, Ronnie's glamorous and sexually charged performance belies her precarious position in a male-dominated business. Ronnie *is* the trapped fly, about to be crushed by male tyranny—new love for the Brundle Fly or old flame for Stathis Borans, her boss at *The Particle*. Jealous, possessive, patronizing, and contemptible, Borans appears to be the fly from which Ronnie recoils in one scene in order to embrace the misshapen Brundle. SOBs they all prove themselves to be: Brundle, Borans, and Bartok, the "bitch" now being the telepod. Bartok, a mere symbolic name in Cronenberg, materializes as a vicious patriarch in *The Fly II*. The finale in Cronenberg enacts the fairy tale rescue of the distressed damsel: Borans manages to fire his phallic double-barreled shotgun at the last moment to save Ronnie from being fused with the Brundle Fly. Instead, the Brundle Fly now merges with the telepod itself, a monstrosity of human, insect, and machine. Although Ronnie pulls the trigger to relieve the monstrosity of misery, the nightmare is to be continued through the seeds in her womb. The seeds and the future are foretold in Brundle's musing between insect-like tics: "I am an insect who dreamt he was a man and loved it. Now the dream is over and the insect is awake," a philosophical formulation in poetry harking back to "The Butterfly Dream" by Zhuangzi (369?-286? B.C.). Cronenberg has consistently employed such dream states to destabilize reality and fantasy: the female impersonator in *M. Butterfly* (1993) debunks gender; and the junkie protagonist in *Naked Lunch* (1991) wonders about drug-induced reality in the Arabic Interzone

Granted, no audience would mistake *The Fly*, with superhuman ability, for one of the comic superheroes. Batman, Superman, and even the insect-related Spiderman assume their superhero roles by means of the costume they don: they wear their roles via the pointy-ear mask, the Big S, and the spider web jersey. Under their costumes, the fundamental human form remains intact. These superheroes exercise total control of their split selves: bug and man, or Superman and Clark Kent, are inviolable entities willingly adopted for specific occasions. By contrast, the Fly is bug and man mongrelized, the process fixed and irreversible. The other sci-fi horror scenario is a complete takeover of the human body and mind by a nonself. In *Aliens* (1986), Sigourney Weaver battles what is essentially a queen bee laying numerous eggs that require human bodies as hosts for gestation. Human bodies are turned into raw materials for the propagation of aliens or, in *The Matrix* (1999), into the source of energy for the postnuclear holocaust era. Accordingly, what emerges from the cocoon of the human torso is not a butterfly but a grotesque alien, which splits asunder many a chest, to the revulsion of moviegoers mesmerized by Arnold Schwarznegger's *Total Recall* (1990), Cronenberg's *Naked Lunch*, and other horror films. In addition to futuristic sci-fi films in the West, bugman is no stranger to the genre of thrillers about sociopathological serial killers, whose horrific transgressions border on the fantastic, as do the deeds of mad scientists. The degeneration inherent in the insect lends itself to the depiction of criminals, particularly serial killers, whom Victoria Nelson in *The Secret Life of Puppets* (2001) labels as "American mass culture's coded icon of unrepentant evil, secular stand-in for the Devil" (258). These murderous bugmen exhibit masculine paranoia just as sci-fi does. Similar to sexual perversity in the surrogate-mother telepod, serial killers are motivated by such deviancy as impotence and repressed transvestism. As sexuality is key to metamorphosis and reproduction in an insect's life, the longing for regeneration drives both the mad scientist and the serial killer.

Published in 1963, John Fowles's *The Collector* follows a psychotic clerk-killer, Clegg, who uses his pool or lottery prize money to abduct, imprison, and destroy upper-class art student Miranda. The title refers to Clegg's hobby of collecting butterflies, Miranda included. By extension, the insect trope suggests the volatile postwar Britain struggling to shed the traditional cocoon for a new society. The reshuffling of class and money crystallizes in Miranda's alcoholic mother with her aristocratic intonation ("la-di-da" according to Clegg), totally useless in shielding Miranda from the rise of the "New People" (middle and lower middle class). On the other hand, abandoned by his mother, Clegg, in his stunted, regressive psychological state, realizes any teenage boy's fantasy of power over the other sex by utilizing, by chance, the pooled resources from the historically disadvantaged masses. In this novel, severely restricted in its point of view and fictional universe, the cultural elite comprises Miranda and her art teacher, father figure G.P., for George Gaston or, as Clegg speculates when reviewing his captive's secret diary, general practitioner, which is not far from the truth in view of Miranda's emotional dependency on G.P. Consistent with Fowles' subsequent novels, such as *The Magus* (1965), G.P. also comes across as a magician or magus from the East, an impression strengthened by his taste for Indian music and the divan. Moreover, his appearance is said to resemble that of a Turk. In Miranda's diary, the abbreviation G.P. brings to mind the other two alphabets repeatedly used—M and D—for mum and dad. The elite and the despised New People are besieged by a similar fallacy of Freudian imago, idealized images of parents: Miranda hero-worships G.P., a father substitute, and Clegg nurses Miranda as the lost mother. A serial killer, Clegg plans, after burying Miranda, the next abduction of another M or Marian, a shop girl. The psychological conundrum lies in the perversion of "Clegg the Egg," giving birth to what would eventually become a series of stillborn mothers. This is what collectors routinely do, opines Clegg: an imago is killed once it emerges from the cocoon, with its beauty preserved for perpetuity only in death.

Clegg yokes brute force and utter servility, tyranny and submission. The violence of the abduction of Miranda by chloroform is followed by her bondage via bolts, locks, gags, and rope, culminating in her photographic rape, the picture-taking in lieu of phallic penetration from an impotent Clegg. All such indignity takes place in an underground chapel deep inside a castle, as if enacting a sacrificial ritual. Entomologically, Miranda is treated as the queen ant, whereas Clegg is the sexless worker ant attending to the cleaning and cooking. The queen ant is a kept woman, yet her role is no longer to produce offspring, but to be revered as the mother imago, the incest taboo forbidding any intercourse between the queen and the worker. Although sexless, the very nature of the serial killer promises to sire a line of such queen ants. This chillingly evokes M.C. Escher's unending Möbius strip where ants, centipedes, lizards, and other animals circle around while metamorphosizing. The collector Clegg subjects his Miranda to the duality of, as Pamela Cooper puts it, "elevation and debasement," as "goddess and insect, at once superhuman and subhuman" (*The Fictions of John Fowles* 27). But the serial, cyclical movement of the novel suggests that Miranda, an egg hatching in Clegg's dungeon, is Clegg's kindred soul, fantasizing about her father substitute G.P. and the magic of art in her "prison notebook." G.P., in turn, is a collector of young women—their admiration and their bodies, just as Miranda with art objects or as Clegg with butterfly specimens

Psychologically, a collector can be someone who inventories and utilizes thoughts and fancies. If construed as sexual fantasies, the term brings us to Miranda's charge of Clegg as the "masturbating worm" (89). Flung against her tormentor in anger, Miranda's description targets both Clegg, the person who behaves like a lowly bug, and Clegg's penis, a worm-like appendage unable to perform. That he is plagued by impotence means that he may not be able to reach erection and ejaculate, masturbating or otherwise, as Clegg confesses: "I told her I knew I could never do it . . . I dream about it, I said. It can't ever be real" (82). Given that a soft penis, resembling a worm, cannot masturbate itself except through a moving hand or gyrating body, masturbatory autoeroticism always involves the other—sexually arousing objects conjured up by the mind or received by the senses. To compensate, Clegg effects sexual dominance by way of the sadomasochistic bondage of Miranda. Conceptually, however, both Miranda and G.P. are masturbating worms as well, one locked underground and escaping into reveries over G.P., the other voraciously consuming women for sexual gratification and for artistic inspiration. The line between the art of collecting butterflies or beauty and the art of collecting women is blurred indeed.

Horror films never fail to locate evil in sexual depravity, often coupling insect and crime. Through a figurative bug or virus, Clegg kills Miranda when he passes his cold to her, whose cause of death is probably severe, protracted, and untreated pneumonia. In terms of sexuality, the serial killer Clegg's impotence becomes the serial killer Buffalo Bill's transvestism in *The Silence of the Lambs*. Buffalo Bill indulges in the delusion of rebirth into femininity with his cape pieced together from victims' flayed skin. Another masturbating worm, Buffalo Bill in drag videos his nude, heavily made-up and feminine self, with his penis tucked between his legs and the butterfly wings of a cape spread out as if taking flight. The function of the death's-head moth in his victims' mouths portends such ultimate transformation into womanhood. Clegg and Buffalo Bill are brutal men, yet they ironically assume feminine roles in waiting on Miranda or in applying lipstick and cosmetics, let alone seamstressing with human skin. Given that serial killers have come to represent ultimate evil for our secular age, novelists try to veil the diabolism through language. For instance, the invocation of their names is softened by the use of alliteration or deprecating nicknames. Buffalo Bill, who made his reputation from butchering and flaying buffalos now christens the slayer of women. The name Hannibal Lecter, of course, associates the flesh-eating "cannibal" with "lectern" or "lecturer" (teacher, mentor) for Agent Starling and the society at large, enlightening us as to the truth of human appetite and the dark side of civilization (see Mizejewski, "Stardom"). To move away from the Western context, sexual perversity enjoys purchase not just in Western horror. Koji Suzuki's *The Ring* (1991), which inspires the Japanese as well as Hollywood remakes, locates evil in the female ghost Sadako, who lived as a male pseudohermaphrodite characterized by a female body with testes or "testicular feminization" (225).

Beneficial

To be sure, premodern Asia has not always viewed insects as beneficial pets or valorizations of the self. Not to romanticize, one needs to cite at the outset the Chinese term *louyi*, literally ants, but also the masses or masses of nobodies. In the sixteenth-century classic novel, *Journey to the West,* the Spider Women join the gallery of cannibalistic monsters coveting the monk Tripitaka's flesh. Misogyny is located in such representations of women as well as in the common expression *duxie furenxin* ("Venomous scorpions are a woman's heart"). But the preponderance of evidence from classic Asian culture favors insects as the locus of self-transference or self-elimination, affected as much by East Asian ways of thinking as by the linguistic characteristic of subject omission.

In the Chinese tradition, *Shi Jing* (*Book of Songs*), the first collection of courtly poems and folk songs compiled by Confucius (551-479 B.C.), abounds in descriptions of folk life, which involve such insects as the silkworm, cicada, and cricket. The poem "July" dwells on the seasonal movement of crickets: "In May, *Si Zhong* rubs its wings to sing. / In June, *Shuai Ji* flutters its wings to sing. / In July, it sings in the wilderness. / In August, under the eaves. / In September, inside the house. / In October, the cricket is under my bed" (Legge 226-33; unless indicated otherwise, all translations are mine). Both *Si Zhong* and *Shuai Ji* belong to the cricket family. Although cricket raising and fighting are yet to evolve in subsequent dynasties into an intricate pastime in northern China, this poem points to a dispassionate, if not intimate, relationship with crickets and the seasonal changes their migration represents. "July" follows the typical Chinese linguistic style of an absent narrator; no "I" is used other than the possessive "my bed." Consequently, the link between the I-less poem and humanity must be forged by the reader. No sense of repulsion marks the observation that the cricket has entered into the narrator's house. While coming from outside in summer, the chirping is inside in autumn, which signals the end of the cricket's life cycle. What used to be a vibrant force in youth has mellowed to an inward reflection along with aging. The cricket is an objective correlative for seasonal and human passing. A similar supplying of "I" operates in "East Mountain," where the speaker of the poem likens a sojourner's travails to an insect's: "A silkworm is squirming, / Ah, in the wilderness. / Curled up alone, sleeping / Under the cart as well" (Legge 235-38). The reader understands the poem by taking the silkworm as an analogy for the unnamed traveler. The human is once again read into the insect. Such self-transference motivates the famous "Butterfly Dream" with which Zhuangzi concludes *Qiwu lun* ("On Leveling All Things") in *Zhuangzi*. Zhuangzi's philosophy is part of the canon of Daoism, which is founded by Laozi and his *Tao Te Ching* of the late Spring and Autumn Period. The sinologist Herbert A. Giles translated the episode into English and, as Hans-Georg Möller explicates, exerted tremendous impact on Martin Buber, Martin Heidegger, Hermann Hesse, and other Western and, in a reverse flow, Chinese thinkers. Möller points out, quite accurately, that Giles adds the nonexistent subject "I" no less than ten times ("Zhuangzi's 'Dream of the Butterfly'" 440): "Once upon a time, I, Chuang Tzu, dreamt I was a butterfly, fluttering hither and thither, to all intents and purposes a butterfly. I was conscious only of following my fancies as a butterfly, and was unconscious of my individuality as a man. Suddenly, I awaked, and there I lay, myself again. Now I do not know whether I was then a man dreaming I was a butterfly, or whether I am now a butterfly, dreaming I am a man. Between a man and a butterfly there is necessarily a barrier. The transition is called *Metempsychosis*" (439). By identifying Zhuangzi with the narrator "I," Giles neglects the original's detachment of the speaking voice from both the butterfly and Zhuangzi, both the dream and the dreamer. Möller, following the exegesis of Guo Xiang (252-312 A.D.), stresses the importance of the distinction between self and nonself rather than the "relativity of distinction" (440). Nonetheless, the very possibility of distinction seems problematized by the fluidity of the narrator, the dreamer, and the dream. Should all things be equalized and cohered according to Zhuangzi, why does the dreamer exchange identity with one of nature's masterpieces and not with a cockroach or fly? The aesthetic bias is taken for granted in East Asian philosophy and literati culture.

In classical Japanese literature, *Kojiki* (*Record of Ancient Things*, completed in 712 A.D.) locates the origin of Japan in a creation myth that had gone awry much as Adam and Eve of Christianity did. The brother and sister deities of Izanagi and Izanami commit incest and give birth to a leech-child, which is subsequently cast out on "a boat made of reeds," reminiscent of Moses (*Kojiki* 51). That a *piru-go* (leech-child), a "monstrosity lacking arms and legs" (399), is sired stems not so much from the taboo of incest as from the taboo of female transgression, for Izanagi belatedly realizes that "it is not proper that the woman speak first" (51). Female aggressiveness connects with Eve's temptation. As a consequence, God punishes the snake, which is doomed to crawl on its belly, a fate that awaits the leech-child born without limbs. Despite a perfect match in comparative religion and mythology, the banishment from the pantheon is not so complete in Japan. In its returns to wreak havoc, the leech-child is accommodated for its association with childhood obstreperousness and insect harmlessness. The atom bomb-inspired destroyer Godzilla, argues Jerome F. Shapiro in *Atomic Bomb Cinema* (2002), is one such leech-child, an "angry, unwanted child (e.g., Gojira) who returns to Japan to claim the honor he is denied" (280). Godzilla occasionally evolves in postwar Japan into an object of affection fighting dinosaurs and monsters on behalf of humanity. Takao Okawara, in *Godzilla and Mothra: The Battle for Earth* (1992), further spins off from the leech-child image to fashion a marauding, caterpillar-shaped Mothra, which spews silky filaments and emerges from the cocoon a dazzling moth.

In the Heian Period (794-1192 A.D.), the *Tsutsumi Chunagon Monogatari* (*Tsutsumi Chunagon Tales*), a collection of eleventh-century short stories, contains references to insects, including "The Young Lady Who Loved Insects." The story features an idiosyncratic young lady who collects caterpillars. Her eccentricity extends to her appearance: she neither plucks her eyebrows nor blackens her teeth, as aristocratic ladies are wont to do. The society scorns her by equating her with caterpillars, unwittingly reinscribing the wuwo tradition: "How loathsome! Her eyebrows are like hairy caterpillars, and her white gums are nothing but caterpillars with their skins peeled off" (20). The story closes with an exchange of mocking and possibly flirtatious poems between the young lady and the Vice Director of the Imperial Horses of the Right. The Vice Director may yet progress to be a suitor in "Book Two," a sequel promised in the concluding line. Since there is no "Book Two," the young lady's matrimony remains a tantalizing potential, like a caterpillar-in-waiting.

The insect as an alter ego recurs in Chinese and Japanese literati paintings, particularly the genre of *caochong* (grass-and-insect) painting. By perfecting the stylization of birds, insects, and fish amid flowers and plants, the literati, ideally, release themselves from worldly hustle and bustle. Even in the more popularized, mass-produced Japanese prints, the master Hokusai's *Irises and Grasshopper* adopts a perspective that is level with a grasshopper upside-down on a blade of grass, as if the reader squats down near the ground for a close-up of the insect. This technique reminds one of Yasujiro Ozu's postwar films where the waist-level camera height captures, horizontally, characters sitting cross-legged on the tatami. Both angles in the Japanese print and films deny any higher status to the spectator, who is drawn, instead, into the microcosmic insect world or Ozu's family drama.

One of the most prominent insects throughout Chinese history is the cricket. From their appearance in the earliest collection of poetry, *Shi Jing,* crickets have graced poetry and essays throughout subsequent dynasties, culminating in *Cuzhi Jing* (*Book on Crickets*) by the Southern Song Prime Minister Jia Sidao (1213-1275), nicknamed the "Cricket Prime Minister," who continued in the game of cricket fighting despite the Mongolian invasion of the central plains. Jia's monograph details the raising and dueling of crickets, which is elevated to an art form (Meng, *Qiannian qiuxing huacishuai* [*On Crickets for a Thousand Autumns* (1999)]). Among its many appearances, the cricket even shows up in the collection of ghost stories, *Liaozhai zhiyi* (*Strange Tales from a Chinese Studio* [1766]) by Pu Songling (1640-1715) (See *Cuzhi* 329-32). Contextualized by this northern Chinese hobby over crickets, the sixth-generation filmmaker Zhang Yang makes the film *Xizao* (*Shower* 1999). Zhang takes leave of the fifth-generation's penchant for epic panorama and extreme conditions, imbuing *Shower* with a bittersweet nostalgia for the vanishing old Beijing and an elegy for shattered masculinity. The set is a traditional, communal bathhouse, a gathering place for "geezers." This culture of yesteryear is coming to an end with the imminent demolition of the neighborhood for a modern shopping mall, the sudden death of the bathhouse owner, the violent backlash from his mentally retarded son, and the dispersal of the old customers. Also gone is the male bonding at the bathhouse practiced through cleansing, massaging, relaxing, enjoying Beijing operas on the radio, and cricket dueling. Specifically, two old-timers at the bathhouse perpetually spar with words and with their pet crickets. As the bathhouse is about to be razed, they lament, while soaking in the bath, that they would have to move to high-rise apartments where no crickets can survive due to the separation from *diqi* (earth air). Such an elegy of the other—their doppelgänger, to boot—is always self-elegy, bemoaning the end of the old Beijing and themselves. This sentiment is expressed by old Beijingers living in *hutong* in real life as well (Brubach, "Raze High the Roof

Beams, Comrade" 84; Meyer, *The Last Days of Old Beijing*). The finale shows the two old-timers riding a tricycle around the neighborhood to document on the camcorder the coup de grace of the wrecking ball. By means of the bugmen's self-elegy, Zhang diagnoses male anxiety on the threshold of modernity and urbanization. Yet Zhang's film is far more nuanced than a wholesale dismissal of modernity, the old and the new closely intertwined. Both tools, a dilapidated tricycle and a new camcorder, are required to record the demolition, just as Zhang captures with his camera a vanishing world. The last image in Zhang's film by way of the bugmen's shaky camcorder is the idiot character singing "O Sole Mio!" to his Walkman headphones, another mechanic messenger bringing the Western aria to comfort a Chinese soul. The insect motif is echoed by a TV program on nature on the heels of the owner's death. His retarded son sits staring at the TV screen as a beetle rolls a ball of dung where the young are to emerge, the program punctuated by the high-pitched Beijing dialect typical of any public announcement, so crisply enunciated and so charged with sorrow as to be maudlin. Is the son escaping from the pain of bereavement or is he mourning by projection onto the insect world? If the latter, the faked empathy of the narrative voice-over contrasts sharply with the son's grief. The contemporary dubbing strikes one as an affected pose, a corruption of the traditional wuwo or losing oneself in nature embodied by the tiniest, lowest insect

Ideally aesthetic and philosophical, bugman in China stems from a leaning toward the old, the pre-industrial, and the archaic. Zhuangzi sets up the archetype in his famous dream of a butterfly. The interchangeable subjectivity between human and insect bespeaks the human position within nature rather than above nature. Beyond philosophical discourse, bugs permeate Chinese culture. The folk romance of Liang-Zhu, also known as the butterfly lovers, resembles that of Romeo and Juliet, except the Chinese twin deaths climax in a pair of butterflies rising out of the grave. On the other hand, Li Shizhen (1518-1593), in his magisterial *Bencao gangmu* (*Compendium of Materia Medica*) on Chinese herbal medicine, focuses on insects in four out of its forty-two volumes, totaling thirty-eight kinds of insects for medicinal purposes. Such a thriving culture as cricket raising in Beijing influences even Westerners. In the very first Western film shot on location in the Forbidden City in the wake of the Cultural Revolution, Bernardo Bertolucci in *The Last Emperor* (1987) adroitly deploys crickets for a touch of magic. During the crowning ceremony, the utterly bored child emperor Pu Yi follows the cricket sound to find the symbol of his child-like innocence. At the end of the film, when the last emperor has long been struggled against and reformed as an old, stooping gardener in the People's Republic of China, Pu Yi rediscovers his pet cricket behind the throne, as if his reign of innocence remains intact. Bertolucci's film is soon joined by Disney's *Mulan* and many other Orientalist representations involving crickets as a sidekick for comedy and exoticism.

The Japanese counterpart to Chinese cricket fighting may well be the famed firefly hunt featured in Japanese puppet theater and modern Japanese literature. Junichiro Tanizaki 's *Sasameyuki* (*The Makioka Sisters* 1946-1948) includes many *miai*, the traditional matchmaking meetings between prospective partners and their families. One particular miai is disguised as a seasonal firefly hunt. From the narrative perspective of the second Makioka sister Sachiko, Tanizaki first evokes *Bunraku* or the puppet stage when the puppets "Miyuki and Komazawa murmur[] of love as they sail[] down the River Uji" (341). *Bunraku* is one of the foci for Tanizaki's return to the traditional Japan and one he integrates into his 1928 novel *Some Prefer Nettles*. Through Sachiko's eyes, Tanizaki describes the scene:

> In the last moment of light, with the darkness creeping up from the water and the moving plumes of grass still faintly outlined, there, far as the river stretched—an infinite number of little lines in two long rows on either side, quiet, unearthly. Sachiko could see it all even now, here inside with her eyes closed. . . . A firefly hunt has none of the radiance of a cherry-blossom party. Dark, dreamy, rather—might one say? Perhaps something of the child's world, the world of the fairy story in it. Something not to be painted, but set to music, the mood of it taken up on piano or koto. And while she lay with her eyes closed, the fireflies, out there along the river, all through the night, were flashing on and off, silent, numberless. Sachiko felt a surging inside her, as though she were joining them, soaring and dipping along the surface of the water, cutting her own uncertain track of light. (342)

Arising at dusk, between light and darkness, themselves flickering "on and off," fireflies symbolize the ambiguity of union. Only against night can the mates "in two long rows" find each other, which is the purpose of miai, its pretense notwithstanding. Although matchmaking for the third Makioka sister Yukiko, the traditional beauty mysteriously unwedded, Tanizaki manages to skew the romance genre through the youngest Makioka sister Taeko, dissolute, decadent, and sadomasochistic. If Yukiko stands for the old Japan beyond reach, then Taeko is the modern Japan. The aesthetics in the firefly hunt and miai veil an unseeming undercurrent of sexuality. Seen by Sachiko in her mind's eye, the past, crystallized in fireflies, revisits, fleeting mental constructs more fittingly represented by the intangible music. Sachiko closes with her urge to join the fireflies, an impulse recurring in Zhuangzi, Hokusai, Zhang Yang, and many East Asian texts.

Fireflies flare up in dream-like reminiscences, betokening momentary repossession, followed by oblivion. Mirroring the daytime cherry-blossom viewing, the firefly hunt has at its core a wistfulness over the transience of all things, with the viewing self merging with the cherry petal falling to its death and the firefly a mere apostrophe amid deepening darkness. Along similar lines, Yoshiaki Kawajiri's anime Ninja Scroll (1993) projects a female ninja's fear and despair onto fireflies. Almost violated by a monster, she kneels down holding herself, while a single firefly lights up on a blade of grass as if in response to her muted sob, as if to keep her company. The anime director Isao Takahata draws from this Japanese sensibility over fireflies more extensively in his antiwar Grave of the Fireflies (1988), where spirits of dead children return with thousands of dancing, glistening lights. The anime maestro Hayao Miyazaki also creates fireflies' shadows in dust balls scurrying into crevices of a traditional Japanese wood house in Totoro (1988) and soot fairies in Spirited

Away (2001). Despite their indistinct shade and shape, both dust balls and soot fairies are delightful familiars in children's wonder worlds. The animation most relevant to bugs may be Miyazaki's Nausicaa of the Valley of the Wind (1984). As a result of ecological devastation, toxic jungles in Nausicaa spread on earth to threaten human survival. The messenger of ill tiding happens to be Ohmu, which Miyazaki identifies as larvae: "Even when they become adults, they remain larvae. They die as larvae. They are such strange organisms. They are in their pre-metamorphic state" (interview with Hayao Miyazaki). Part of nature, Ohmu remains regressive due to human destruction of the environment. That Ohmu heals the heroine Nausicaa, a Christ figure, signals Miyazaki's artistic vision that nature, given time and due respect, will restore the human world.

Aberration

Through cross-cultural pollination and immersion, writers and artists come to imbibe characteristics of another culture. Bertolucci has done that with Chinese crickets in the Forbidden City; many more will do so in the twenty-first century marked by globalization. With regard to bugman, aberrations occur when the other's prevailing ethos is adopted, or when Westerners view bugman—"it"—as beneficial pet and Easterners view "it" as injurious pest. A prose stylist and one-time journalist fascinated by the exotic in New Orleans and the West Indies, Lafcadio Hearn (1850-1904) traveled to Japan in 1890, married a Japanese woman, and became a Japanese citizen with a Japanese name, Yakumo Koizumi. His works from Japan are littered with poems, fairy tales, and folk stories featuring insects drawn from Japanese and Chinese sources. As Hearn read none of the Asian languages, he must have relied on native informants. Hearn's practice of presenting Haiku and Japanese poems romanized, followed by parenthetical renditions in English, merits close analysis of cross-cultural communication—its effectiveness and dubiousness—as a precursor to the multilingual global culture one century later. With the exception of bilingual speakers, most readers simply skip the nonsensical romanization, which, nevertheless, lends an aura of authenticity to Hearn's "translation" of East Asian insect culture. It awaits competent bilingual and bicultural critics to study Hearn's forays into bugman. In *Exotics and Retrospectives* (1898), Hearn exults on "Insect Musicians" or "night-singers" (42). *In Ghostly Japan* (1899) contains a piece, "Silkworms," which leaps from Japan's silkworm keeping to human spirituality suggested by the insect's life cycle. *A Japanese Miscellany* (1901) has an essay on "Dragonflies," combining scientific categorization of the insect and poetic allusions. In *Kwaidan: Stories and Studies of Strange Things* (1904), Hearn includes "The Dream of Akinosuke" on a Zhuangzi-like dream of ants. *Kwaidan* concludes with "Insect Studies," which moves from the aesthetic, haiku-filled, fairy-tale "Butterflies," to the pseudo-scientific "Mosquitoes" based on a Dr. Howard's book of the same title, and finally to "Ants," poised between Asian aesthetics, on the one hand, and scientific findings on the ant colony of a number of Western researchers, including the philosopher

Herbert Spencer, on the other. Hearn seems to be striking a balance between Eastern aesthetic and Western scientific leanings.

One of the Beat Poets influenced by Eastern philosophy, Gary Snyder, translates the Tang monk-poet Han Shan in *Riprap and Cold Mountain Poems* (1990). *Cold Mountain Poems* was originally published in 1958, one of which opens with "There's a naked bug at Cold Mountain." The allusion to "naked bug" comes from *Li Ji* (*The Records of Li*), one of the Five Classics of the Chinese Confucian literature. In Mandarin, "bug" or *Chong* (insect, worm, or being) has long been used to refer to all living beings, hence negating the hierarchy of the animal kingdom espoused by Western science. *Li Ji* states: "There are three hundred and sixty kinds of worms with feathers, and the Phoenix leads them; there are three hundred and sixty kinds of worms with hairs, and the unicorn leads them; there are three hundred and sixty kinds of worms with shells, and the divine tortoise leads them; there are three hundred and sixty kinds of worms with scales, and the dragon leads them; there are three hundred and sixty kinds of naked worms, and the sage leads them." The historical genealogy behind Han Shan's "naked bug" is not readily apparent; Snyder may be more taken by the jolting of consciousness from the contrast between nakedness and cold than that between human and bug. Rather than a mere figure of speech, Han Shan's "naked bug" is literal, at least in mythological terms.

By contrast, Kobo Abe's existentialist *Woman in the Dunes* (1964) regards human life in a Sisyphian routine, much like M.C. Escher's ants crawling along a Möbius strip. The cultural borrowing has been noted by critics such as Christopher Hollingworth in *Poetics of the Hive*, albeit in a haphazard way with numerous factual errors. Abe's protagonist is an amateur entomologist, Niki Jumpei, who arrives in a seaside village to collect insects under dubious circumstances in that he seems subconsciously orchestrating a permanent severance from society. A self-fulfilling prophecy, Jumpei is trapped in the sand dunes by villagers who make him rid excess sand every night in order to halt the advance of the sand dunes. Succumbing to the villagers' threat of cutting off his water supply, Jumpei turns into a sand-boring insect. A Japanese household, of course, is defined by the concept of cleanliness and boundaries: shoes are removed at the entrance and the floor is meticulously mopped daily. Yet in Jumpei's wood shack sunken in the dunes, sand is everywhere, outside as well as inside, pasted on Jumpei's skin as well as swallowed with food and water. Jumpei complains to his captor—the unnamed woman who is herself a captive—that his saliva tastes of sand. Hiroshi Teshigahara's black and white film based on this novel contains numerous close-ups of parts of the woman's body, shot so microscopically that they resemble an insect's mandible or gullet bejeweled with grains of sand. Another existentialist obsession, nausea, also marks Jumpei's experiences. Plagued by ennui and disgusted with the world, characters in Sartre and Camus purge themselves by expelling food and foreign objects. In the image of insects, Jumpei repeatedly and instinctively secretes saliva in the dunes. That vomiting fails to cleanse him, culminating in the "yellow gastric liquid" (144) he throws up when he swallows sand to extract water, illustrates that Jumpei is part of the nauseating world, the line between humans and bugs, living and death, entirely blurred. This obfuscating hinges on water, a key symbol in Abe. So close to the sea, Jumpei is deprived of water; briny water, at any rate, will not sustain Jumpei. With his discovery of the capillary action of sand, Jumpei chances upon an epiphany of sorts, namely, that the sand *is* the water. The dry, life-denying sand dune turns out to be pregnant with life-giving water. Teshigahara's film has prepared for this Zen moment through the opening credits where wind-swept ridges of sand fade into water ripples. This enlightenment does not explain away Abe's ambiguous ending, though: the woman suffers an extra-uterine pregnancy and is taken to the hospital. The irregularity of their life style is reflected in the abnormal, life-threatening conception. Believing that "he was still in the hole, but it seemed as if he were already outside" (235) and that he acquired "a new self" (236), Jumpei may be in denial that his new life in the hourglass of sand, literally, is as fraught with problems as his old life in the city. Her mis-conception outside the womb equals his mis-conception outside of human society.

Egg

Faced with modernity, West and East adopt various coping strategies: one projects fear over demasculinization onto bugman that dehumanizes the self; the other retreats, nostalgically, into nature and insect, an idealized egoless state. The West maximizes and deifies the modern self so much so that it falls from the Godhead to a headless fly, whereas the East evacuates the self to a minimalist insect, yet the aesthetic impulse in the arc of a beautiful butterfly or a firefly remains essentially human and even egotistic. Nonetheless, both try to absorb the impact of collision among machine, nature, and human through reconceptualization, mind games that either pretend to see through a fly's compound eyes or pretend there are no eyes at all. I have, so to speak, cross-bred Zhuangzi with Brundle, wondering what the new species would look like. Incidentally, such operative words as "futuristic," "fantastic," "aesthetic," and even "horrific" in the preceding pages share the suffix "(t)ic," intimating that the bugman is an involuntary tic in Western and Eastern cultures. The march of science and technology in both hemispheres are inexorable, any self-doubt relegated to moments of suppressed glitches. Cinematically, Brundle-Goldblum's facial and muscular twitches increase as his metamorphosis to a fly is nearly complete. These tics are the pathology endemic to the mad scientist tales, such as Dr. Jekyll's violent convulsions in his transformation to Mr. Hyde as John Barrymore performs it in the 1920 silent film classic. Asian literati tradition, on the other hand, is dusted off for a comeback in contemporary nostalgic, aesthetic revivals of self-transformation. The high order of wuwo (no self), however, remains an Eastern dream to elude the tight grip of modernity and late capitalism.

Chapter Seven

Kim Ki-duk's Nonperson Films

Korea's national dish or side dish, kimchi, has made only cameo appearances in Kim Ki-duk's corpus of over a dozen films, for instance, in *3-Iron* (2004), where the trespassers into empty houses (*Bin-jip*, the original Korean title) claim the homeowners' dinner table as their own. Indeed, kimchi rarely occupies a place in Kim's staged meals because in miming—pun intended—the lives of marginalized, taciturn protagonists, the filmmaker never has much use for regular Korean meals with multiple bowls of meats and vegetables, kimchi included. While such a plentiful, everyday menu constitutes a staple scene in the Korean Wave's family drama, a global cultural phenomenon at the dawn of the twenty-first century, it connotes a quotidian life that ill-fits Kim's estranged universe. Kimchi's absence notwithstanding, each of his films reeks of the pungent, spicy smell of fermented Chinese cabbage and other ingredients. I do not mean to slight kimchi's side effect of body odor mixing garlic, green onion, chili pepper, and whatnot, as I am a kimchi lover myself, initiated, alas, much too late in life. Rather, kimchi serves as a perfect metaphor for what I call Kim Ki-duk's nonperson films.

Both the making and the consuming of kimchi pivot on transforming physical pain into pleasure, physical and transcendent. Traditionally considered a feminine task, each housewife, as the kimchi lore goes, prides herself on a special kimchi recipe passed down matrilineally. The making of kimchi is labor intensive and arduous: the lengthy preparation of vegetables makes the shoulders sore; the cutting of green onions brings tears to the eyes. In addition, the production does not end in instant gratification. In olden times, earthen jars containing kimchi were buried underground for fermentation and dug out for winter vegetables. Even with modern refrigerators, kimchi requires days of sitting. This process of fermentation allows a chemical change induced by yeast to alchemize raw vegetables into mouthfuls of burning ecstasy, the euphoria of which arrives in the wake of a range of nearly unbearable stimulations to taste buds. Sucking cool air, wiping away snivel, the connoisseur has finally reached nirvana, Korean style. Similar to a sauna, a Turkish bath, a massage, acupuncture, endurance sports, and perhaps sadomasochistic foreplay, physical pain fashions and maximizes pleasure.

The other definition for ferment is "agitation and tumult," which suggest the instability caused by kimchi in terms of sensations and by the Korean Wave in terms of viewer reception. Just as the extreme tastes of kimchi challenge the threshold of pain, the Korean Wave delves into extreme human condition of nonperson. The state of nonperson does not simply equate with dehumanization in the usual sense of the word; rather, dehumanization must be taken to accentuate humanity, since only humans can be subject to it. Therefore, the person in nonperson is simultaneously denied and affirmed, the pain of humiliation mixed with joy, occasionally of a masochistic vein. Psychologically, nonpersonhood appears to be the way to shed human bondage. By abandoning the self, one reaches for a higher plane of consciousness in the same manner that raw, inedible vegetables are turned into fermented kimchi. Should the kimchi dynamic of pleasure and pain be part of the Korean identity, nonpersonhood and the subsequent fulfillment or even transcendence of humanity provide a tentative answer to the question, "why do we consume the Korean Wave?" From Korean to Asian to global, the Korean Wave's nonperson person appeals to the audience in different ways: Koreans attracted to, among other things, the reprise of the traditional sentiment of *han* (historical suffering and the elation of overcoming grievances or simply outliving them); Asians drawn to Western modernity that, paradoxically, alienates; Westerners in search of exotic alternative entertainment that echoes their sense of atomization (Chung, "Toward a Strategic Korean Cinephilia"; see also Ma, *East-West Montage* ch. 7, "The O of *Han Ju*," and ch. 8, "Tradition and/of Bastards in the Korean Wave").

Nonperson and the Korean wave

The term *nonperson* is used in sociology to indicate individuals whose personhood has been diminished or cast in doubt, mostly due to appearance, exemplified by burn victims. An array of loaded terms is often used to signal nonperson: monster, hunchback, cripple, retard, freak, and more. David Lynch's *The Elephant Man* (1980) demonstrates how a deforming disease dooms a Victorian Englishman to a life of misery at the freak show. More "genuinely," *Freaks* (1932) features a cast of characters with disabilities, from a limbless, worm-like torso to Siamese twins. Recent disabilities studies addresses the very issue of discrimination against those viewed as subhuman or nonpersons. In addition, nonperson treatment against others is at times socially sanctioned vis-à-vis, for instance, misbehaving minors receiving silent treatment, waiters and butlers (Stevens in *The Remains of the Day*), panhandlers and drunks. Intriguingly, the last category segues into the Korean Wave, where drinking and drunkenness are part of the master narrative. Otherwise, Western understanding of the nonperson would have difficulty relating to its Korean counterpart.

The Korean sense of han results not so much from physical disabilities as from an inferiority complex, the residual of a history of (neo)colonization by China, Japan, and the West as well as the repression of its persistent divided state of North versus South Korea. This inferiority complex swings—in a drunken state, an emotional outburst, or a surge of passion—into self-inflation so oblivious to others that it verges on the superiority complex. The two opposites complement each other within the tightly knit Korean society. In a hierarchical, patriarchal culture where relations to others are defined by the very language used, alcohol charts a perfect escape route. Similar to the Chinese maxim of *Jiuhou tuzhenyen* ("true confession comes after wine"), a tongue loosened by alcohol confesses deeply buried truth or long-suppressed love; wobbly gait and outrageous mannerism metamorphose the social, exterior self into the real, inner self. Granted, excessive drinking dulls reason, disrupts social order, and renders the drinker dysfunctional. While the intoxicated is not his or her usual self, a nonperson insofar as driving, decision making, and working are concerned, individuality or the true self erupts like night-blooming cereus, breaking down social conventions. Drunken transgressions would wither like the cereus's petals into lame excuses and hangover the following morning. Given that the nonself, nonperson excesses materialize and vanish, inner thoughts are both articulated and silenced, an Asian dialectic between nighttime manifestation and daytime suppression.

This dialectic of self arises not only in drunkenness but in moments of towering, maniacal rage. Lashing out against perpetrators, however, often turns inward, into self-tormenting, suicidal impulse. The nonperson internalizes social stigma; the revenge undertaken cuts both ways—out as well as in. This interpretation is consistent with han, as Chong-hwa Chung and Brother Anthony of Taize describe it: "the force of anger turns inward and burns, a flame of intense unhappiness, leaving life full of bitter ashes of frustration and disillusion" (Translators' Introduction, Yi Mun-yol, *The Poet* x-xi). Among many other artistic expressions of han, Chul-Soo Park's *301/302* (1996) attests to this paradox. The film shows two female protagonists traumatized by patriarchy: an anorexic writer molested by her stepfather; a chef betrayed by her husband. The writer rejects the world in the form of food and the male, both threatening to invade her body, culminating in the suicidal wish of self-disintegration. The chef channels sexuality into the compulsive activity of cooking and eating. Despite the apparent differences, the two women are döppelgangers. The writer and the chef are equally food-obsessed, oral-fixated nonperson wannabes, either wasting oneself away or gorging oneself with foreign objects. blinded by the futile rage against masculinity, they turn against themselves, against femininity. As the chef complies with the writer's death wish, dismembering and cannibalizing her, they wed each other. Unable to challenge the patriarchy, women gain humanity by means of a heinous crime against their own bodies, a monstrosity that transforms pain into pleasure, self-denial into self-aggrandizement, nonperson into a perfect specimen of femininity.

Chul-Soo Park's take of Freud's *Totem and Taboo* is much too ghastly for the mainstay of the Korean Wave, family melodrama, which turns to other means to exploit the same nonperson abyss. Romance comes to be thwarted repeatedly by physical and mental problems that somehow do not blemish performers' facial and physical perfection. Accordingly, the Korean Wave favors blindness and amnesia as tropes for nonpersonhood. Both handicaps rob a lover of full humanity, while preserving intact the "look." Period dramas, on the other hand, resort to yet another nonperson option within the historical context: *nobi,* or slaves, a fate plaguing male and female protagonists in *Shan Dao* (The Tao of Business), *Yi Dao* (The Tao of Medicine), *Dae Jang Kum,* and many more television serials (Kim, "Unheard Voices").

Kim Ki-duk

Kim's films are not alone in exploring nonperson persons. Many Korean texts interrogate similar issues. For example, in Mun-yol Yi's 1992 historical novel, *The Poet,* there is this: "the moment his grandfather had been sentenced, he had become a non-person, had lost all identity" (59). Yi's poet-protagonist realizes that once his grandfather sided with the rebels led by Hong Kyong-rae in 1811-1812, his family turned instantly into pariahs. Not succumbing to the arranged marriage, Hye-sok Na's early feminist protagonist in her 1918 story, "Kyonghui," is sneered at by her father: "Nonsense! You're just a nobody!" (83). Both Yi's and Na's characters sink to the worthless, nonperson undertow in the Korean consciousness. Nonetheless, the protagonists find a way to rise from the abject bottom assigned by the patriarchy, ultimately reaching a state of being that transcends not only nonpersonhood but personhood. The nadir happens to be where the soul takes flight, a convergence of opposites deep within the Korean and Asian psyche. Glancing at his exiled, emaciated father on the hill, the poet experiences a sudden vision: "Ah, now father's going to fly away!" (31). The poet himself accomplishes that in the finale, disappearing into nature, as his son reports: "A poet tied down by nothing in the whole world . . . moved beyond the brushwood gate of the inn and stepped on to the grassy forest trail; at that very moment he vanished completely" (198). The apotheosis in Yi is made possible by the premodern, historical-aesthetic context.

Unmoored from that historical context, thrust amid modernization, Na's protagonist cannot afford a transcendent denouement. Na's closure, instead, shows the heroine Kyonghui experiencing, simultaneously, two epiphanies: one based on Western Enlightenment that moves toward self-realization; the other based on a traditional religious, specifically Zen, awakening that entails self-obliteration. Marrying according to her father's wishes contradicts her Western training on independence, yet to assert herself as a human being above all "beasts," as she puts it, is undercut by self-incineration in her mind's eye: "Kyonghui suddenly felt her hair stand on end. She felt as though her broad face, large mouth, and lanky limbs had all vanished and felt as though she had glimpsed something like a flame floating in the air—like a spark at the tip of a small wheat straw" (84). The "nobody" designation turns literal in her vision. Rather than a degrading nonperson status assigned from top down, Kyonghui embraces and consecrates it from the bottom up, from the feminine task of lighting the stove with wheat straws, which produces food and sustains life. This illumination is closely followed by a scientific analysis of her surroundings, particularly domestic animals: "These were beasts, that is, animals of the lower order, as Kyonghui had learned in zoology" (84). Scientific hierarchy coexists with religious and Buddhist equalizing. Unresolved throughout the story, Kyonghui's tension between individual identity and nonpersonhood continues in Ki-duk Kim's allegorical films, nearly a century later. Kim's oeuvre seems shot through by the struggle toward idealized bodilessness evidenced in Yi's closing and in Na's momentary vision.

Kim's art-house films enjoy quite a following in the West, but they are not all that popular in his home country. His perhaps most famous film, *Spring, Summer, Fall, Winter, and . . . Spring* (2003), appears to embody the quiescence and pensiveness of the East. It continues, nonetheless, a number of Kim's controversial themes, themes of nonperson torment effecting transcendence, of pain inducing pleasure. These themes include physical violence against males, sexual violence against females, and voicelessness or bodilessness. One is immediately struck by the fact that sexual violence is never perpetrated against males. If repeated beatings and copious bleeding so predictable in Kim aim to undo characters' manhood, why do they not culminate in the ultimate form of emasculation: homosexual anal penetration that turns a man into a woman? That homosexuality never occurs despite overwhelming physical violence among males suggests the integrity of masculinity even within Kim's iconoclastic dramaturgy. On the contrary, physical violence against males without sexual subjugation serves paradoxically to highlight machismo. *Spring*, true to its title, progresses in seasonal, circular segments, with the film set in concentric circles that infinitely expand and shrink. The floating temple where the action unfolds occupies the center of a lake, surrounded by rocky mountain peaks covered with trees. In the middle of the temple's wooden deck is a pond with koi. Inside the temple is a stone Buddha statue, sitting in a basin of water also with koi. Interwoven into one are water, wood, and stone, as well as Buddha, man, and beasts—fish and other animals that populate the temple in different seasons. Such fluidity is echoed in the spatial arrangement of the temple. A boat ferries the master and his young novice, anonymous personifications of stages in life, to the lake shore, where a creaky wooden door painted with the twin door gods is all that that separates the temple's watery grounds from the outside world. The small temple is likewise compartmentalized by doors with no walls beyond door frames. But the only time the novice circumvents these symbolic doors, in the "Summer" segment, is when he engages in youthful dalliance with a woman, which leads to his leaving the temple, marrying her, and murdering her out of jealousy and hate in the ensuing "Fall" segment

Returning to the old monk in "Fall," the murderer carries within his bag the blood-stained knife and the stone Buddha that he made away with. Unbeknownst to him, the Buddha has never left him, even at the moment of killing. He comes to repent his sins and attempts suicide by suffocation. Writing "shut" on rice paper, he pastes five pieces over his six facial orifices, closing himself off from life. But the gasps for air suggest a reluctance to end his life, the heaving noise alerting the master, who begins cudgeling him, a favorite Zen strategy leading to sudden awakening, followed by an elaborate contrivance whereby the novice is hung midair with welts and scars over his body, while a candle slowly burns the rope. The corporal punishment does effect a change: the drained novice shaves his head, embarking upon the atonement of carving Prajnaparamita (The Heart Sutra) on the wooden deck with the murder weapon throughout the night, with bleary eyes, bleeding hands, and police detectives waiting to take him into custody. This sequence recurs, like the cycle of seasons, as the aging master readies himself for self-immolation. Covering his orifices with identical rice paper with "shut," the master cremates himself on a drifting and slowly flooding boat. As the middle-aged novice returns in the "Winter" segment after having apparently served his prison term, the penance continues in his wintry martial arts training and self-flagellating climb uphill, burdened by a stone mill and the stone Buddha. Kim choreographs these sequences of hardship, if not self-inflicted then at least welcome by the sufferer. These scenes consist of serene, deliberate step-by-step planning, executing, and enduring of physical and mental torment, all unfolding with minimal soundtrack, muted except for natural sounds and theme music, definitely without dialogue. The drawn-out procedure aestheticizes suffering, best illustrated by the multicolored Prajnaparamita after the night-long carving and calligraphic tracing. The counterintuitive wooing and savoring of physical pain turn these sequences into rituals of violence which maximize pain to the extent that pain gives way to rapture, an alchemization aided in no small measure by the severing of human voice from human body. Robbing the body of voice both deprives it of humanity and calls into question the very idea of humanity as a union of body and voice or mind. Granted, words give shape to our thoughts but they are utterly useless beyond our limited conceptual framework. The human body is enabling as well, but who can deny that it is also a mobile solitary confinement? Herein lies the ambiguity of a voiceless, traumatized nonperson and true personhood beyond physical form and expression. By the same token, Kim's ritualization of violence dangles between sadomasochism that debases and reifies human beings and mysticism that negates demarcation of human and nonhuman.

Unlike the nauseous sadomasochism in films such as *The Isle* (2000) and *Bad Guy* (2001), *Spring* tones down sexual violence. Within the context of the Asian patriarchal, masculinist culture, women are nevertheless assigned minor roles: in "Summer," the novice's lover has few lines other than moans during intercourse; in "Winter," a veiled, guilt-ridden mother has no face. Voiceless and faceless, both come across less as characters than as tropes. The lover serves as the object of desire to consummate not only the novice's sexual longing but his enlightenment; the mother's sin of abandoning the child and drowning in the water hole serve to consummate the novice-master's enlightenment. Insofar as the novice and the master are the same person, the lover and the mother appear to be allegorical personifications of the female sex. Consistently, masculinity in Kim represents humanity in totality, whereas femininity the opposite to humanity, or nature. In this equation, women are nonhuman natural forces, to which humanity embodied by male protagonists struggles to return.

Gender is closely tied to the recurring motif of the waterlogged boat, flooded and barely afloat, in Kim Ki-duk's films. Boats, like the temple and the ferry in *Spring*, crystallize human or man's alienation, albeit buoyant in the watery womb.

Water is outside and inside the boat, as male and female elements intertwine. *The Isle* features a fishing manageress, both the innocent, prelingual nature's child, who never speaks, and the cursed, predatory water elf. She runs the fishing rental business on a lake dotted with isle-like floats, provides sexual services on demand, and exacts vengeance on male perpetrators against not her sexuality but her dignity. The film closes with the woman and her lover sailing away on one of the floats to elude the law and human society. Her lover then wades midstream into a clump of tall grass, which, in the subsequent long shot, metamorphoses into her pubic hair as she lies, nude, in a submerged boat. He hides in her private parts; she floats in a male boat; the sperm-boat bobs in the womb; the boundless water is contained by a male filmmaker's cinematic frames. Likewise, this "prop" materializes mysteriously in *Samaritan Girl* (2004), when the father and the daughter visit the mother's gravesite in the Korean countryside. That this sighting of a boat is eerie and entirely out of place—in the mountains far away from bodies of water and the hulk holding water from a faucet—accentuates the allegorical nature of revisiting the tomb or womb. Leaving Seoul and the underage daughter's seemingly promiscuous activities, entering the deceased mother's embrace in rural Korea, the father bestows a new life onto the daughter. Even her dream of demise in the hands of her father and the burial in a recently dried riverbed repeat the theme of rebirth through water.

The Bow (2005) reprises the water spirit of a vulnerable, mute young woman, probably abducted a decade ago by a boat owner, now an old man looking forward to marrying her when she comes of age, yet potent in her sexuality and mystical power as a fortune teller. Here and elsewhere, numerous scenes of calculated ritualization bear the stamp of a male filmmaker, specifically the objectification of femininity: the old man's active role in the fortune telling and his interpretation of her whispered messages in *The Bow*, the father's preparation of sushi for the late wife in *Samaritan Girl*, his subsequent burying of the sinning/sinned daughter, and more. Accompanied by theme music alone, these highly stylized and elaborately staged moments stem as much from an unconscious patriarchal ideology as from Kim's obsession with male spiritual transcendence by means of female bodies, oftentimes identified with nature. A case in point: *The Bow* ends with a variation of Kim's signature sadomasochistic relationship. The young woman leaves with a young man, while the old man makes a noose from her boat's mooring rope. As she pulls away, the noose tightens around his neck, his eyes bulging and bloodshot, a physiognomic contortion harking back to the "hooked," emotionally entangled and literally via fish hooks, protagonists in *The Isle.* The young woman is moved by the old man's suicidal attempt, aborted unbeknownst to her, and marries him in a traditional Korean wedding. The Korean tradition in nearly every film by Kim heals characters physically and spiritually. Rather than intimacy, their wedding ceremony culminates in the old man playing on his bow-adapted instrument heart-wrenching theme music to a bride spread out in a pure white undershirt. The theme music is a traditional-sounding piece with Chinese *Er-hu*, a two-stringed, violin-like instrument played vertically, yet this "Korean" instrument is supported by a chorus of Western music instruments, a musical potpourri Kim is to repeat in *3-Iron*, where romance unfolds with Arabic-sounding music. Kim's constructed, essentialized Koreanness integrates non-Korean and Western elements, a hybridity similar to his France-inflected filmmaking on the alleged Koreanness with an impressive following—in the West. At the climax of his performance, the old man shoots his arrow straight up into the sky and leaps into the waves. In the bride's slumber, however, her legs part to begin a series of spasm, reaching an orgasm or a childbirth, virginal and parturient blood smearing her white undershirt as the arrow whizzes back to pierce the deck between her thighs. The man is spiritualized against the virgin's body, his boat fast sinking into the amniotic ocean in the finale. The voiceless woman gives an immaculate birth to and completes the apotheosis of the man, now bodiless.

Even without the final beatification, males in Kim formulaically achieve a fuller humanity by virtue of women's physicality. Women abuse their bodies and their bodies are abused in a misogynist and sadomasochistic way. Kim Ki-duk's treatment of Korean women is fundamentally different from the erasure of Korean femininity vis-à-vis Chinese and Japanese female characters examined by Hye Seung Chung and David Scott Diffrient in "Interethnic Romance and Political Reconciliation in *Asako in Ruby Shoes*." The angry artist in *Real Fiction* (2000) lashes out against his girlfriend and the woman with a camcorder from the experimental theater documenting his rage, the cause and the trigger of his pent-up hate. *The Isle* distributes masochism evenly between the manageress and her lover, caught in a tumultuous relationship of carnal possession and platonic perversion worthy of Dostoyevsky. While he swallows multiple fish hooks to terminate his voice or communication with the world, she hooks them inside her vagina when he rows away. As she is mute throughout, the mangling of her vocal chord is not as symbolic as that of her maidenhood. Her personhood lies in her sexual organs, the maiming of which comes closest to self-annihilation.

Kim's women routinely debase themselves for men's sexual needs and, intriguingly, spiritual amelioration. *Bad Guy* (2001) depicts a pimp becoming obsessed with a college student, orchestrating her fall into the red-light district. Gazing at her through a one-way mirror as she sells her body, he maintains a chaste relationship. After much hardship, hers localized in her lower body and his in his face and upper body, they are inexplicably reunited through a déjà vu photograph of them as lovers on the beach. The photo's woman dressed in red drowns herself, in order to be reborn as the student turned prostitute. The pimp undergoes a similar resurrection after near-death experiences on death row and, subsequently, being stabbed in the stomach. Submitting the male body to violence and the female body to sexual abjection somehow allows the two nonpersons to retrieve their true selves from a previous incarnation, which they reenact now as pimp and prostitute. Kim assigns the voiceless role to the pimp, who, in a severe beating, utters his only line in a high-pitched, broken, and almost falsetto voice due to, it is implied, a damaged or severed vocal cord. Qualitatively, the voiceless women, all youthful and attractive, are different from this scarred, morose, hostile pimp. Only in *3-Iron* is there a strikingly good-looking yet silent male on a par with female mutes. Only in this silent male can voicelessness sublimate to bodied bodilessness, whereas female mutes continue to be defined by their bodies

Before we get to the "silent" film *3-Iron*, there is the "talky" *Samaritan Girl* that also came out in 2004. Structurally, *Samaritan Girl* reflects the unresolved tension since Na Kye-sok, drawing simultaneously from the Indian Vasumitra in part 1 and the Christian Samaritan in part 2. Both exemplars in feminine virtues vis-à-vis males in distress, Vasumitra plays a decisive role in shaping the two high-school protagonists' sexual ventures. To purchase airplane tickets for Europe (yet another Western sign looming off-screen), they embark on their escort service, innocent child play to the ever-smiling, seemingly family-less Jae-young, the body that provides sex, but depraved and dirty to Yeo-jin, the voice that phones male clients, whose father is a police detective. Ambivalently lesbian, they become one when Yeo-jin assumes the other's identity after Jae-young's death. In the opening shots, Jae-young advises Yeo-jin to call her Vasumitra, the Indian prostitute-deity who converts her customers to Buddhism through "happy sex" and "maternal love." Such Tantric miracles are echoed in the detective father's stories of Christian wonders during each morning drive to Yeo-jin's school as well as in the daughter's symbolic rebirth in the closing moments

In addition to the East-West dichotomy, another tension pulls the film taut: mystical-transcendent versus realistic-societal readings of female sexuality, or, specifically, how males versus fathers view young girls as sexual beings. What Jae-young insists is spiritual liberation from the body and social trappings is to others, Yeo-jin included, seedy cyberporn and illicit pedophilia. That Yeo-jin would continue in Jae-young's stead, giving not only her body but money back to the clients, can conceivably be viewed as mourning gone awry, a Korean version of *Psycho* (1960) and the cross-dressing Norman Bates. Promiscuity, to a bereaved Yeo-jin, keeps the sex goddess Jae-young alive. Invariably, the romantic depiction of these trysts ends with the clients mending their ways, thus fulfilling the Vasumitra legend, until the second half of the film when the detective father and the realistic realm he represents intrude into the symbolic and mystical context, when the father intervenes with tremendous violence to save his daughter who purportedly saves men's souls. The film undergoes a seismic change as the father, investigating the case of a murdered young woman, looks out from the window of one of the shady motels and sees his own daughter entertaining a client. He begins to stalk his daughter and obstructs, with increasing brute force, any liaison, finally escalating to the suicide of a family man shamed at the dinner table and a murder, perpetrated by the detective himself with some help from police handcuffs. He blurs his professional skills in protecting the public, including minors, with a father's outrage over his daughter's fall. Throughout the curses, slaps, punches, and kicks he inflicts on men who partake of his daughter's body, he continues to behave as the gentle, tender father to his daughter, if slightly more subdued and tormented. The film revolves around multiple ironies: paternal affection gives vent to brutality; external violence is introduced to seemingly peaceful human transactions; pleasure and sensuality turn criminal in the father's (society's) eye; and feminine mercy allegedly blesses all males, while hurting the closest male—the father.

Also released in 2004, *3-Iron* evinces equally poignant ruminations through another set of marginalized, "half-human" protagonists: the thief, Tae-suk, who breaks into houses when the owners are on vacation and the abused wife, Sun-hwa, who used to be a nude model. Both voiceless throughout the film, Sun-hwa does scream into the telephone at her husband early on and concludes the film with "I love you" to her by then phantom lover Tae-suk. To Sun-hwa's abusive husband, the golf-playing master of the house, her remark is intended for him. They appear resolved and embrace, while Sun-hwa steals a kiss from Tae-suk behind her husband's back, literally. The poster accompanying the US release is the film still of the three characters' embrace and kiss, which, coupled with the title *3-Iron*, suggests a triangular relationship or even ménage à trois. In addition to the titillating threesome implied by the film's "name and face" as it is known in the US, which Kim Ki-duk approves of in his running commentary, *3-Iron* borrows from the universal symbol of golf as a sign of affluence. The original Korean title of *Bin-jip* or *Empty House(s)* is reinvented in the global market in such a way as to downplay the philosophy of nonperson nothingness in favor of concrete, sexuality-laced advertising strategies

A house is a vessel, seemingly constant and durable, whose inner space is occupied by different owners at different times (a vessel, of course, means both a container and a boat, which circles back to Kim's favorite prop). By the same token, a body offers an empty space wherein any given self—happy, angry, and so forth—is manifested. While proprietorship of a house or a body seems solid and incontrovertible, boundaries are easily breached, demonstrated by Tae-suk's break-ins and Sun-hwa's bruised face and body. A key difference, however, separates the two violations. Tae-suk resembles a Houdini-type escape artist, with no family, minimal personal history, as the police discover, and no attachment other than the photos he takes in various houses, at times against the owners' family pictures on the wall. In the end, Tae-suk succeeds in fleeing altogether from the prison of his own body—Kim's ideal of bodied bodilessness. Sun-hwa, on the other hand, *is* her body, owned and used by her husband like the luxurious house with modern Western interior design as well as the statue of a half-nude Venus and the golf practice area on the well-manicured lawn. Previously a nude model baring herself to the world, Sun-hwa's career remains unchanged after marriage, except she is stripped naked and traumatized by one man and the patriarchal ownership he symbolizes.

Humans are territorial animals, marking their space through objects, particularly family pictures hanging on the wall. While owners are away on vacation, the empty house continues to be suffused with their images. Into such sharply defined spaces ventures Tae-suk, whose "crime," however, resembles child play in its harmlessness and, frankly, user-friendliness: he fixes electronics, waters the house plants, tidies up rooms, and does the laundry, always in the traditional way of squatting and kneading on a washboard, never the washer and dryer. By taking on such feminine house chores conscientiously, Tae-suk looks like a house sitter rather than a criminal. His youthful look, accentuated by a near-religious adherence to silence, contributes to his increasingly positive image in the audience's eye. As Sun-hwa joins Tae-suk's escapades, they conduct their wordless love by playing with the patriarchal symbol of golf. Their courtship follows a golf ball rolling back and forth between them. The rescue of Sun-hwa from her husband is accomplished with the help of a golf club. Golf balls are henceforth unremittingly deployed as a tool of violence: the corrupt police officer knocks on Tae-suk's head with a golf ball; the husband avenges himself by hitting the balls into a handcuffed Tae-suk; Tae-suk later returns the favor to the police officer. Not yet awakened from the dream of social status and power, Tae-suk does copy the lifestyle of the rich through golf practice. Sun-hwa instinctively tries to stop that emulation, but in vain, resulting in the injury of an innocent woman.

Against Western modernity, Tae-suk and Sun-hwa's love unfolds by way of traditional Korean tropes. Their first touch via their feet barely visible under the table takes place in a house with Korean-style architecture and furniture and a courtyard with miniature lotuses floating on an old earthen jar. The owners of that house wear traditionally inflected dress and show hospitality to Sun-hwa, a total stranger. The simple tea ritual at that house amounts to a private wedding ceremony, sealing their love. The high point of their love is the traditional Korean burial they perform for an elderly man in one of their break-ins, the ceremonial care given to the shroud enough to convince a policeman of their respect for the dead. The dead man's son and family happen to be on vacation in Cheju Island, unaware of their elderly father's apparently late-stage lung cancer. The love expressed through Koreanness is shattered once it encounters modernity. The son suspects them of murder and calls the police on his cell phone. Modern technology enables lightning-speed communication that overwhelms the protagonists' nonverbal communication in the burial and their love beyond words. Thrown into jail, Tae-suk continues his golf practice sans clubs and balls that is, sociopathologically, a sign of growing mental illness or, mystically, the warm-up to the final leap beyond all physical forms. After all, Tae-suk has long been the invisible man, entering houses, in a manner of speaking, behind residents' backs. Tae-suk now perfects his skill of lurking in the 180 degrees behind the prison guard, after countless beatings, a filmic staple attesting to masculinity in Kim Ki-duk and in the Korean Wave in general. Tae-suk's first round of visits to houses and apartments are paid while owners are absent; in his second round after being released from prison, he is a phantom, a haunting presence felt but not seen by the owners. Only Sun-hwa could arrest this shadow of a man. Both weightless beings, as the final shot of the scale on which they stand indicates, Sun-hwa spies him silhouetted against screen doors, reflected in mirrors, and she finally corners him against her own nude picture on the wall. In yet another of Kim Ki-duk's ambiguous endings, she may well be imagining a union with her ghost lover, or their love may have indeed freed them from their bodies. In Kim Ki-duk's oeuvre, nonetheless, such transcendental moments largely spiritualize male protagonists beyond their bodily form, in such scenes as the vanishing into the woman's pubic hair in *The Isle*, the father's departure and symbolic death in *Samaritan Girl,* the master's self-immolation in *Spring*, and the dive into the ocean in *The Bow*. Unique and iconoclastic within the Korean Wave, Kim Ki-duk's recipe has grown slightly repetitive. Considering how prolific and creative the filmmaker has been, Kim Ki-duk is sure to surprise us with kimchi-flavored nonperson experimentations that promise new sensations to our palates. As Kim reaches deep into his midlife fermentation for new visions, we shall gather and feast at his table for years to come, laughing through tears and crying from the deep joy of the heart.

Chapter Eight

Nakazawa's A-bomb, Tezuka's *Adolf,* and Kobayashi's Apologia

"The twentieth century began with a futuristic utopia and ended with nostalgia," writes Svetlana Boym in *The Future of Nostalgia* (xiv). This zeitgeist of looking backwards materializes in Japanese manga and anime as a belated rendezvous with World War II, as a gaze across half a century into the Rising Sun and the invariable averting from the blinding rays of wartime history. Japanese comic's "return of the repressed" entails a coming to terms with the collective trauma that allegedly ended in 1945, yet this yearning to engage a specific past of great pain is adulterated by the human instinct for pleasure and a withdrawal from pain. After all, any gaze into the sun results in a turning away, lest blindness or madness set in. Instead of staring into the sun himself, Vincent Van Gogh lets, maintains Georges Bataille, his sunflowers do that ("Sacrificial Mutilation"). Bataille further casts this paradox of attraction and revulsion of the sun in the image of Icarus: "the summit of elevation is in practice confused with a sudden fall of unheard-of violence. The myth of Icarus is particularly expressive from this point of view: it clearly splits the sun in two—the one that was shining at the moment of Icarus's elevation, and the other that melted the wax, causing failure and a screaming fall when Icarus got too close" ("Rotten Sun" 58). Drawn to the best and the worst of times of imperial Japan, the three manga artists— Keiji Nakazawa in the 1970s, Osamu Tezuka in the 1980s, and Yoshinori Kobayashi at the turn of the century—manage to capture, in the words of Bataille, either "the preceding sun (the one not looked at) [which] is perfectly beautiful" or "the scrutinized sun [which] can be horribly ugly" (57). Rather than dwelling on Japan's historical responsibility over the war, Nakazawa's *Barefoot Gen* represents the tragedy of the atom bomb from the lone perspective of a pacifist family, Tazuka's *Adolf* gives vent to a bizarre anti-Semitic Hitler myth, and Kobayashi's *On Taiwan* peddles his right-wing apologia for Japanese militarism. Either from the left or the right of the Japanese political spectrum, the wartime Rising Sun is viewed obliquely like Hokusai's famous "One Hundred Views of Fuji."

In order not to gaze unblinkingly at the sun or the Japanese wartime history, both Nakazawa and Tezuka locate their subject matter in the pacifist minority during and immediately after the war. Favoring left-wing liberal politics, the two manga artists make possible the English-speaking reader's sympathy and even identification with the antiwar position of the protagonists, who are, needless to say, victims of conservative, militaristic forces of the time. Who can argue with the tragedy of *hibakusha* (explosion-affected persons) in Nakazawa, except to say it is not balanced by any representation of Japanese aggression and atrocities? Indeed, there is no representation at all of Japanese oppression of its colonies other than one Korean character forced into hard labor in Japan. Tezuka weaves his version of the Hitler myth by means of, likewise, an antiwar protagonist. From Nakazawa's A-bomb testimony, Tezuka moves into the controversial realm of "imagining Hitler" (see Rosenfeld, *Imagining Hitler*). Yet the witness and the daydreamer are replaced on the threshold of the twenty-first century by Kobayashi's virulent reactionary polemic. The antiwar position shifts into its nemesis, or Kobayashi's diatribe advocating a revival of the Japanese spirit symbolized by militarism. Composed for the Japanese domestic market as well as, strangely enough, a sizeable market in Taiwan in Chinese translation, Kobayashi's *On Taiwan* was not and will most possibly never be translated into English. By contrast, in English translation, Nakazawa appeals to a global readership in terms of the antinuclear peace movement and Tezuka by way of the fascination for Hitler. Not only are the three artists looking, obliquely, at the sun, but the global audience does the same in English, Chinese, and other translations.

Nakazawa's *Barefoot Gen*

Six years old at the time of the atom bombing of Hiroshima, Keiji Nakazawa in his early career as a cartoonist refrained from the subject altogether, "hat[ing] the very mention of the word." Nakazawa continued to reminisce in "Introduction: My Hope for *Barefoot Gen*" in *Barefoot Gen: Out of the Ashes*, which was the fourth and last of the series: "But in October 1966—twenty-one years after the bomb—my mother died. . . . When her body was cremated, I discovered something that made me tremble with rage: nothing was left of her bones. Usually the bones remain after cremation, but radioactive cesium had eaten my mother's bones away, and they had turned into ash. The A-bomb had taken everything from me, even my precious mother's bones" (x). Nakazawa's rage over the belated incineration and total erasure of his mother propelled him to confront the bomb. A classic return of the repressed, the cartoonist might have attributed to the bomb what is possibly a case of osteoporosis, with little physical remains after cremation and a lifetime of calcium loss. This autobiographical detail makes all the more significant the episode in *Barefoot Gen* when the protagonist Gen Nakaoka retrieves his father's and two siblings' bones from the ruins after an extended period of denial of their deaths. After all, the survivors of the Nakaoka family do not revisit the site of their house for the remains of the dead until volume 3, *Barefoot Gen: After the Bomb*, when they have long perished at the end of volume 1, *Barefoot Gen: A Cartoon History of Hiroshima*. The entire second volume, *Barefoot Gen: The Day After*, manifests Gen and his mother Kimie in various stages of psychological denial. Contrary to Christ's advice, only the living can bury the dead. Gen's family begins the return to reality once they come to accept the fate of the loved ones.

In 1972-73, Nakazawa serialized *Barefoot Gen* in *Shukan Shonen Jampu*, the largest weekly comic magazine in Japan. Art Spiegelman describes Nakazawa's "draftsmanship [as] somewhat graceless, even homely, and without much nuance, but it gets the job done. . . . The drawing's greatest virtue is its straightforward, blunt sincerity. . . . It is the inexorable art of the witness" (Foreword vii). Compared to Art Spiegelman and other graphic novelists of the same caliber, Nakazawa's drawings appear to be artless, yet the simplistic, unadorned style befits the testimonial mode of bomb survivors. The story revolves around the survival of the Nakaoka family, the father's antiwar stance turning them into scapegoats for wartime misery. Indoctrinated by propaganda and patriotic jingoism, the Nakaokas' neighbors and the children's classmates and teachers label them traitors, subjecting the pariah family to discrimination and violence. The only exception seems to be the decent Korean neighbor Mr. Pak, sympathetic because he himself is an oppressed minority. The metaphor of wheat, "push[ing] its shoots up" despite "winter frost" and human trampling, as the father explains in the opening panel, becomes the key to rejuvenating the surviving Nakaokas. Gen (meaning "root") inherits this undaunted spirit, forever resourceful and of good cheer, particularly after the father, the oldest daughter Eiko, and Gen's younger brother Shinji are consumed by the conflagration in the wake of the bomb.

The motif of death and rebirth repeats itself in the manner of a fugue from the wheat imagery to numerous "reincarnations." Gen and the mother Kimie survive the blast purely by chance, protected by a concrete wall and on the attic. Having witnessed three members of her family burned to death, Kimie gives birth to Tomoko amid the rubble, yet Tomoko dies in her infancy due to either malnutrition or the radiation aftereffect of cancer. Gen also rescues a Shinji's look-alike, Ryuta, and an Eiko substitute, the novice dancer Natsue. Gen's pluck notwithstanding, Ryuta is forced to join the ruthless postwar underworld and Natsue is unlikely to realize her dream as a performer with her keloid-scarred face. Even the invalid painter Seiji is, figuratively, pulled back by Gen from the jaws of suicidal depression. Regeneration graces Gen himself in the concluding pages when he finds a fuzz of hair covering his bald head, parallel to the wheat seedlings after the bomb where the land is purportedly to stay barren for sixty years. This gallery of monstrosities, physically as in the case of hibakusha or socially as in the case of thieving orphans of Ryuta and his gang, illustrates Gen's picaresque journey through hell. These supporting characters around Gen emerge and vanish in the narrative without much logic, akin to the chaos in Hiroshima.

What remains constant is the grotesquerie and agony of survival. Numerous reportages and testimonies of the atom bomb have familiarized twenty-first century readers with the nuclear horror, yet to see, page after page, the walking dead with peeled-off skin dragging behind, with the flesh torn clean off the bones, with melted faces, with maggots squirming in the wounds and flies feasting on corpses is so nauseating that the reading induces, as Robert Jay Lifton argues in *Death in Life* (1967), compassion fatigue. Although John Hersey's *Hiroshima* (1946), Michihiko Hachiya's *Hiroshima Diary* (1955), Masuji Ibuse's *Black Rain* (1970), Kenzaburo Oe's *The Crazy Iris* (1985), Akira Kurosawa's *Dream* (1990), and a host of others have shared their mushroom vision, either survivors' close-ups or artists' long shots, with us for decades, the rawness of Nakazawa's art still assaults our senses. Nonetheless, the cartoonist balances the nightmarish images with comic conventions of physical slapstick and humor, courtesy of the indomitable Gen, the combination of which proves to be a saving grace to sustaining not only the Nakaoka household but also the reader.

The choice of wheat as a central metaphor is intriguing. Throughout the four volumes, the Nakaoka family teeter on the verge of starvation, from wartime rationing to postwar collapse of the economy, particularly for a refugee family, to the US military "foodstuffs" Gen risks his life to steal from trigger-happy American guards. Such cans turn out to contain packs of playing cards and rubber balloons, an ironic reference to condoms and the sex industry accompanying the American GIs wherever they go. The never-ending search for food focuses on the staple of Japanese diet, rice, against which is the Nakaoka icon of wheat, as if the cartoonist deliberately chooses an atypical Japanese food to embody the antiwar, dissenting spirit of the Nakaokas. The erstwhile un-Japanese sentiment comes to be embraced wholeheartedly in postwar Japan.

Imaging Hitler in Japan

Lionized as the "God of Comics" and "God of Animation" in Japan, Osamu Tezuka the manga artist had a long career that boasted of 500 titles of manga and animations and about 150,000 drawn pages. His most representative works include, in chronological order from the 50s to the 80s, *Metropolis*, *Jungle Emperor*, *Tetsuwan Atom* or *Mighty Atom*, *Phoenix*, *Ribon no Kishi* or *Princess Knight*, *Black Jack*, and *Adorufu ni Tsugu* (*Adolf*, or more precisely, *Tell Adolf*) (Bird, "States of Emergency"). Tezuka's five-volume *Adolf* (subsequent references use volume number and page number) was serialized in the Japanese magazine *Shukan Bunshun*. Though *Adolf* was the first book by Tezuka to be translated into English, perhaps on the merit of its sensational subject matter more than anything else, *Jungle Emperor* might be the one most familiar to the American public, thanks to its 60s and 70s resurrection as the TV animation *Kimba, the White Lion*, which in turn inspired Disney's *The Lion King*. Despite Disney's denials, the resemblance of Kimba and Simba and that of a host of other characters and episodes underline the derivativeness of global cultural productions, Tezuka's *Adolf* included. As Jean Baudrillard declares of the postmodern age, "we live in a world where there is more and more information, and less and less meaning" (*Simulacra and Simulation* 79). The voluminous information on the Third

Reich obtained by Tezuka, evidenced in the year-by-year comparative time line of World War II appended to many chapters, gives way to the most sensationalizing, slanderous, and anti-Semitic hoax about the mass murderer, namely, that Hitler was, to borrow Sander Gilman's coinage, a self-hating Jew. His artistic imagination seems captured not so much by the actual deeds of Hitler as by the large liberties promised to him by the free association of the first name, Adolf. Put another way, Tezuka pirates the given name of the mass murderer as a loaded "logo" to advance his "action thriller." Just as Disney plagiarizes his *Kimba,* Tezuka borrows from the Hitler kitsch. In so doing, the history of World War II constitutes merely the backdrop to a highly improbable plot involving three Adolfs.

In addition to Adolf Hitler, the other two Adolfs are Adolf Kaufmann, born in Kobe of a German consular official and his Japanese wife, who is sent back to Germany and eventually becomes a ruthless German officer; and Adolf Kamil, the son of a Jewish-German refugee couple who ran a bakery in Kobe. All three Adolfs have something to hide. Hitler tries to conceal his alleged Jewish ancestry, for which he sends Kaufman on a mission back to Japan. A member of the Hitler Youth and later of the SD, Kaufman denies his Japanese, hence non-Aryan, blood. The Kamils flee the nazis to Japan and the Jewish boy believes that he is entirely Japanese, even though his playmates call him "whitey." The two younger Adolfs are childhood friends turned deadly enemies.

Not only does racial passing occur but cultural and generic boundaries are also crisscrossed: the five-volume story spans Japan, Germany, and the Middle East; in terms of genre, the Holocaust seems too weighty a topic for comics. The vehicle for breaching borders of race, culture, and genre proves to be the narrator, Sohei Toge, a former college track-and-field star turned newspaper reporter. He covered the 1936 Berlin Olympic Games for a Japanese newspaper and his communist brother passed on to him the documents of Hitler's birth. Toge is pivotal to *Adolf* because, unlike the three namesakes who are either murderous or angst ridden, Toge is funny. Upright and unsophisticated, Toge provides a great portion of the gaffes and laughs central to the appeal of comics. On the other hand, Toge offers a frame for the story befitting the grave, ponderous nature of the subject matter. The opening of the first installment *Adolf: A Tale of the Twentieth Century* (12-14) and the conclusion of the last installment *Adolf: 1945 and All That Remains* (253) hook up like the two ends of a full circle as Toge visits Kamil's grave at an Israeli cemetery. Similar to the conclusion of Spiegelman's Pulitzer Prize-winning *Maus I* (1986) and *Maus II* (1991), with the tombstone of his Holocaust survivor-parents, Tezuka captures the dirge-like quality of the Holocaust. But Toge's interior monologue, repeated at the beginning and the end of the story, spells the problematics of imagining Hitler or, put another way, of translating the Holocaust: "This is the story of three men named Adolf. Each Adolf lived a life that was very different from that of the other two . . . Yet the three of them were bound together by a single twist of fate." In the last pages of the fifth volume, Toge proceeds to remark that the story he is leaving behind "will be read by millions of 'Adolfs' all over the world" (5: 251). Adolf becomes everyman who becomes Hitler. A chilling implication, Tezuka perpetuates Hannah Arendt's theory of the banality of evil, except that the cartoonist ups the ante of the case study from Eichmann to Hitler.

While the hidden ideology is irresponsible and reprehensive, it is lightened considerably by Tezuka's mastery of the medium. His techniques of storytelling enable him to traverse nations and time periods with great ease, albeit with many coincidences that require suspension of disbelief. Action and mystery, which Tezuka manages to maintain well over a thousand pages, testify to his power as a comic artist, but they jar against the somber, lamentational opening and ending. The plot revolves around the struggle over the possession of documents proving Hitler's racial background, including Hitler's birth certificate and letters written by his mother to his Jewish grandfather. Both the Japanese and German secret agents, Adolf Kaufman among them, attempt to rob Toge of these documents. Toge, on the other hand, risks everything to protect the documents, which he repeatedly claims would "bring down Hitler." This brief sketch suffices to demonstrate the anti-Semitic drift of Tezuka's text. The Holocaust is attributed to Jewish self-loathing. In other words, by annihilating Jews from the face of the earth, Hitler denies, in effect, his own Jewishness. A viciously ahistorical interpretation of *Endlosung*, this approach finds eager advocates among modern artists trying to contain the genocide in individual psychosis, such as George Steiner's *The Portage to San Cristobal of A.H.* (1981) and W.D. Snodgrass's *The Fuhrer Bunker* (1977). Anti-Semitic rhetoric also rears its head in Tazuka's character of Frankenburger, Hitler's wealthy Jewish grandfather, who is said to have raped his German maid and to have sired Hitler's father. This follows the racist stereotype of lascivious Jewish males coveting Aryan women (2: 36). Another stereotype of Jews surfaces in the Jewish girl Eliza's father, an opportunistic businessman. In order to survive, he not only collaborates with the nazis but he encourages Eliza to befriend the Hitler Youth member, Adolf Kaufman, as an "investment" against any impending catastrophe.

The translator Yuji Oniki writes, in his introduction to *Adolf: An Exile in Japan,* that "the story revolves around the secret of Adolf Hitler's Jewish ancestry. The historical validity of this premise is less important than the fact that each Adolf in Tezuka's story represents not a particular race or nationality, but a particular 'mixed' circumstance" (n. pag.). Such a casual dismissal of the anti-Semitic thesis from a then Ph.D. candidate in comparative literature at the University of California at Berkeley is disturbing. It is tantamount to saying that the official whitewashing in Japanese history textbooks of the Rape of Nanking in 1937 is "less important than the fact that" atrocities take place in every war due to multiple causes. The translator's fashionable discourse of universalism obfuscates historical responsibility and memory; his promotion of a global village of mixed races and cultures makes possible amnesia over past traumas and contributes to ever-increasing racial and ethnic strifes. The translator's sentiment is echoed by the editor. Annette Roman, the editor of the *Adolf* series at Cadence Books, agrees that the plot is "somewhat contrived" (Introduction, *Adolf: Days of Infamy*) but adds that "I am a child of survivors, but in a sense all of us are survivors of some kind." Roman's father is a Hungarian Jew who survives forced labor camps, but her mother is a Protestant German who acquires survivor status, in Roman's view, as a result of having endured the Allied bombings. Though of different generations and nationalities, Tezuka, Oniji, Roman, and perhaps many of their readers share in the willful abuse of terminologies, in the erasure of collective memories.

Conceivably, fans of manga would defend Tezuka's shift from the historical Hitler to the fictitious Adolfs on grounds that Tezuka is, after all, Japanese, removed from the European continent where the drama of the extermination of Jews unfolded. Such apologists would surely contend that any such representation of the Holocaust is bound to be a translation. A survivor's memoir such as Elie Wiesel's *Night* (1956) and Primo Levi's *Survival in Auschwitz* (1959) is certainly closer to the collectivity of human tragedies we have come to call the Holocaust than a fictitious work such as William Styron's *Sophie's Choice* (1979), D.M. Thomas's *The White Hotel* (1981), or Sylvia Plath's various poems on her suicidal wish. The distance between *Endlosung* and its various translations—autobiographical or imaginary—may be one in degree rather than in kind, though. Even Spiegelman's *Maus,* based on the life story of his survivor father Vladek, remains a representation of the Holocaust, as I argued in "Mourning With the (As a) Jew": "what a reader holds in the hands is several removes from the actual event—from the incomprehensible totality known as the Holocaust, to the fraction experienced and then selectively recalled by Vladek, to Art Spiegelman's 'doodle drawings' based on the shaky recall of that fraction, and eventually to mass-produced, market-oriented 'facsimiles' of Spiegelman's originals. The contrived spelling of *Maus* exemplifies at the outset the comics' artifice and, therefore, its removal from the reality of that animal" (118). Yet, even as a Japanese artist transcribing his wartime experience onto the half dozen pages of *Adolf* on the Japanese Royal Army's atrocities against the Chinese, Tezuka's representation is well intentioned yet woefully inadequate. The artist's indulgence in fantasies over Hitler sharpens his failure in confronting Japan's own historical responsibility in the Chinese theater and elsewhere. The emphasis on Japan itself, furthermore, lapses into a self-congratulating reiteration of the sacrifices of dissidents in Japan, such as Toge and his leftist friends, whose efforts, revealingly, concentrate on the outlandish scheme of exposing Hitler's Jewish ancestry rather than on the sabotaging of the domestic war machine. After all, instead of *Adolf,* why did Tezuka not draw comics titled *Hiro* after the Japanese emperor Hirohito? Why does he expend so much ink—and Tezuka is meticulous in his drawings—on a foreign devil, Hitler? Perhaps the Japanese readers prefer an escape into the fantasy land of the Third Reich, hyped by the grotesque mass destruction. Even as fervent a manga critic as Frederik L. Schodt concedes that *Adolf* may have inspired the popular trend in Japan marked by "bizarre, fantastic theories about Jews . . . With subject matter ranging from recycled American and European anti-Semitic tracts, to claims that Jews are a superior race and (guess what?) that Japanese—not Europeans—are actually the true Jews" (*Dreamland Japan* 252). Through the English translation of *Adolf,* Tezuka extended his influence from the Pacific Rim to the US and around the world, educating the young on the plasticity of history and the thrill of imagining Hitler.

The translation and publication of *Adolf* for the English-speaking, hence world, market are underwritten by the "colonization of the mind" already manifest in the Japanese texts. Tezuka's trademark of Japanese female characters with Caucasian facial and physical features have undoubtedly endeared his postwar readers' longing for the beauty and power embodied by the West. Accordingly, the geisha Kinuko (Sachi Honda) (1: 131) in fact resembles Rosa Lampe, a German Barbie doll with an unrealistically-proportioned body and an impeccable face (1: 45). With exactly the same face, Kinuko has slightly darker pupils and wears a geisha's hairdo and kimono. Japanese women in the Western image have cloned themselves in manga and other forms of cultural production. The economic superpower of Japan continues to fantasize itself in terms prescribed by Western media and icons.

Kobayashi's *On Taiwan*

As manga and anime fans around the globe are enamored by the fantastic rather than political nature of the genre, Yoshinori Kobayashi is not as well-known a figure as Osamu Tezuka or Hayao Miyazaki. Nonetheless, Kobayashi's manga enjoys a considerable domestic market, particularly among right-wing conservatives and, further afield, pro-Japan Taiwanese. When the Chinese translation of Kobayashi's *On Taiwan* was published in Taiwan in 2001, an uproar raged over its apologia for Japanese militarism during World War II, for colonization of Taiwan and other parts of Asia, and for postwar nationalism in Japanese and Taiwanese politics. Protests erupted over the representation of the "benevolent" Japanese colonization of Taiwan and, in particular, over the claim that Taiwan's aboriginal military units and comfort women "volunteered" their service to Japan. While the historical entanglement and political intricacy of the controversy has escaped the attention of global fans, Kobayashi's manga has touched a raw nerve in Japan and Taiwan, unleashing furious debates in public discourse.

Undoubtedly, Kobayashi is the spokesperson for Japanese discontent over postwar liberal democracy, indulging in the golden past of Japanese colonialism, perpetuating a revisionism of the war. Along with right-wing politicians, Kobayashi has even contributed to the diluting of the history of the war in Japanese textbooks. Kobayashi stands for a revolt against what he sees as "masochistic" liberal guilt over wartime aggression and atrocities. In addition, he embodies the fear of the rise of China in the twenty-first century, reacting to which he raises the specter of Japanese nationalism. Breathing new life into the revisionist project in *On Taiwan*, the cartoonist buttresses his case by virtue of prominent pro-Japan personages in Taiwan, including ex-President Teng-hui Lee, industrialist Wen-lung Hsu, and long-time Taiwanese independence activist Mei-ling Jing. The Nipponphile chorus from Taiwan is lauded by Kobayashi as the last sanctuary of the good old Japanese spirit, preserved like a time capsule among many Taiwanese over the age of sixty who were educated and came of age during the Japanese colonialism of Taiwan in 1895-1945, uncorrupted by the left-leaning culture in Japan proper. The Taiwanese writer and critic Ying-chen Chen quotes the historian Guojun Dai in attributing Lee's and other Japan zealots' motives to an "accomplice structure" (8). Chen contends that these pro-Japan Taiwanese have been so implicated in Japanese interests and their sense of identity so inextricably bound to Japan that they must idolize Japan and turn a blind eye to its historical faults ("*Taiwan lun zi baoyen jiqi gungfeng gozhao*" ["The Violent Rhetoric and its Accomplice Structure"]).

In terms of Taiwan's history, Lee and his cohort find in Kobayashi's comics an echo for their nostalgia for the past, prior to the island's takeover by Chiang Kai-shek's nationalist troops in 1949. In this shared pro-Japanese sentiment, Lee and like-minded Taiwanese forge a common identity against Chiang and the "mainlanders," the occupying force that brought the white terror, such as the February 28 Incident, during which Taiwanese dissidents were persecuted. The exponential growth of the Chinese economy and Chinese might across the Taiwan Strait further fuels Taiwanese paranoia over the mainlanders' affiliation. Taiwan independence becomes a rallying cry against unification with China, alleged to be the mainlanders' dream. Owing to such political faultlines in Japanese and Taiwanese domestic politics as well as to international tensions among China, the US, Japan, and Taiwan, *On Taiwan*, despite its narcissistic kitschiness and distasteful diatribe, bursts open Taiwan's silence over Japanese militarism.

Delving into topics somewhat serious for comics, Kobayashi even attempts to chronicle Taiwanese history and political struggle. But he often willfully distorts historical facts. A case in point: the Taiwanese resentment against the arrival of Chiang's nationalists is aptly captured in the Taiwanese saying at the time: "dogs leave; pigs come" (145). "Pigs" refer, of course, to nationalists, whereas Kobayashi seems to feign ignorance over the meaning of "dogs"—Japanese colonists. In general, Kobayashi presents a simplistic version of complex social issues. He even gets basic statistics wrong: he claims that mainlanders constitute 16% of Taiwan's population, Taiwanese 82%, aborigines 2-3%, leaving out the Hakanese altogether, as if this large minority does not exist. With all his trouble, Kobayashi's agenda is self-serving. His sycophantic hero worship of Teng-hui Lee and his discovery of the Japanese spirit in certain Taiwanese are tautological and ultimately bestow honor on the old Japan. If Lee and Wen-lung Hsu embody the "warrior" or "samurai" tradition, then they are neither Taiwanese nor Chinese (206). Rather, they are the real Japanese long vanished in postwar Japan.

Working in cahoots, the cartoonist and pro-Japan Taiwanese attribute to Japanese colonialism nearly all the modern amenities on the island, from its unique species of rice, the irrigation system, the Sun-Moon Lake, the railroads, the infrastructure for electricity, the sugar industry, and whatnot. Kobayashi even compares Japanese colonization favorably with British India, with the former bent upon improving living standards on Taiwan. In his narcissistic and polemical style, Kobayashi is the protagonist in *On Taiwan*, marked by the ant-like antennae of hair overhanging his forehead. Seeking a verisimilitude of real people, Kobayashi tends to blow up the characters' faces and heads. With political idols such as Teng-hui Lee, Kobayashi invariably draws Lee as looming large, godlike, over the panel. Kobayashi also resorts to actual photographs for key moments in this loosely organized travelogue across Taiwan and memorable audiences with Taiwanese luminaries. Unlike Nakazawa and Tezuka, whose comics lend themselves to the tastes of different segments of manga fans globally and are hence translated into the lingua franca English, Kobayashi is translated into Chinese and marketed in Taiwan only, for his right-wing reactionary Japanese politics is not embraced elsewhere. The three manga artists cast the Rising Sun during WWII in varying light to perpetuate their respective artistic and ideological interpretations. Ultimately, massive sufferings such as the Holocaust and wartime Japanese atrocities are perhaps too weighty for comics and even for literature as a whole, resulting in gazes that are all somewhat oblique.

Chapter Nine

Orientalism Goes to War in the Twentieth Century

Orientalism does not go to war; Orientalism is war, with East and West pitted against each other ideologically, if not militarily. In war, one engages the enemy to inflict maximum injury, to do away with the other altogether, at least its will to wage war. Orientalism as a Western imaginary that subjugates the East, hence, befits the aims of war perfectly; war, in turn, culminates the Orientalist urge of domination. As Carl von Clausewitz notes, war is "nothing but the continuation of policy with other means" (*On War* 69), Orientalism in wartime is, at the very least, an extension of Orientalism in peacetime. Furthermore, if war is marked by its terrifying unknowability, where one vacillates between supreme power over the other's life and death and utter powerlessness in one's own possible demise, then it resembles the stereotypically inscrutable Orient, forever polarized between the aesthetic and the abominable, attracting and repulsing the West at once. Linking the two—war and the Orient—means linking the trio—God, death, and the Orient. Not to mince words, death becomes the East, which signals a metaphorical death or the cessation of consciousness and rationality, the self-designated provinces of the West since the Enlightenment. Defined yet constricted by such logocentrism, the West secretly covets its opposite—an insensate oceanic feeling—that is projected onto the Orient.

With the Cold War filling the gap between the hot wars of World War II, the Korean War, and the Vietnam War, the latter half of the twentieth century witnesses a relentless power struggle in East-West relationships, which periodically erupts into armed conflicts. A wide swath of Western literature and history of the previous century is hereby covered: during World War II, the Japanese were the enemy in the Pacific theater, replaced in the Korean and Vietnam Wars by communism. While each war is distinct, I concentrate in these texts on the shared presence—friend or foe—of the Orient, without on the battlefield as well as within in the Orientalist mind. I thus investigate fictions and films featuring whites in war-ravaged Asia or amid Asian bellicosity. The number of texts selected is small; there are simply far too many war narratives, especially war movies, to be inclusive. Western characters in these texts dangle between their power as (neo)colonial Gods and their paralysis, a death-like trance induced by the yellow peril (Rohmer), the futility of violence and racism (Mailer), illegal substances and eroticism (Greene), brainwashing (*The Manchurian Candidate*), black humor (*M*A*S*H*), escapist reveries (O'Brien), and postmodern affectlessness (Ballard). In the multitude of scenarios, the godlike West is a given, a constant, but its proverbial omnipotence often comes across as a delusion of grandeur. The West aggrandizes itself so wantonly that it flees into the Orient, a fetishized mental construct for the West to assert as well as disavow itself. An arc from repulsion by to attraction to the Orient marks the dots from Sax Rohmer to J.G. Ballard, from the West's self-affirmation to self-abnegation.

War stories become, ironically, as much an averting as a confronting of the trauma of war. There coincides a need to share and confess about the terrors of war and the antithetical pull away from it. Freudian transference squarely motivates Western texts' ambivalence over war. Freud analyzes the paradox of war trauma in *Beyond the Pleasure Principle* (1920), where shell-shocked veterans of World War I experience repetition compulsion, such as nightmares, while consciously shying away from memories of the battlefield. To resolve the apparent contradiction between his theory of the pleasure principle and the displeasure repetition compulsion inevitably brings, Freud links Eros (sex drive) with Thanatos (death drive). Freud first defines the pleasure principle as "a tendency operating in the service of a function whose business it is to free the mental apparatus entirely from excitation or to keep the amount of excitation in it constant or to keep it as low as possible." He follows it up by positing the ultimate goal of this drive for "all living substance" being "to return to the quiescence of the inorganic world" (76). Traumatic experience recurs in part due to the appeal inherent in the death drive, particularly when such recall proceeds in projection or transference—relocated behind the veil, so to speak. Cathy Caruth further elaborates that "The pathology [of trauma] consists, rather, solely in the *structure of its experience* or reception: the event is not assimilated or experienced fully at the time, but only belatedly, in its repeated *possession* of the one who experiences it. To be traumatized is precisely to be possessed by an image or event" (Introduction, *Trauma* 4-5). Caruth continues to maintain in *Unclaimed Experience* (1996) that in trauma narratives there is a "double telling, the oscillation between *a crisis of death* and the correlative *crisis of life*" (7). Accordingly, the twentieth-century war tales "double back" to the hell of war in such a way as to contain and even neutralize the hellishness. This reliving of war years in symbolic forms satisfies the psychic imperatives both to survive and to die, albeit imaginatively. As Freud draws not only from war veterans but train accident survivors and his one-and-a-half-year-old grandson for evidence of repetition compulsion, one is struck by how trauma projection and transference from self to other, from violence to peace, from brokenness to intactness can seem so downright, for lack of a better word, infantile, a psychological defense mechanism so basic that it is deployed by adults and children alike. Ironically, in depicting the aggressiveness of a war, novelists invariably lapse into childish regressiveness and "play soldiers" like any neighborhood kids firing toy guns, only to fall and writhe in death throes, only to rise again—the repetition of simulated violence culminating in an inert corpse. This pattern of "play God, play dead" characterizes literary Orientalism on war-torn Asia. The Orient unfolds as a perplexing spectacle in the image of a Chinese box or a play within a play, through which the West conjures up extravagant dreams, ending predictably with death.

That the Orientalist mentality resembles that of a child at play is evidenced by the persistence of simplistic, dualistic stereotypes. Evil Fu Manchu of the yellow peril joins hands with the good, comical Charlie Chan in Western subconsciousness. The two Orientals' physical differences merely veil the Western mastermind's psychological projections of paranoia and the ensuing overcompensation (Wu, *The Yellow Peril* 176). The two are so closely entwined that they are given a kinship in stories concocted by the West. Jachinson Chan quotes Marvel Comics' *Master of Kung Fu* to demonstrate the parricide attributed to the Asian American psyche, that is, to abandon Asia for America. Shang-Chi, protagonist of *Master of Kung Fu*, denounces Fu Manchu: "I swore to oppose you . . . Now, my father, you die!" (*Chinese American Masculinities* 3). Jachinson Chan proceeds to associate Shang-Chi with both Bruce Lee's martial arts and Charlie Chan's probity. What seems missing here, however, is the fact that Sax Rohmer imposes the Oedipus complex, yet another of Freud's hypotheses, onto the Orient. Rohmer, of course, has on more than one occasion proudly announced that he knows "nothing about the Chinese" (qtd. in Van Ash, 72), indicating his sense of superiority over his subject, which, in retrospect, is both ignorant and childish. Yet Rohmer's colonial attitude is passed down to Norman Mailer in the extreme prejudice of the prosecution of war against the "Japs" in *The Naked and the Dead* (1948).

Orientalist stereotypes make possible, with absolute impunity, escapism from the harsh reality of war, but they readily beg the question of and sorely test Orientalist willfulness. The evolution from the near-total erasure of "Japs" and racism in Mailer to the imaginary fraternizing with the Vietcong in Tim O'Brien's *Going After Cacciato* (1975) to Clint Eastwood's counterpointing pseudo-Japanese perspective in *Letters of Iwo Jima* (2006) on the basis of a second-generation Japanese American's rewriting of General Kuriyashi's posthumous *Picture Letters of the Commander in Chief* charts a gradual decentering of Western collective consciousness, where the enemy is allowed to emerge as something more than a menacing phantom. This is due as much to the exigencies of globalization—the erstwhile enemy is now one's neighbor and trading partner—as to the history of the United States. The United States has, after all, undergone a baptism of fire from the triumph of World War II to the stalemate on the Korean peninsula to defeat in Vietnam. This century-long baptism has to some extent singed from the Western psyche the old-fashioned masculinity that tends to feminize the East into emasculated Asian males and hyperfeminine Asian females—the latter manifested in the pair of Madame Butterfly and Dragon Lady, reincarnated in Zhang Ziyi and Gong Li of *Memoirs of a Geisha* (2005). In terms of Asian masculinity, however, Orientalist war narratives see fit to portray, albeit begrudgingly, Asian resistance, its passive effeminate attributes substituted by dynamic strength.

Norman Mailer frames the war story in *The Naked and the Dead* with character profiles that offer a panorama of the American society, from the privileged New England upper class to the disenfranchised working class, from the Midwestern small town to the South. Without a single point of view, Mailer moves ceaselessly from one character to the next, a multiperspective that is, nevertheless, entirely from the American side. Consequently, Mailer shifts between the battle plan of General Cummings and his personality clashes with his assistant Lieutenant Hearn. As incredulous as it may sound in view of the military hierarchy, Mailer arbitrarily adopts an ideological angle to interpret conflicts, be it the conservative fascist Cummings versus the ineffectually liberal Hearn, or the fascist Japan versus US interests. Beyond the outlandish test of will of the two officers, Mailer also narrates through the eyes of the "bad" Sergeant Croft and those of the GIs in his platoon. Croft is the quintessential killer-soldier, the archetype of a tyrannical father who is routinely eliminated to make way for a happy ending of sorts, such as the killing of Sgt. Barnes (Tom Berenger) by Private Taylor (Charlie Sheen) in Oliver Stone's *Platoon* (1986). This archetype projects evil, intrinsic in any war, onto a certain American character in the same manner Dr. Jekyll dissociates himself from Mr. Hyde or the Freudian ego from the id. Tim O'Brien does exactly that with the bad officer Sidney Martin, stickler to rules or standard operating procedures (SOP), and the "badass" Oscar, allegedly from inner-city Detroit in *Going after Cacciato* (1975). Croft is so irredeemably evil that he plays with a Japanese captive like a cat plays with a mouse before shooting him in cold blood; moreover, he has his commanding officer Hearn murdered by withholding information of an enemy presence. One salient feature of Mailer's exclusive American perspective is Jewish characters, who evoke the long history of anti-Semitism and the Jewish role as scapegoat. One Irish American GI Gallagher, for instance, immediately blames the "Yid doctor" upon learning of his wife's death during childbirth. The American culture is fighting the enemy without—the Japanese—as well as the enemy within—anti-Semitism.

Like *Catch-22* (1961), the war against the Japanese is absurd: the battle on Island Anopopei is won by accident by a Major in General Cummings's absence, whereas Lt. Hearn's reconnaissance mission, ordered indirectly by Cummings out of a petty vendetta against his subordinate, goes awry, resulting in heavy casualties, including Hearn's. The reconnaissance turns out to be unnecessary since the battle has already been won. Having done away with Hearn, Croft leads the platoon on a single-minded pursuit of a mission, which is aborted by a nest of hornets. In the wake of the hornet attack, Croft's last thoughts, practically the book's as well, are on the insurmountability of Mt. Anaka, which obstructs the mission. Both Cummings and Croft appear to wield supreme power over others; Cummings, in fact, likens himself to God. But their command comes to a preposterous end. The deadliness of the war game only makes it so much more ridiculous.

The Japanese name of the mountain range, Mt. Anaka, symbolizes the impossibility of comprehending the Japanese, their defeat notwithstanding. Japanese soldiers make cameo appearances in killing Americans and in being killed. Understandably, communication between the opponents is minimal and often over a battlefield. The first Japanese voice, "Yank. We you coming-to-get, Yank" (149), rings across the front line of a river. The first description of a Japanese soldier's face and the only close-up occurs right before he and his comrades are blown up by a grenade and the sole survivor is summarily executed by Croft (189). The only sustained enemy presence is through the diary of a dead Japanese officer, whose last words are mediated through the army's Japanese American translator Wakara. Having volunteered for the army so as to leave the internment camp and now besieged by military racism, Wakara feels for the humanity inherent in the diary's poetry, yet he echoes the Orientalist rhetoric of the duality of beauty and voidness made famous by Ruth Benedict in *The Crysanthemum and the Sword* (1944): "Behind the beauty [of the diary entries and Japanese culture] it was all bare, with nothing in their lives but toil and abnegation. They were abstract people, who had elaborated an abstract art, and thought in abstractions and spoke in them, devised involuted ceremonies for saying nothing at all" (248). Mailer pontificates supposedly with the inside knowledge of a Japanese American character Wakara, who is but a mouthpiece to hide the novelist's lack of understanding of the other. The subtleties of Japanese culture are dismissed as abstract and nothing, a cliché gesture to justify Orientalist arrogance.

The West's haughtiness improves little in the hands of a Briton writing on the conflict between the colonial French, aided by the US, and Vietminh, the predecessor to Vietcong. Graham Greene, in *The Quiet American* (1955), sets up a fundamental East-West divide, with the latter split into the young, "quiet" American spy Pyle and the older, world-weary British journalist Fowler, suggesting that the American empire is poised to take over the old colonial power. Despite Fowler's repeated claim, "I'm not involved," Pyle and Fowler fight over not only symbolic control of Vietnam but of Fowler's mistress Phuong, for Phuong, whose name means "Phoenix" with the mythical association of reincarnation from ashes, is the war-torn Vietnam. A triangular romance among, pardon the expression, the old King of Europe, the young Duke of America, and the whore of Vietnam unfolds. With such bald-faced stereotypes, it is surprising that Greene critics remain as blithely indifferent to Orientalism or racism in general as Greene was. These critics attend more to traditional Euro-American literary studies. Neil Sinyard raises the biographical ménage à trois among Greene, Catherine Walston, and her husband Henry to elucidate the tension in the fiction (*Graham Greene* 66). Harvey Curtis Webster quotes Greene's letter to the *New York Times* to prove Greene's anti-Americanism: American foreign policy in Indochina and elsewhere is dominated by an innocence that is "like a dumb leper who has lost his bell, wandering the world, meaning no harm" ("The World of Graham Greene" 23). Gwenn R. Boardman reports that the novel is based on "four visits of three months each between March 1952 and June 1955 . . . as a correspondent" (*Graham Greene* 101). A. A. DeVitis finds "Sartrean existentialism" at the heart of *The Quiet American* (*Graham Greene* 116). None of these critics sees beyond the tradition of and the split within the West to investigate the equally split personality attributed to the Orient.

Given that the name of Phuong signifies both annihilation and rebirth, her naiveté further counterbalances with her scheming elder sister. Granted, Fowler at one point self-reflexively muses that perhaps Phuong is a figment of his making: "'she won't scratch, she'll only decay.' But even while I made my speech . . . I knew I was inventing a character just as much as Pyle was" (124). A postmodernist turn, it does not last long amid this problematic text fraught with extreme, ultimately dehumanizing, delineations, such as this one on the Vietnamese guards on a watch tower: "They looked like schoolboys, but with the Vietnamese age drops suddenly like the sun—they are boys and then they are old men" (84). Rather than accepting at face value the judgment of "schoolboys" versus "old men," we witness a sophisticated, middle-aged Fowler giving vent to juvenile imperiousness, where the other is either alive or dead, either an endearing toy or discarded. The rare moment of lucidity over Phuong's constructedness is overshadowed, above all, by Fowler's death wish, the yearning for oblivion through an immersion in the East. Fowler confesses that "it's better to die like this. That's why I came east. Death stays with you" (113) and "I came east to be killed" (119). Before the literal death prosecuted by the Vietminh, such as the rusted bayonet in Pyle's chest, Fowler seeks the metaphorical death or the suspension of selfhood by means of opium and sex, both serviced by Phuong, a métisse prostitute, a brothel called "House of 500 Girls," or Vietnam as a (w)hole.

Nor does the moment of lucidity manage to shed light on the hackneyed racial binarism: the Red horde comes into contact with Fowler through the journalist's assistant Dominguez, a Gandhi-like Indian from Goa. The saintly, hybridized Dominguez is in touch with the shadowy, violence-prone Chinese communists. Fowler locates a Mr. Chou's junkyard in the city's Chinatown, recommended by Dominguez. The junkyard is a mere front for Mr. Heng, a communist operative bent upon stopping Pyle's meddling at all costs. The junkyard and the family inhabiting it constitute a site of utter chaos of objects, rituals, and "race," the height of Oriental incomprehensibility. Yet what appears to be trash and nonsense to Western eyes camouflages a conspiracy that will eventually turn Vietnam red. Fowler and Pyle are, of course, deceptive in their own ways as well: Fowler hides his imminent transfer and his wife's refusal for a divorce in order to keep Phuong longer; Pyle masks his identity as a spy. Although not intended as such, Greene may have stumbled upon a "defensive masquerade" in the character of Pyle, as Michael Rogin explains that the countersubversive Cold Warriors often adopt the subversives' tactics, becoming de facto the subversives, on the grounds that "the world [is] divided between a defensive good and a pervasive, conspiratorial, and 'demonic' evil" (qtd. in Nguyen, *Race and Resistance* 71), and the only way to outwit conspirators, so goes the countersubversives' rationale, is to be even more conspiratory.

The master of disguise surfaces at the height of the Cold War. Set in the early 1950s, *The Manchurian Candidate* (1962), directed by John Frankenheimer, is a complex thriller which epitomizes cold war paranoia. It not only reflects the tension of the Korean War a decade ago but the abiding paranoia in the year of the Cuban missile crisis, a year that leads to assassinations, civil rights disturbances, and the

Vietnam debacle. Paranoia suggests a subject plagued by insecurity, besiegement, and gnawing suspicion of conspiracy against himself. One sure way to cope with paranoia is concealment or psychological transference, which *The Manchurian Candidate* accomplishes via a throwback to the Korean peninsula. Similar transference takes place in Robert Altman's 1969 film *M*A*S*H*, based on Richard Hooker's novel of the previous year, and continued as a TV series from 1972 to 1983. To circumvent the ongoing trauma of the Vietnam War, Altman transposes from the Vietnam on the television set in the late sixties to black humor in Korea in the early fifties. Daily evening news of the battlefield are shrouded by black comedy and bawdy jokes revolving around a military mobile hospital, collective suffering softened as individual fun and game.

If laughter is Altman's anesthetic for the viewers' anxiety, *The Manchurian Candidate* attempts the opposite, ratcheting up fear to the point of hysteria over losing one's faculties to communist brainwashing. Both hilarity and hysteria insulate the masses by eliciting either emotional release or defensive loathing and hatred. The myth of mind control springs from the coupling of two sources: Pavlovian behaviorism and communist China's campaign of thought reform (*xinao* ["brainwashing"]). Ivan Petrovich Pavlov (1849-1936) is a Russian physiologist whose experiments centered on the conditioned reflex. A pioneer of modern experimental psychology, Pavlov is recognized for bridging physiology and psychology, linking the body with the mind, for which he received the Nobel Prize in 1904. Pavlov performed surgeries on dogs and measured their salivary and gastric juices upon stimulation with food, either consumed or suggested, and herein lies his theory of conditioned reflex. Marxist materialism sees in Pavlovian theories a confirmation that animal behavior results from brain function. Thus behavior and thoughts are all traced back to brain cells and the nervous system. Nevertheless, there is no evidence that Pavlov extends his experiments from dogs to human beings. And for *The Manchurian Candidate* to present a Chinese scientist, Dr. Yen Lo, from the Pavlov Institute, presiding over the brainwashing, it requires a leap of faith in Soviet and Chinese scientific breakthroughs, which were nonexistent at the time. Moreover, this paranoia over conditioned assassins stems in part from the apparent mass defection of American POWs during the Korean War, believed to have buckled under intense and prolonged interrogation by their communist captors.

In Richard Condon's 1959 novel, *The Manchurian Candidate,* from which the film was adapted, the Intelligence and Reconnaissance patrol of nine soldiers, led by Major Ben Marco (Marco Polo?), is first infiltrated by Chunjin, Marco's orderly and interpreter, captured by North Koreans, transported to Manchuria, and finally brainwashed by Yen Lo. The brainwashing of the patrol members, particularly Raymond Shaw, played by Laurence Harvey, is accomplished in four short days, from July 8 through July 12, 1951. Being missing in action longer than that is likely to arouse suspicion and blow the cover for Raymond. Yet according to studies conducted in the fifties, thought reform practiced in China lasted months, if not years. Each of the three subjects in Robert Jay Lifton's *Thought Reform and the Psychology of*

Totalism (1961) had undergone over three years of thought reform. The speeding-up of brainwashing relies on drugs and technology, but Condon never bothers to illustrate what kind of techniques are employed. In Frankenheimer's film, the episode on brainwashing is composed of a single demonstration chaired by Yen Lo, who shows off to the Russians and Chinese the end result of his four-day program. Accordingly, the film skips the entire process of brainwashing except the demonstration, which occurs through fragmentary recalls from nightmares suffered by Major Ben Marco, played by Frank Sinatra, and Corporal Al Melvin.

These dream sequences, in addition to the opening shots, are the only representation of the Korean War, since the film is otherwise set in the US. The American soldiers, as these dreams show, are conditioned to experience the demonstration, in which two of their men are murdered, as a boring lecture at the Ladies Garden Club in New Jersey, a group of middle-aged and elderly women discussing plants and gardens. Cinematographically, the switching between past trauma and displaced dream is accomplished through 360-degree pans from the stage to the audience and back, during which American matrons are replaced by communist officers, flowers and plants by guns and deaths. Also in this crucial scene, Frankenheimer carefully interjects race and sex into the novel: the nightmares recalled by Marco and Melvin differ in that the former, dreamed by an Italian American, consist of white ladies exclusively, whereas the latter, dreamed by an African American, consist of black ladies. More importantly, the ruthless tyranny imposed by alien patriarchs such as Yen Lo and other male communist officers is disguised as a tiresome party of matron-like characters from Marco's and Melvin's respective lives. Yen Lo the puppeteer hides behind the hallucination involving middle(wo)men; foreign penetration of the mind masks itself as an irritable yet harmless pursuit, a feminine hobby for aesthetics. In contrast to Raymond Shaw's Oedipus complex, Marco and Melvin suffer from patriarchal control (Yen Lo) in drag or disguised as conservative, bourgeois matriarchal conformity (Ladies Garden Club).

But the brainwashing proves, ultimately, a failure, for they repeatedly wake up screaming at the moments of the nightmare when Raymond, following Yen Lo's orders, strangles a comrade and shoots another. These recurring nightmares, driven by conscience and guilt, are the undercurrent to minds which are otherwise perfectly dominated. Major Marco subsequently battles out of conditioned reflexes through the domestic help of a nurturing, Nightingale-like Janet Leigh and the support of the US Army. Hence, patriotic, red-blooded American parents join hands to defeat subversive, "red" parents. Likewise, while foreign intervention denies Raymond independent thinking and emotions, camaraderie and true love from fellow Americans such as Ben Marco break this spell, leading him to avenge his loved ones. The film declares that whereas Marxist control reduces human beings to animals with conditioned reflexes, American ways elevate individuals into higher love and sacrifice.

The killings during Yen Ho's demonstration take place at the whim of communist participants seeking concrete evidence of mind control. However, these chance executions establish a pattern of placid, automaton-like facial expressions and behavior in the American soldiers while prosecuting abominable crimes against their own. Since none but Raymond continues to revert back to this robotic state in the United States, it is essential for these scenes to showcase all nine American soldiers behaving uniformly, under the influence of brainwashing. Dictated by forces beyond their control, all of them appear to be entranced. Such possession is taken to be inherent in the Orient: the Orient *is* a trance, whether pseudo-scientifically engineered (*The Manchurian Candidate*) or opium and sex induced (Rohmer and Greene). Another alternative to manufacturing Oriental trances is Francis Ford Coppola's myth making in *Apocalypse Now* (1979), where Marlon Brando's Kurtz plays a deranged God in the Southeast Asian jungle after his sudden illumination. To his would-be assassin Willard, played by Martin Sheen, Kurtz attributes his awakening to Vietcong brutality. "And I remember," Kurtz recalls, "I was shot with a diamond bullet right through my forehead." Kurtz has figuratively died, leading an afterlife, resurrected by the grace of the Vietcong or the Orient.

As opposed to a General's panoramic view in Mailer, Tim O'Brien's *Going After Cacciato* is told from the limited perspective of the "common grunt" (198), filled, like any other war narrative, with scenes of bureaucratic absurdity and farce. As opposed to the transference of *M*A*S*H* and the mythologizing of *Apocalypse Now*, O'Brien opens his novel with an unflinching "threnody," what Mark A. Heberle describes as "O'Brien's most distinctive stylistic device, the mundane catalog or list that evokes significance through understatement" (*A Trauma Artist* 115). O'Brien recalls eight fallen comrades, with his elegy continuing in the form of the specifics of each casualty throughout the first forty-one chapters (116). This gaze at the horror of war triggers, in time, its own elaborate "escape clause"—a fantasized trek across the Orient to reach Paris, nominally in pursuit of a deserter, Cacciato. Indeed, as the epigraph of Siegfried Sasson's poetry says, "soldiers are dreamers," an ironic twist to what soldiers do—kill. This escapist reverie provides, on the one hand, the wish fulfillment of a Vietnamese lover and a Vietcong friend and, on the other, the projection of anxiety when an Iranian deserter, like Cacciato's pursuers or followers, is executed. (Yet another projection of anxiety of the post-Vietnam, civil rights era is the African American character Oscar Johnson, who leads the fragging against their inflexible commanding officer. Johnson is portrayed in the intimating black stud image associated with inner-city Detroit.) Occupying between nineteen to twenty out of the forty-six chapters, this pursuit takes the reader through Vietnam; its border with Laos; a Vietcong tunnel; Mandalay, Burma; Chittagong, Bangladesh; Delhi, India, via the Delhi Express; Ovissil, Afghanistan; Tehran, Iran; Ankara and Izmir, Turkey; Piraeus and Athens, Greece; Zagreb, Yugoslavia; Austria; Germany; Luxembourg; and, voila, Paris. The latter half from Turkey to Luxembourg is a whirlwind with scanty details in comparison to the richly textured first half of the journey. The interest in the peoples and cities of Asia is prompted by personal involvement in the Vietnam War, whereas O'Brien fast-forwards the narrative once the patrol reaches Europe, no longer the exotic Orient. "The rest is easy" alludes to the familiar European setting (5). Heberle calls this journey "an exotic, Americanized tour of the world that reflects popular stereotypes and Hollywood adventure films," adding that "'The Road to Paris' included one way or the other in twelve of the nineteen quest chapters echoes Hope-Cosby musical comedies" (131) and that this pursuit "frequently parodies the typical World War II GI prison escape film" (139).

Scholars and critics disagree on exactly how to categorize the three strands of the novel. Heberle finds the imaginary pursuit in nineteen chapters, the protagonist Paul Berlin's thoughts while on voluntary all-night shift on the observation tower at the edge of the South China Sea in another ten, and the eight deaths in ten more (114). Tobey C. Herzog divides up the "tripartite" structure more precisely: ten of the forty-six chapters on "Observation Post"; sixteen "fact chapters"; and twenty on the trip to Paris (*Tim O'Brien* 82). The reason for this difference of opinion may well be that toward the end of the novel, O'Brien increasingly mixes the fantasy of the journey, the memory of deaths, and present reality. Both critics allude to certain reviewers' dissatisfaction about the journey chapters. Heberle cites John Updike, who "found O'Brien's vignettes of battlefield trauma extremely powerful writing but complained that the book lost focus and force by continuingly shifting to the fantasy quest after Cacciato, which seemed by comparison an adventure story" (113). Herzog writes that Updike labels the 8,600-mile odyssey "picaresque interludes" (91). While critics may not see eye to eye with Updike, they seem to concur in downplaying the significance of the grand tour through the Orient. Instead, critical opinions multiply on "us" Americans, ignoring "them," the repressed Orient.

The protagonist Paul Berlin is named after one of Christ's apostles. Berlin, on the other hand, is a divided city, betokening a character torn between desertion and duty, fear and courage, fantasy and standing guard, wetting pants and spilling blood (Kaplan, *Understanding Tim O'Brien* 83). The cause of the fantasy journey throughout the night guard lies in Berlin's own shameful soiling of pants when a comrade accidentally sets off Cacciato's smoke bomb to warn off the hunt. Berlin's inability to hold in check his bodily functions leads him to spin off a discourse entirely under his control. To suggest this is to regard the road to Paris chapters as a compensation for losing control of his bowels, a regression to infancy. However, the journey can conceivably be taken as a letting go, a release from mental shackles, and a wish fulfillment that brings joy. The reverting to incontinence signals, psychologically speaking, shame as much as intensified, hyperactive imagination to elude the war. Fouling oneself heralds deliberately fouling out of the war game; the escapist reverie ejects from the body politic soldiers who dream of going AWOL (O'Brien writes in the nonfiction *If I Die in a Combat Zone, Box Me Up and Ship Me Home* that he could not go AWOL for fear of shaming family and community in Minnesota [73], a sentiment echoed in *Going After Cacciato* [264]). Put another way, the paradox of the novel converges on the title of "going after," which points to pursuing a deserter as well as imitating him. The key word is "going," which commences the chase as well as the urinating.

Given the duality of body functions and of psychological turns within the West, it is egregious that O'Brien consistently essentializes the Orient. Having conjured up unremitting flights of fancy of the Orient, Berlin remains named after a Western city. The nomenclature fails to do justice to the doublespeak intended by the protagonist, who should be called, for lack of a better term, Paul Orientalist. The same problem plagues the character of Cacciato. Seemingly of Italian descent, he is described thus: "See how the eyes slant? Pigeon toes, domed head? My theory is that the guy missed Mongolian idiocy by the breadth of a genetic hair" (8). Moreover, Cacciato keeps smiling like the proverbial dumb Oriental in comics and movies; his "round face" suggests the full moon face of Mongoloids (26). The Oriental subtext, however, is avalanched by Christian symbolism; Cacciato turns into the squad's conscience or a Christ figure in rejecting the "fragging" or fratricide of Lt. Sidney Martin. Existentially, Cacciato's initial brings to mind the convict or condemned. As the squad plots against a dangerously rigid West Pointer, Cacciato fishes in "the Lake Country," also evoking Wordsworth's "The Child is father of the Man" ("My Heart Leaps Up When I Behold"). Cacciato's inaction or passivity in the face of a seditious act echoes Christ's prior to the betrayal. In the vagaries of Berlin's night thoughts, Cacciato also serves as a guide and a rescuer—literally, from an Iranian prison where the team is stranded for desertion.

When Orientals do come around in O'Brien, they are, alas, readily recognizable as stereotypes in the vein of Graham Greene's pairs: the erotic Phuong and her repugnant elder sister; schoolboys and old men. Berlin fantasizes the squad chancing upon Sarkin Aung Wan and her ugly aunts. The name "Sarkin Aung Wan" recalls the fictitious Southeast Asian country of Sarkhan in *The Ugly American* (1958). Tobey C. Herzog sees "Wan as a representative of an American male's romantic vision of idealized Asian women—a 'mother and lover'" (95). Her aunts' water buffalo, Nguyen, is killed by the squad's trigger-happy scout and the two crones continue to moan and sob at day and wail at night, for Nguyen is implied to have been "breastfed" as a calf (52). Orientals are deemed regressively "oral": either the desirable Sarkin Aung Wan licks Paul Berlin's wound like a dog (122) or the undesirable aunts suckled their pet animal. Both scenarios cross humanity and bestiality, maternity and male fantasy. In crisis, Sarkin Aung Wan further rises to the occasion like the legendary Guan Yin, goddess of Mercy, whereas the aunts drop from the narrative as haphazardly as they materialized, their banishment as incredulous as their earlier role as extras.

This narrative crisis arrives when the squad finds itself, like Alice tumbling down the rabbit hole, falling into a Vietcong tunnel, managed by a Li Van Hgoc, who turns out to be a Vietcong deserter—once again echoing the escapist anxiety—condemned to underground imprisonment. In view of the horrifying tunnel that resulted in the deaths of two comrades and the murder of the officer who ordered the two searches, Berlin feels compelled to envision what lies inside the tunnel and imagine a reconciliation of sorts between the combatants. This psychological imperative entails not only familiarizing himself with the death trap but fraternizing with the Vietcong, who is like "us," trapped between absconding and serving. Typical of Orientalists who seek transcendence over, shall we say, the dead body of the nonself, O'Brien vests a mystical vision in Van's interpretation of the land (*Xa* in

Vietnamese). The unintelligibility of the foreign word gestures toward a meaning beyond English and the existing paradigm, thus making some sense of a senseless war waged on a strange land allegedly exhibiting "features [telling] of the personality, but whose personality was untelling. The underground, the smiling man [Van] said, was the literal summary of the land, and of mystery contained in it; a statement of greater truth could not be made. *Xa Hoi*, the party, had its vision in *Xa*, the land" (86). With his inane smile, his vacuous statement in the superlative degree, and his tautological and circular rhetoric equating the land and the people, the Oriental spiritual guide is bound to disorient and, ultimately, disillusion, formulaically manifested in abrupt aging: "Suddenly the man [Van] sagged. His smile was gone . . . His pith hat fell to the floor and spun like a top. The man's hair was white" (95). Similar to Greene's use of old men on the watch tower, O'Brien intends to shock with the vision of sudden death. At the very moment of illumination, the Orient is snuffed out. Both novelists play God and play dead by masterminding an Orientalist discourse and its "sudden death." Philip Caputo engages in similar maneuver in *A Rumor of War* (1977). The memoir records, first of all, a young, invincible Caputo "playing God." But this idealism of 1965 quickly deteriorates with the escalating war, to the point of spiritual morass in the latter half of the book, particularly Caputo's own court martial for ordering the murders of two innocent Vietnamese.

Seemingly at variance with previous texts, J. G. Ballard's *Empire of the Sun* (1984) is narrated from child protagonist Jim's perspective of the war and subsequent internment by the Japanese army at the Lunghua Camp near Shanghai. This novel is based on, as the foreword announces, the young Ballard's experience of internment from 1942 to 1945, with certain major revisions. One is that, contrary to the novel's lone child, the Ballards, including the parents, stayed together at the Lunghua Camp (Ballard, *A User's Guide to the Millennium* 283-94). The point of view of a young teen from the age of eleven to fourteen rather than that of soldiers, journalists, and medical personnel in no way exempts the horror of war. The war trauma, in fact, intensifies to such a grotesque level that it numbs the reader. This is, after all, Ballard's intention. While Ballard is primarily known as a science fiction writer, *Empire* is often categorized as a World War II novel; this work and his *The Kindness of Women* (1991) are, as Roger Luckhurst puts it, "detached from [Ballard's] oeuvre in their generic shift; both can be read as new additions to an honourable 'confessional' mode, thus escaping the derogatory appellation of 'science fiction'" (*"The Angle Between Two Walls"* 154-55). The generic shift notwithstanding, Ballard's style of postmodern affectlessness and flattened interiority informs *Empire* as much as any of his novels and short stories. Arguably, the protagonist's survival by way of deadening his sensibility turns even more unnerving in *Empire* because of its semi-autobiographical and historical setting as opposed to the futuristic, post-Holocaust one. Jim's detached survivalist mindset can be traced back to Ballard's style of clinical description of futuristic ruins, the death of affect, and Gothic humor. Ballard appears to imbue, retroactively, this novel on an early adolescence in China with a temperament steeled in subsequent decades in England and (science) fiction writing.

Or the other way around. It is tempting to follow Peter Brigg's lead in attributing Ballard's stylistic keeping at "arm's length" his subject matter of catastrophes to "a childhood spent beyond the European-American axis" (*J. G. Ballard* 11-12). Brigg claims that the novelist's outsider perspective "came about partly from a childhood lived in the Far East" (12-13). David Punter echoes this view in attributing a "Freudian *Nachträglichkeit*, a postponement or deferral of meaning" to Ballard's oeuvre, where *Empire* offers "a kind of key to [Ballard's] symbolic landscape" (*Modernity* 136). Early trauma, in Freudian terms, creates the paradigm of a fragmented world and psyche that Ballard is doomed to repeat in science fiction. The Orient in this view is the originary yet repressed wound, belatedly surfacing in *Empire*. This seems to be born out by the conclusion of *Empire* when Jim, leaving for England, reflects that "only part of his mind would leave Shanghai. The rest would remain there forever, returning on the tide like the coffins launched from the funeral piers at Nantao" (279), which eerily circles back to the opening paragraph where "the tides that raced up theYangtze and returned to this gaudy city all the coffins cast adrift" (3). However, Ballard does it with so much sardonic relish and so devoid of any moral center that somber trauma theories run aground with a writer who resonates well with Jameson's depthlessness, Baudrilliard's simulacrum, and postmodernist playfulness, all of which drive Ballard to test the limits of evil. Within the context of *Empire*, Ballard situates the reverse of postmodern utopianism in the specific site of war-ravaged China. The urban ruins are described precisely, meticulously, even clinically, without any emotion, as if through the lens of a camera rather than human eyes.

Granted, much of Jim's reactions at the camp can be chalked up to post-traumatic stress disorder (PTSD), such as the Stockholm syndrome whereby Jim identifies with his Japanese captors, creating in the last days of the war a doppelgänger in a young kamikaze pilot. Faced with such moral vacuity, critics never cease to supply a "lesson." In the vein of Robert Jay Lifton's psychological studies, Andrzej Gasiorek sees Jim's shutting down of "ethical vocabulary" as leading to "psychopathology" (*J. G. Ballard* 148). Jim's adaptability, Gasiorek observes, "relies on a numbing of affect, which permits him to accept the inverted values of camp life as normal" (147). Peter Brigg echoes this ethical assessment by pointing to his affinity with surrealism, marked by "'the death of affect,' the twentieth-century condition in which the sheer weight of the horror of violence and the confusions of the emotional life have deadened human reactions, a survival mechanism negating the values of classic humanism. The increasingly bizarre and exaggerated images of the human condition in Ballard's own work are efforts to shock readers into an awareness of this state and to move them so powerfully that reactions are reawakened" (16). Whereas Brigg's initial sentence seems apt, the second sentence risks simplification in that Ballard's dehumanizing universe is so numbing that readers are lulled into the same waning of emotions. Only when readers are bored with the macabre, chilling repetition do they realize their own complicity. Only then will the shock of no longer being in shock dawn on readers.

With neither British nor US combatants, *Empire* appears to skirt the province of "Orientalism Goes to War," yet it embodies the issue most fully. The novel opens with a cast of privileged Western civilians served by a squadron of Chinese domestics within Shanghai's foreign concession in the 30s and 40s. Colonial racial hierarchy informs Jim's surroundings. Jim shouts at his Chinese Amah: "I'll kill you!" at the least provocation, but is filled with amorous fantasies over his White Russian governess, a euphemism for babysitter. Such godlike characters are immediately reduced at the Lunghua Camp to starving inmates on the brink of death. Deemed a "war child" by the selfless humanitarian Dr. Ransome, the "good father," Jim at Lunghua increasingly immerses himself in the war and "Japaneseness," assisted in no small measure by the opportunistic, survivor par excellence Basie, the "bad father." In place of Eliot's "hollow man," which is at least three dimensional with a subjectivity to be filled, Jim is flat, an object without interiority. However, Jim's self-alienation and desensitization is not exclusively the result of wartime trauma.

Even in prewar Shanghai, in the luxurious prison of the foreign concession, reality enters into Jim's mind like a film: "The whole of Shanghai was turning into a newsreel leaking from inside his head" (5). Jim feels that the commentator on the newsreel "boomed in his head" (4) and his family chauffeur Yang once worked as a film extra. Lived reality and the equivalent of today's virtual reality intertwine. The battle raging outside, on the newsreel, or inside Jim's head are one and the same, a loop that never ends. The bedlam on the streets of prewar Shanghai, "this electric and lurid city" (23), is viewed with the same kind of disinterestedness as Jim witnesses the crater-filled rubbles and war atrocities, all evolving into postwar chaos. Typical of postmodernism, space substitutes for time. Ballard's aesthetics of urban wasteland seems inspired as much by the Shanghai of the past as by the postnuclear holocaust dreamscape of the future. Since time is more or less rendered obsolete, that the historical setting would forbid the sci-fi motif of cyborgization does little to keep Ballard from infiltrating Shanghai life with technology, as if machines are implanted in living organisms. Jim's mental constructs, needless to say, come in the metaphor of newsreels. Foreign expatriates' lifestyle of endless parties revolves around automobiles and other modern amenities. Aircrafts are Jim's obsession, from a balsam wood model airplane to a Japanese Zero. About to die of hunger in the postwar confusion, Jim is saved by manna from the sky packaged in three layers of steel: cans of Spam and powdered milk in canisters dropped by B-29 Super fortresses. Metal and technology in the form of guns and bombs gobble up China, but they sustain Jim, one of their own, in the dark days.

Technology is surely not the purview of the West alone, as Japanese colonial machinery subdues the subcolony of China and British colonies such as Hong Kong and Singapore. Yet even ferocious Japanese soldiers can be temporarily mistaken for stereotypically effeminate Orientals. The two figures at his old home's entrance porch, Jim surmises, are women wearing "white gowns with deep sleeves that floated from their arms. Jim was sure that his mother had come home and was greeting one of her guests." The momentary lapse lands Jim, Basie, and his American partner

Frank in Japanese hands, for soldiers "in kimonos were running from the house [to seize them], like a party of outraged women fresh from their baths." As Frank is being bludgeoned to death, Jim still hears the sound from "his mother's picnic gramophone," sustaining and perhaps mocking the fleeting illusion of feminine Orientalism (80). Not just the vice of Orientalist stereotypes persists in a war, so does the yearning for transcendence. Jim's life is spared because of the intervention of a Mrs. Philips, a devout Christian, who offers Jim her potato, and of a Mr. Maxted, who beseeches Jim to play dead to survive the death march perpetrated by the Japanese. Both Mrs. Philips and Mr. Maxted die soon after their last offering to Jim, but Jim's warped mind suspects their intentions. In a "dream-wake" state induced by extreme physical and mental conditions, Jim turns Mrs. Philips into "Death, with her mother-of-pearl skin, [who] had almost seduced him with a sweet potato" (197). Not only does Jim feel no guilt, for he has no affect, but also his defense mechanism demonizes his guardian angel, so to speak. Notwithstanding Jim's increasing blurring of dream and wakefulness, self and other, peace and war, and living and dead, one discerns the human longing for something nobler, perhaps even a religious impulse.

Ballard chooses to climax neither in Orientalism nor religiosity. Rather, the book ends with the bang of a complete switch of life and death. Finding his kamikaze pilot doppelgänger dead, Jim reaches a near-crazed mental state. As he eats from a can of spam, "the greasy flesh was still alive, as if carved from the body of the breathing animal. Its lungs and liver quiver in the can, still driven by a heart." Deciding that "living flesh was not meant to feed the dead," Jim feeds the dead Japanese instead for the obvious reason that the Japanese is believed to be alive. Incredibly, the pilot's "chipped teeth closed around his finger, cutting the cuticle" (270). Dead or cornified epidermis around fingernails, the clinical term "cuticle" replaces "skin" that would associate more with the living; rather, the word choice highlights the "dead" within the living. This ghastly scenario is posited on two pieces of dead meat—spam and the kamikaze pilot. The pilot is but a corpse for the raising, as Jim, "by prizing his teeth apart . . . had made a small space in his death and allowed his soul to return" (271). This trope reflects Ballard's ultimate Orientalist fallacy: the omnipotent Japanese, like prewar Western nationals, are but props in his war novel, subject to Jim's and, ultimately, Ballard's, power of animating. Akin to *Empire*, all the texts analyzed here consistently feature the Orient as a prop, a set, or a minor motif, despite the irony that it takes two to have a fight. Since all these wars take place on Asian soil, that the East remains marginal to the conflict bespeaks the very nature of Orientalism, which erases the other. With the ongoing war on terror in the twenty-first century, one witnesses the identical pattern from the Bush administration on down "playing God, playing dead," the opening salvo of "shock and awe" settling into a deathly pall of despair over the American Goliath.

Chapter Ten

Hyperreal Beijing and the 2008 Olympics

The Beijing Olympics commenced on 8 August 2008 with great fanfare in the opening ceremony orchestrated by the fifth-generation filmmaker Zhang Yimou, aided by Steven Spielberg (before he quit to protest China's policy on Darfur) and what the *People's Daily* dubs the "five-tiger generals," including such a Chinese celebrity as the "fireworks" artist Cai Guoqiang ("Zhang Yimou" 1). The number 888 is pronounced "bu, bu, bu" (as in "but") in Cantonese and is considered close to "fu, fu, fu" (as in the f-word) for "prosper, prosper, prosper." A Cantonese habit long adopted by the whole country, the auspicious date of 888 was deliberately chosen for the game that would purportedly demonstrate China's prowess to the world. Sports, after all, have long been the proving ground, literally and metaphorically, for Asia to showcase modernity vis-à-vis its adversary the West. Dominated by Western (neo)colonial powers, the East during the Cold War and the contemporary global era resorts to the seemingly nonconflict, nonviolent athletic arena and tropes to prove its worth. Hence, the lingo of track and field competition suffuses East-West rivalry. During the Cold War, the nuclear race and the race to the moon were watershed events. Chairman Mao's disastrous Great Leap Forward of the 1950s touted the slogan "Surpass England and Catch Up with America" in a few short years. The Sino-US relationship in the 1970s was channeled into the game of "ping-pong diplomacy," far friendlier than late-Qing "gunboat diplomacy." Ping-pong diplomacy stood both parties in good stead: China made contact from a position of strength; the US downplayed and belittled the outcome of this "mini-sport." In good time, amid recalls of Chinese products and the US economic downturn, the ping-pong ball pickled into *Balls of Fury* (2007), after Bruce Lee's *Fists of Fury* (*Tangshan daxiong* [1971]), with Christopher Walken, a caricature of Fu Manchu, in quasi-Qing wardrobe and pompadour hair style, plus a queue. Christopher Walken's wardrobe and pompadour hair style make him an androgynous character, consistent with the stereotype of castrated and effeminate Oriental males. Back in the late 60s and early 70s, the Little League Baseball championships won by Red Leaf and other Taiwanese teams in Williamsport, Pennsylvania, boosted national identity for the island beleaguered internationally. In other parts of East Asia, the equation of sports with national pride applied as well. Professional baseball arose in postwar rubbles to restore Japan's self-image. The 2002 World Cup semifinal appearance of the host South Korea led to high expectations and the crushing defeat of the 2006 game in Germany. Recently, Asian exports such as the Houston Rocket's Yao Ming and New York Yankee's Wang Chien-ming became celebrities on both sides of the Pacific, a transnational promise yet to be realized in reverse flow by the American export Michelle Kwan and the like.

Translated back into English, however, "fu, fu, fu" sounds like the repetition of an expletive. Indeed, Beijing's official triumphalism revolving around 888 meant the city's underbelly was, pardon the expression, "fucked up." The Olympic hype spelled the end(game) for the old Beijing, literally, as old *hutong* ("alleys"), *siheyuan* ("single-storied courtyard houses"), and other infrastructure of hundreds of years were peremptorily dug up to make way for (post)modernist sports venues and relevant facilities of steel and fiberglass, for instance, the National Stadium ("Bird's Nest"), the National Aquatics Center ("Water Cube"), the CCTV station poised to broadcast the competition, and the giant egg of the National Grand Theater adjacent to the Forbidden City, all designed by Western architectural firms. Any aerial shot of the neighboring National Grand Theater and the Forbidden City would confirm the jarring juxtaposition of the old and the new, except the "old" here is deemed the everlasting, the forever young. The other, "truly" old Beijing does not show up in such aerial views; it needs to be excavated from below.

The opening date signals how tightly controlled public discourse over the Olympics was. Mass media—newspapers, television channels, billboards, public campaigns and activities—strove to ensure a successful international event that brought nothing but joy. The effusive propaganda and advertising over the Olympics saturated the public domain, so much so that a virtual net/work was cast by the regime and big corporations. This net/work constituted an immersion experience of images and sound bites similar to virtual reality. Physical constructions with mammoth cranes and tractors coincided with mental constructions with words and events. The Olympics was given a three-pronged mission, named respectively as *keji aoyun* ("Science and Technology Olympics"), *luse aoyun* ("Green or Environmental Olympics"), and *renwen aoyun* ("Humanities or People's Olympics"). A site for such propaganda was the *People's Daily* Overseas Edition, which brought, every Friday since at least 2006, if not before, a number of pages devoted to "The Press for the Games of the XXIX Olympiad." The header for this weekly report was distinctly identified through the logo of "Beijing 2008" called "Chinese Script, Dancing Beijing," which consisted of the Chinese script for "jing" ("capital" as in Beijing) drawn as a runner with curved, apparently galloping, legs and open arms. The header often included a countdown to the opening day of the Olympics. The logo is an ingenious design, absorbing a sports event into the host city, the world into a single Chinese word. This sinologizing or nativizing of the Olympics was repeated in some of Friday's editorial series entitled *wuhuan qixia* ("under the five-ringed flag"), the Olympic symbol remade to evoke the communist China's *wuxing hongqi* ("Five-Star Red Flag," the national flag of the PRC). Contributors to wuhuan qixia included Hung Shen ("Red Deep," a pen name loaded with communist ideology). Indeed, all the articles and reports in "The Press for the Game" yoked together Olympics with China, be it the Great Wall, folk art, ongoing city construction, military exercises, emergency drills, or whatnot. Each Friday, a foreign diplomat, usually an ambassador, was featured as she or he congratulated the nation for its preparation for the Olympics.

The overwhelming campaign to promote the Olympics recalled the Maoist tactics of *xinao* ("brainwash") and *sixiang gaizao* ("thought reform"). Similar to those campaigns of a bygone era, the slogan of Beijing's Olympics, "One World One Dream," proved ultimately self-defeating, since there exist as many dreams and parallel universes as there are participants. Ideological conformity that can be traced back to Maoism is uncannily complemented by its opposite, the Western import of pleasure-seeking modernity. The model for such mass manufacturing of the sensation of pleasure is, of course, Disney. European and Latin American critics have long critiqued Disneyland as the height of hyperreality. Umberto Eco bemoans the fact that the absolute fake at Disneyland and across the American landscape has become absolute real or hyperreal (*Travels in Hyperreality* 8). Baudrillard equates simulation with the hyperreal: simulation "is the generation by models of a real without origin or reality: a hyperreal" (*Simulacra and Simulation* 1).

The Disneyification of Chinese style created a hyperreal Beijing, both in the cityscape and in the virtual space, a discursive hyperbole inscribed architecturally and virtually. In fact, the facelift in virtual reality preceded the real, as countless cybertours presented in computer-generated images the Olympic venues long before their completion. But just as various construction projects moved past the exterior phase less than a year before the Olympics, actual photographs of the exterior never replaced their virtual images, except for a series of progress photographs chronicling the rise of the "Bird's Nest" out of the "yellow earth" of northern China. One assumes they eventually will, although virtual images prove rather conducive to cybervisitors' fanciful flights. To illustrate, many images are "night shots" of phantom structures, structures yet to be completed. The two anchors of the Olympic Green (the Olympic Park), endearingly nicknamed the "Bird's Nest" and the "Water Cube," are prominently rendered as night scenes. Not only are they hyperreal representations but hyperreal of a certain kind—the darkness of night creating a magical aura over the brightly lighted venues. Even in "day shots," lighting bathes the buildings in a similar halo. Such manipulation is but the tip of the iceberg of the concerted sales pitch of 888 that puts off even the designer of the Bird's Nest. The Canadian Broadcasting Corporation reported on 11 August 2007 that the Beijing designer of the Bird's Nest, Ai Weiwei, the son of the poet Ai Qing, had castigated the showbiz surrounding the Olympics: "I hate the kind of feeling stirred up by promotion or propaganda . . . It's the kind of sentiment when you don't stick to the facts, but try to make up something, to mislead people away from a true discussion" (qtd. in "Artist behind Beijing's 'Bird's Nest' Stadium Boycotts Olympics"). Witnessing how his brainchild had been corrupted into "a shining symbol of China's march towards modernism," he called it a "pretend smile." The misleading "pretend smile" is the hyperreal Beijing that has come to supplant the real. Other voices from outside China have also criticized the demolition of the old Beijing (Lung, "Zhushi yige gudu de reibian" ["Gazing at an Ancient Capital's Metamorphosis"] A12). Beyond the Bird's Nest and the Water Cube, the Olympic Green flanking the Fourth-Circle Road, extending north from the axis centered at the Forbidden City, was repeatedly compared by the media to the shape of a Chinese dragon on the basis of the lakes and waterways in the terrain. Evoking ancient mythology and the custom of feng shui, where dragons are embroiled with water, editorials and reports in the *People's Daily* on 15 December 2006, for instance, situated the dragon head in the lake on the north side of the Olympic Green, its body meandering down, with its tail curled around the Bird's Nest. Virtual hyperreality, such as "night shots" of ghost stadiums, finds its soul mate in the mythical dragon hidden in the man-made channels, not far or not so distinct from underground or open sewages of yesteryear.

The halo of hyperreality surrounding the Olympics and the capital city is symptomatic of the nation as a whole. This rush toward modernity characterizes China's overall development in economy and technology, most evidently borne out in the quintessential form of production of modern fantasy—films, particularly those set exclusively or partly in Beijing. Fifth-generation filmmakers have manifested the modernizing and Westernizing drive, ironically, in their nostalgic revisit of the martial arts genre in recent years. Soaring swordsmen come to resemble futuristic, sci-fi cyborgs, both mythologizing a humanity in pursuit of, yet also bound by, science and technology. Although swordsmen allegedly accomplish their feat via kung fu, a range of filmmaking technology—special effects, computer-generated sequences of fights, cinematography and editing, even low-tech wirework—render the martial arts films of Zhang Yimou, Chen Kaige, and Feng Xiaogang the next of kin to anime's and sci-fi's fantasy world. Chen's *The Promise* (*Wuji* 2005), in particular, has been roundly criticized as cartoonish, and rather crudely made at that. Indulging themselves in such hyperrealism, these fifth-generation directors, joined by the Hong Konger Tsui Hark, occasionally give vent to the opposite impulse of representing the hyporeal, or the unpleasant reality to be repressed and forgotten, a coinage inspired by such pairs as hypertension and hypotension, hyperthermia and hypothermia. The dynamics of the two can be complex, exemplified by Feng Xiaogang's *Cell Phone* (*Shouji* [2003]), which dovetails nostalgic, romanticized rural China into his Beijing stories of real people in real time. In *Cell Phone*, Feng shuttles between the protagonist's extramarital affairs and his roots in the countryside, the backward hyporeal that acquires a magical aura to heal urban malaise. Feng attributes to this hyporeality the source of modern China and a nostalgic past that China ought to recapture in spirit.

The hyperreal seeks, in principle, to copy what alleges to be Western modernity. However, Baudrillard theorized that the original for simulacrum is absent, which partly explains the fifth-generation's ambivalence toward the Western model, alternately idolizing and dismissing it. Zhang's corpus is marked by nothing short of schizophrenia. Pitted against his early, self-Orientalizing "red films"—*Red Sor-*

ghum (1987), *Ju Dou* (1990), and *Raise the Red Lantern* (1991)—are Zhang's semi-documentary, neorealist works, *The Story of Qiu Ju* (1992), *Not One Less* (1999), and *Happy Times* (2001). As much as the red films exoticize the old China for the global cinema, the later works reverse to a realistic depiction of contemporary "little people." Granted that stars do appear in his later works, they seldom do so in their stellar selves: Gong Li in *The Story of Qiu Ju* is made up to look like a country bumpkin speaking in rustic accent; both the comedian Benshan Zhao and the rising star Jie Dong in *Happy Times* depict marginal characters—a retiree desperate to get married and a blind girl. These little people diverge dramatically from the mythical, even archetypal characters of his red films; the everyday quandaries of little people are a far cry from the broad strokes of human drama in feudal China.

In particular, critics have found the representation of Chinese *lao guiju* ("old customs") in Zhang's red films "absurd and excessive," catering to the global cinema eager for exoticism from the "primitive" Orient and third world. Most sensationalizing are the *diandeng chuijiao* ("lighting the lanterns; massaging the feet") in *Raise the Red Lantern* and *lanlu dangguan* ("blocking the way of the coffin") in *Ju Dou*. The former details the titillating foot massage administered on a concubine before a night with the patriarch. The massage harks back to the fetish of bound feet, so eroticized that the fondling of the feet is in itself foreplay. The latter consists of forty-nine rounds of blocking a coffin to demonstrate the survivors' grief. Even *Ju Dou*'s torture scenes and self-exhibitionism are suspiciously ethnographic, as if through a peephole to spy on what is allegedly Chinese. The flaying of prisoners in *Red Sorghum* crystallizes the "redness" of Zhang's early career—blood and violence as well as passion and communist ideology. Such dehumanization in feudal China unfolds in landscapes and sets that are breathtakingly beautiful. Whatever the location, Zhang's ingenious cinematography puts a magical touch to the sorghum field and the arid land in *Red Sorghum*, to the classical compound in *Raise the Red Lantern*, and to the dye shop with long stretches of multicolored cloths in *Ju Dou*. The duality of the aesthetic and the abject lies at the core of Zhang's "red" films. These "quotes" of feudal China are, schizophrenically, yoked with "quotes" of the West in Zhang and other Chinese filmmakers. In his return to the rural China in *Not One Less*, Zhang introduces a single can of Coca-Cola, a synecdoche of Western luxury and decadence, which the poor schoolchildren pass around for a tiny sip after a long day's work at the brick factory. Signifying modern amenities, the West is embedded in both a boom box and a modern hotel's revolving door, which disorient retirees in *Happy Times*. Likewise, Chen Kaige in *Farewell My Concubine* (1993) features the old China's beauty in the Beijing Opera and its depravity of opium addiction and homoerotic longings. Chen's "citation" of the West emerges most conspicuously in *Together* (*He ni zai yi qi* [2002]), where violins and Western music epitomize culture and an exit from a life of deprivation in China.

Departing from their predecessors, many sixth-generation filmmakers devote their entire careers to the hyporeal—little people falling through the cracks of modernization and urbanization. Accordingly, Zhang Yang's *Shower* (*Xizao* [1999]) bemoans the vanishing of the old Beijing in the demolition of traditional neighborhoods of hutong, communal bathhouses, and male bonding amid modernization. Just as *Cell Phone* opens with the rural "epigraph," the hyporeality in *Shower* features an epigraph of a futuristic roadside shower facility, a comic cross between public restroom and carwash, in a sequence accompanied by modern electronic music. Neither Feng Xiaogang nor Zhang Yang forgets to include the dialectic antithesis to the hyperreal or hyporeal filmic universe. In Zhang Yang's nostalgia, surrogates of the West pose challenges at various points. In addition to the epigraph, the revolving door of a modern skyscraper, once again, confuses a mentally challenged character. Although the West epitomizes omnivorous progress razing the old and the unfit, a bittersweet and heart-warming film like *Shower* refrains from outright condemnation of the foreign invasion. Among the aged, the ailing, and the disabled, a certain "bathhouse tenor" succeeds in performing "O Sole Mio," made famous by Luciano Pavarotti in the wake of his 1986 China tour, only in a shower. Despite wistfulness for the old, Zhang Yang breaks down the boundary between the premodern China and the modern West: a young Chinese Pavarotti frequents a crumbling bathhouse to sing an Italian folksong in a Western-style shower, with an idiot character—the embodiment of the diminishing Beijing—as his most devoted fan. When plagued by stage fright in a neighborhood variety show, the tenor is saved by the idiot who recreates a shower by spraying on him with a garden hose. Magic is borne out of disabilities and imminent demise.

Turning the camera from the dying old to the emerging young, Wang Xiaoshuai in *Beijing Bicycle* (*Shiqi sui de danche* [2001]) zooms in on the "lost generation" of urban youth, cast adrift by rapid growth and the disintegration of family and neighborhood. One of millions of migrant workers swamping China's cities, seventeen-year-old Guei from the countryside is happily employed by an express delivery service in Beijing after leasing to own a bicycle for transportation. In one of his deliveries to an elite health club, which evokes Zhang Yang's traditional communal bathhouses, his bicycle, now his own, is stolen. In desperation, he tries to steal a bicycle and is arrested and summarily fired. The plot thus far recalls Vittorio De Sica's neorealist *The Bicycle Thief* (1948). But Wang diverges from the Italian classic by introducing a double: Guei believes his bicycle is now ridden by a Beijing high schooler Jian. Jian turns out to have purchased the bicycle from the black market. A tug-of-war begins between Guei and Jian and his friends, reaching a compromise of sorts when they share the use between Guei's work and Jian's, for lack of a better word, "play," for a bicycle is the equivalent of the American high school student's automobile, symbol of prestige. Mocked for his lackluster bicycle, Jian loses his girlfriend to a bike gang leader, who performs stunts on his mountain bicycle, in dyed hair and flashy athlete jerseys, a cigarette dangling from his lips. The finale is shot in the warren of Beijing's hutong, dusty and narrow tenements of bricks and cement. Jian's revenge begins as he follows the lovers into a hutong, while the waist-level close-up focuses on Jian's hand picking up a brick from the dilapidated wall. With that brick, Jian knocks down the biker off-screen, typical of Wang's style of intimating rather than graphically portraying violence, deploying off-screen sounds as well as long shots. When Jian returns the bicycle to Guei in the last hand-over, for Jian claims that he is done, the bike gang arrives. Both Guei and Jian become prey in the ensuing chase in the labyrinth. Although Guei is not involved, he fails to find a way out of the unfamiliar hutong and is badly roughed up along with Jian. The senseless violence even extends to the bicycle, after the gang leaves. Pleading with the last of the gang members to stop mangling his bicycle, the docile Guei repeats Jian's earlier revenge and knocks down the gang member with a brick. In slow motion and with wistful theme music, the closing shot captures a bloodied Guei, the beat-up bicycle on his shoulder, crossing the crowded street. Reminiscent of Lao She's *Rickshaw* (1936-37), the young laborer from the countryside is ensnared as much by the old Beijing as by modernity. Even his urban counterpart, the Beijinger Jian, is alienated from his broken family crammed into a rundown siheyuan. Under the assault of the new, the old offers no sanctuary. Rather, the old both entraps and enables revenge, vulnerable to the onslaught of modernity, while rising up in revolt through the hands of the wrathful "twins."

One recurring motif in these films intertwines the hyperreal with the hyporeal. Animated interludes and special effects are strewn almost incongruously across comedies and neorealist dramas, but such intrusions portend heightened fantasy tantamount to wish fulfillment. A case in point: animated characters in flight or in constant motion eerily link sensibilities as diverse as Feng Xiaogang's tragicomedies (*Big Shot's Funeral* [*Dawan* (2001)] and *Cell Phone*) and Jia Zhangke's muted tragedies (*The World* [*Shijie* (2004)] and *Still Life* [*Sanxia haoren* (2006)]). The hyperreal is employed to create light comedy as well as to assuage, futilely of course, the yearning for freedom of the hyporeal, seen, for example, in migrant laborers in the city. In *Big Shot's Funeral*, characters are treated to an animated dramatization of a "comedy funeral" for the American film director in a coma at the Beijing hospital. The reincarnated filmmaker is a baby flying over the city, with his race or skin color being revised along with the ongoing discussion. Feng's wit and satirical sensibility ensure that the film beyond this animated episode retains a fantastical quality, nutty and funny. While Feng permeates his films with a cartoon-like fancy, Jia Zhangke, with his opposite temperament, contrasts the animated hyperreal with the live action hyporeal. Even the poster for *The World* illustrates this discord. Perhaps a rung above Beijing's migrant laborers from her home province of Shanxi, the female protagonist Xiao Tao is a performer at a theme park at the outskirts of the capital city. The poster features her anxiously looking down at her cell phone, trying in vain to reach her boyfriend, who is enamored with an exporter of women's clothing and accessories. What is striking is that Xiao Tao is in Japanese kimono and hairdo for one of her roles, against a backdrop of cartoon drawings of the sights at the theme park, drawings of mock-ups of the Eiffel Tower, the Pyramids, the Sphinx, the Tower of Pisa, and the tram encircling the park. Cartoon imitations of imitations in plaster and concrete, the poster shows images twice removed from the reality of such tourist attractions (in addition, the park also has Big Ben of London, the Acropolis, the twin towers of World Trade Center, and many more). Floating above it all is the protagonist in a flight attendant's uniform, an imaginary exit from her worries. Yet the hyperreal of cartoon drawings only accentuates the desperation of the hyporeal.

By the same token, the very existence of the Disneyland-style theme park modeled after famous sights around the world highlights Chinese visitors' escapist angst. Jia manages to vest each single frame of *The World* with the quiet desperation of a hyperreal society, from the opening credits to the fade-out over two hours later. The opening credits conclude with an old garbage collector standing still in the foreground against the park's Eiffel Tower silhouetted in the smog-filled dawn. The garbage man belongs to the hyporeal or waste matter expelled by the hyperreal in the background, a spiritual wasteland. This tableau is preceded by the jerky hand-held camera tracking through a frenzy backstage preparing for the next show. The camera turns out to trail Xiao Tao's shrill voice asking if anyone has a band-aid, apparently for her bruised heels. The show must go on, despite her pain, because the theme park offers, shall we say, a band-aid for the soul (or soul-less). As the show opens with Lin Qiong's haunting electronic music, all backstage chaos and individual agony are glossed over on the glitzy dance stage. Moving through a gallery of the hyporeal—a migrant construction worker crushed to death, a theme park guard who steals, a dancer turned manager through her intimacy with the troupe director, and Xiao Tao's Russian friend Anna who becomes a call girl, the film closes without any closure. After a falling-out, Xiao Tao and her boy friend, Taisheng, spend a night together at a friend's dormitory. Whether reconciled or committing a double suicide, they are found poisoned from a gas leak, common accidents in the freezing city in winter. As their bodies are laid side by side in the light snow, the film slowly fades out, with the following voice-over, in their Shanxi accents laced with drowsiness, either from sleep or from thickening carbon monoxide:

> Taisheng: "Are we dead yet?"
> Xiao Tao: "No. We have just begun."

This suggests that their thwarted love is to blossom, magically, in afterlife. Through these last words either before expiration in the dorm room or before the camera tilts away from the corpses in the snow, Jia appends what approximates a dream sequence to the tragedy of the hyporeal, as if to defy the tyranny of neorealist film-making, as if Jia himself seeks, like Huck Finn, "light out" for the hyperreal to flee the hyporeality that dooms his characters. Sheldon Lu, in *Chinese Modernity and Global Biopolitics* (2007), maintains that the lovers "are inadvertently poisoned by gas in their apartment. They nearly died." (153). The accident, if indeed it was, takes place at a friend's apartment, not theirs. And to say "they nearly died" is to misread the ambiguous ending.

Jia's next feature, *Still Life*, traces two hyporeal protagonists in slow and painful searches for their spouses amid the construction of the Yangtze River's Three Gorges Dam. The construction has totally devastated residents along the river, their houses demolished and whole villages submerged in rising water. Although the film is devoid of any animated element, Jia continues to inject wish-fulfilling touches as one of the protagonists, deadpan-like, witnesses a ball of light—an UFO—descending on the mountain ranges near the river. Subsequently, a bizarre postmodernist tower, presumably the UFO, blasts off from what is left of the pastoral scene. Totally out of place in the neorealist film, these moments bear out the shock and resentment over invasive modernity, be it the miniature replica of the Eiffel Tower outside Beijing, the futuristic UFO over the Three Gorges Dam, or anywhere else in the hyperreal China. Echoing these filmic narratives, the yoking of the hyperreal of "prosper" and the hyporeal of "fucked" manifests itself in the 2008 Olympics. The representation of this spectacle dangled between Chinese nationalist and Western defensive, somewhat xenophobic extremes. Amid the Chinese hoopla on August 8, 2007 marking the year-long countdown to the Olympics, the 2001 Pulitzer winner Ann Telnaes of *CWS/NYTS* published an editorial cartoon in newspaper syndicates across the US. Telnaes's cartoon shows a Beijing Olympics reviewing stand where Hitler-like figures, complete with communist five-star armbands and Hitler moustaches, raise their arms in the nazi salute, a volatile merger of Beijing and the Berlin of 1936. Telnaes's fellow editorial cartoonists published in the same month works satirizing Chinese exports. Steve Breen of the *San Diego Union-Tribune* punned on the word "junk" for Chinese flat-bottomed boats of old and for present-day shoddy products on cargo ships. Mike Luckovich of the *Atlanta Journal-Constitution* drew a spread-eagled Santa Clause, apparently dead of lead poisoning with Chinese-made toys scattered all around his person. This war of words, from Ann Telnaes's numerous China cartoons to recalls of "Made in China" products to Chinese retaliation, foreshadowed contestation not only in track and field but also in the field of representation. What happened to the hyperreal Beijing, as the 2008 Olympics has come and gone? This may be a moot question, now that the shadow is the city.

Works Cited

Abe, Kobo. *The Woman in the Dunes*. Trans. Dale Saunders. New York: Knopf, 1964.

Akinari, Uyeda. *Tales of Moonlight and Rain: Japanese Gothic Tales* (*Ugetsu Monogatari*). 1769. Trans. Kengi Hamada. Tokyo: U of Tokyo P, 1971.

Altman, Robert, dir. *M*A*S*H*. Hollywood: Twentieth Century Fox, 1970.

Anagnost, Ann. "Scenes of Misrecognition: Maternal Citizenship in the Age of Transnational Adoption." *positions: east asia cultures critique* 8.2 (2000): 389-421.

Animal Encyclopedia. New York: Dorling Kindersley Books, 2000.

Aponiuk, Natalia. "'Ethnic Literature,' 'Minority Literature,' 'Literature in Other Languages,' 'Hyphenated-Canadian Literature': Will it Ever be 'Canadian'?" *Canadian Ethnic Studies* 28.1 (1996): 1-7.

Arendt, Hannah. *Eichmann in Jerusalem*. 1963. New York: Viking, 1966.

"Artist behind Beijing's 'Bird's Nest' Stadium Boycotts Olympics." *cbc.ca* (11 August 2007): <http://www.cbc.ca/arts/artdesign/story/2007/08/11/beijing-artist-stadium.html>.

Ba, Jin. *Family*. 1931. Trans. Sidney Shapiro. New York: Anchor, 1972.

Bacho, Peter. *Dark Blue Suits and Other Stories.* Seattle: U of Washington P, 1997.

Ballard, J.G. *Empire of the Sun*. New York: Simon and Schuster, 1984.

Ballard, J.G. *A User's Guide to the Millennium: Essays and Reviews.* New York: Picador, 1996.

Bataille, Georges. *Death and Sensuality: A Study of Eroticism and the Taboo*. Trans. Mary Dalwood. 1962. New York: Arno, 1977.

Bataille, Georges. "Rotten Sun." *Visions of Excess: Selected Writings, 1927-1939.* Trans. Allan Stoekl, C.R. Lovitt, and D. M. Leslie, Jr. Minneapolis: U of Minnesota P, 1985. 57-58.

Bataille, Georges. "Sacrificial Mutilation and the Severed Ear of Vincent Van Gogh." *Visions of Excess: Selected Writings, 1927-1939.* Trans. Allan Stoekl, C.R. Lovitt, and D. M. Leslie, Jr. Minneapolis: U of Minnesota P, 1985. 61-72.

Baudrillard, Jean. *Simulacra and Simulation*. Trans. Sheila Faria Glaser. Ann Arbor: U of Michigan P, 1994.

Benedict, Ruth. *The Chrysanthemum and the Sword: Patterns of Japanese Culture.* New York: Houghton Mifflin, 1946.

Benjamin, Walter. "The Work of Art in the Age of Mechanical Reproduction." *Illuminations.* Trans. Harry Zohn. Ed. Hannah Arendt. New York: Schocken Books, 1969. 217-51.

Berger, Ludwig, and Michael Powell, dirs. *The Thief of Bagdad*. Perf. Conrad Veidt and Sabu. Hollywood: United Artists, 1940.

Bergman, Ingmar, dir. *The Seventh Seal.* New York: Janus Films, 1957.

Bernds, Edwards, dir. *Return of the Fly*. Hollywood: Twentieth Century Fox, 1959.

Bertolucci, Bernardo, dir. *The Last Emperor*. Morton Grove: Criterion, 1987.

Bertolucci, Bernardo, dir. *Little Buddha*. Santa Monica: Miramax, 1993.

Bhagwati, Jagdish. "Made in China." Rev. of *The Writing on the Wall*, by Will Hutton. *New York Times Book Review* 18 Feb. 2007: 25.

Bird, Lawrence. "States of Emergency: Urban Space and the Robotic Body in the *Metropolis* Tales." *Mechademia 3: Limits of the Human* (Fall 2008): 164-91.

Blodgett, E.D. "Towards an Ethnic Style." *Postcolonial Literature: Theory and Practice / Les Litteratures post-coloniales. Theories et realizations.* Ed. Steven Tötösy de Zepetnek and Sneja Gunew. Thematic Issue *Canadian Review of Comparative Literature / Revue Canadienne de Litterature Comparee* 22.3-4 (1995): 623-38.

Boardman, Gwenn R. *Graham Greene: The Aesthetics of Exploration*. Gainesville: U of Florida P, 1971.

Boym, Svetlana. *The Future of Nostalgia.* New York: Basic Books, 2001.

Breen, Steve. Editorial cartoon. *Lansing State Journal*. August 24, 2007. 7A.

Brigg, Peter. *J. G. Ballard.* Mercer Island: Starmont House, 1985.

Brontë, Emily. *Wuthering Heights*. 1847. New York: Routledge, 1988.

Brooks, Peter. *The Melodramatic Imagination: Balzac, Henry James, and the Mode of Excess.* New Haven: Yale UP, 1976.

Brown, Norman O. *Life Against Death: The Psychological Meaning of History*. Middletown, CT: Wesleyan UP, 1959.

Brown, Norman O. *Love's Body*. New York: Random House, 1966.

Browning, Tod, dir. *Dracula.* Hollywood: Universal City Studio, 1931.

Browning, Tod, dir. *Freaks*. Beverly Hills: Metro-Goldwyn-Mayer, 1932.

Brubach, Holly. "Raze High the Roof Beams, Comrade: Mourning China's Lost Horizons." *The New York Times Style Magazine: Design* (Spring 2008): 84, 86.

Bulosan, Carlos. *America Is in the Heart*. 1943. Seattle: U of Washington P, 1973.

Burgin, Victor, James Donald, and Cora Kaplan. Preface. *Formations of Fantasy.* Ed. Victor Burgin, James Donald, and Cora Kaplan. New York: Methuen, 1986. 1-4.

Byun, Hyuk (Daniel H. Byun), dir. *Juhong geulshi* (*The Scarlet Letter*). Seoul: L.J. Film, 2004.

Caputo, Philip. *A Rumor of War*. New York: Holt, Rinehart and Winston, 1977.

Carroll, Lewis. *Alice in Wonderland.* 1897. Ed. Donlad J. Gray. New York: Norton, 1992.

Carroll, Lewis. *Through the Looking Glass*. 1871. New York: St. Martin, 1977.

Carroll, Noel. *The Philosphy of Horror or Paradoxes of the Heart.* New York: Routledge, 1990.

Caruth, Cathy. *Unclaimed Experience: Trauma, Narrative, and History*. Baltimore: The Johns Hopkins UP, 1996.

Caruth, Cathy, ed. *Trauma: Explorations in Memory.* Baltimore: The Johns Hopkins UP, 1995.

Chan, Jachinson. *Chinese American Masculinities: From Fu Manchu to Bruce Lee.* New York: Routledge, 2001.

Chan, Jeffrey Paul. "A Chinese in Haifa." *Aiiieeeee!: An Anthology of Asian American Writers.* Ed. Frank Chin, Jeffrey Paul Chan, Lawson Fusao Inada, and Shawn Wong. Washington: Howard UP, 1974. 70-92.

Chan, Tony, dir. *Combination Platter.* New York: Koch Lorber Films, 1993.

Chang, Eileen. *The Rice-Sprout Song.* 1955. Trans. Eileen Chang. Berkeley: U of California P, 1998.

Chao, Lien. *Beyond Silence: Chinese Canadian Literature in English.* Toronto: TSAR, 1998.

Chaplin, Charlie, dir. *Modern Times.* Hollywood: Warner Home Video, 1936.

Chen, Kaige, dir. *Farewell my Concubine.* Santa Monica: Miramax, 1993.

Chen, Kaige, dir. *The Promise* (*Wuji*). Hollywood: Warner, 2005.

Chen, Kaige, dir. *Together* (*He ni zai yi qi*). New York: United Artists, 2002.

Chen Ying-chen. "Taiwan lun zi baoyen jiqi gungfeng gozhao" ("The Violent Rhetoric and Its Accomplice Structure"). *Sanjiaozai* (*Three-legged Thing*). Ed. Li Shoulin. Taipei: Haixia Shueshu, 2001. 6-19.

Cheng, Anne Anlin. *The Melancholy of Race: Psychoanalysis, Assimilation, and Hidden Grief.* Oxford: Oxford UP, 2001.

Ching, Siu-tung, dir. *The Chinese Ghost Story*. Prod. Tsui Hark. Hong Kong: Fortune Star, 1987.

Chu, Louis. *Eat a Bowl of Tea.* 1961. New York: Lyle Stuart, 1990.

Chun, Oxide Pang, and Danny Pang, dirs. *The Eye* (*Gin Gwai*). London: Metro Tartan Distribution, 2002.

Chun, Oxide Pang, and Danny Pang, dirs. *The Eye 2.* New York: Lions Gate Films Home Entertainment, 2004.

Chun, Oxide Pang, and Danny Pang, dirs. *The Eye 10.* London: Tartan Video, 2005.

Chung, Hye Seung. "Toward a Strategic Korean Cinephilia: A Transnational *Detournement* of Hollywood Melodrama." *South Korean Golden Age Melodrama: Gender, Genre, and National Cinema.* Ed. Kathleen McHugh and Nancy Abelmann. Detroit: Wayne State UP, 2005. 117-50.

Chung, Hye Seung, and David Scott Diffrient. "Interethnic Romance and Political Reconciliation in *Asako in Ruby Shoes*." *New Korean Cinema*. Ed. Chi-Yun Shin and Julian Stringer. New York: New York UP, 2005. 193-209.

Chung, Yong-woo, dir. *Hotelier*. Seoul: Korean TV, 2001.

Clausewitz, Carl von. *On War*. Trans. Michael Howard and Peter Paret. Princeton: Princeton UP, 1976.

Condon, Richard. *The Manchurian Candidate.* New York: Signet, 1959.

Conrad, Joseph. *Heart of Darkness*. New York: Hanover House, 1903.

Cooper, Pamela. *The Fictions of John Fowles*. Ottawa: U of Ottawa P, 1991.

Coppola, Francis Ford, dir. *Apocalypse Now.* Hollywood: Paramount, 1979.

Coppola, Francis Ford, dir. *Bram Stoker's Dracula.* Hollywood: Columbia Pictures, 1992.

Corman, Richard, dir. *The Wasp Woman*. Dallas: Reel Media International, 1959.

Cronenberg, David, dir. *The Fly*. Hollywood: Twentieth Century Fox, 1986.

Cronenberg, David, dir. *M. Butterfly*. Geffen, 1993.

Cronenberg, David, dir. *Naked Lunch.* Morton Grove: Criterion, 1991.

De Sica, Vittorio, dir. *The Bicycle Thief.* Morton Grove: Criterion, 1948.

Deeney, John J., Yen Yuan-shu, and Chi Ch'iu-lang, ed. *English Literature Anthology for Chinese Students.* Taipei: Hongdao, 1978.

Demme, Jonathan, dir. *The Silence of the Lambs.* Hollywood: Orion, 1991.

Derrida, Jacques. Exordium. *Specters of Marx*. Trans. Peggy Kamuf. New York: Routledge, 1994. xvii-2.

DeVitis, A.A. *Graham Greene*. New York: Twayne, 1964.

Dimić, Milan V. "Language in Chinese-Canadian Writing: Impact on Interpretation and Reception." *Ariel: A Review of International English Literature* 37.2-3 (2006): 91-110.

Dorow, Sara K. *Transnational Adoption.* New York: New York UP, 2006.

Dostoyevsky, Fyodor. *The Idiot*. Trans. Richard Pevear and Larissa Volokhonsky. New York: Knopf, 2002.

Eastwood, Clint, dir. *Letters from Iwo Jima.* Hollywood: Paramount, 2006.

Ebert-Schifferer, Sybille. *Deceptions and Illusions: Five Centuries of Trompe l'Oeil Painting.* Washington: National Gallery of Art, 2002.

Eco, Umberto. *Travels in Hyperreality: Essays.* Trans. William Weaver. New York: Harcourt Brace Jovanovich, 1986.

Eliot, T.S. *Four Quartets.* 1943. New York: Harcourt Brace Jovanovich, 1971.

Eng, David. *Racial Castration: Managing Masculinity in Asian America*. Durham: Duke UP, 2001.

Espiritu, Yen Le. *Asian American Panethnicity: Bridging Institutions and Identities.* Philadelphia: Temple UP, 1992.

Evans, Karin. *The Lost Daughters of China: Abandoned Girls, Their Journey to America, and the Search for a Missing Past.* New York: Jeremy P. Tarcher/Putnam, 2000.

Feng, Xiaogang, dir. *Big Shot's Funeral* (*Dawan*). Hollywood: Columbia Pictures, 2001.

Feng, Xiaogang, dir. *Cell Phone* (*Shouji*). Hollywood: Columbia Pictures, 2003.

Fenkl, Heinz Insu. *Memories of My Ghost Brother*. New York: Dutton Adult, 1996.

Findlay, John M. *People of Chance: Gambling in American Society from Jamestown to Las Vegas*. Oxford: Oxford UP, 1986.

Fleischer, Richard, and Kinji Fukasaku, dir. *Tora Tora Tora*. Hollywood: Twentieth Century Fox, 1970.

Forster, E.M. *Howards End.* 1921. New York: Knopf, 1943.

Foster, Jenny Ryun. "Once Upon a Time in America: An Introduction." *Manoa* 14.2 (2002-2003): 156-57.

Fowles, John. *The Collector.* Boston: Little, Brown, 1963.

Fowles, John. *The Magus*. Boston: Little, Brown, 1965.

Fox, William L. *In the Desert of Desire: Las Vegas and the Culture of Spectacle*. Reno: U of Nevada P, 2005.

Frankenheimer, John, dir. *The Manchurian Candidate.* Hollywood: United Artists, 1962.

Freud, Sigmund. *Beyond the Pleasure Principle*. 1920. Trans. James Strachey. New York: Norton, 1989.

Freud, Sigmund. *Civilization and Its Discontents*. Trans. James Strachey. New York: Norton, 1961.

Freud, Sigmund. *Civilization, War and Death.* Ed. John Rickman. London: Hogarth, 1968.

Freud, Sigmund. "The Direction of the Psychical Personality." *New Introductory Lectures on Psychoanalysis*. Ed. James Strachey. New York: Norton, 1965. 149-63.

Freud, Sigmund. "Dostoevsky and Parricide." 1928. Trans. James Strachey. *Character and Culture*. Ed. Philip Rieff. New York: Collier, 1963. 274-93.

Freud, Sigmund. "The 'Uncanny.'" *Collected Papers.* Vol. 4. Trans. James Strachey. London: Hogarth, 1953. 368-407.

Freud, Sigmund. *Totem and Taboo: Some Points of Agreement between the Mental Lives of Savages and Neurotics.* Trans. James Strachey. New York: Norton, 1950.

Fruit, Chan, dir. *Dumplings* segment of *Three Extremes*. Santa Monica: Lionsgate Films, 2004.

Garant, Robert Ben, dir. *Balls of Fury*. Hollywood: Universal Studios, 2007.

Garber, Marjorie B. *Vice Versa: Bisexuality and the Eroticism of Everyday Life*. New York: Simon and Schuster, 1995.

Gasiorek, Andrzej. *J.G. Ballard.* Manchester: Manchester UP, 2005.

Gelder, Ken. *Reading the Vampire.* New York: Routledge, 1994.

Gibson, Matthew. *Dracula and the Eastern Question: British and French Vampire Narratives of the Nineteenth-Century Near East.* New York: Palgrave Macmillan, 2006.

Gilman, Sander L. *Jewish Self-Hatred*. Baltimore: Johns Hopkins UP, 1986.

Goto, Hiromi. *The Kappa Child*. Calgary: Red Deer, 2001.

Greene, Graham. *The Quiet American*. 1955. New York: Penguin, 2004.

Griswold, Jerry. "The Disappearance of Children's Literature (or Children's Literature as Nostalgia) in the United States in the Late Twentieth Century." *Reflections of Change: Children's Literature Since 1945*. Ed. Sandra Beckett. Westport: Greenwood, 1997. 35-41.

Gunew, Sneja. "Between Auto/Biography and Theory: Can 'Ethnic Abjects' Write Theory?" *Comparative Literature Studies* 42.4 (2005): 363-78.

Hachiya, Michihiko. *Hiroshima Diary: The Journal of a Japanese Physician, August 6-September 30, 1945.* Trans. Warner Wells. Chapel Hill: U of North Carolina P, 1955.

Hade, Daniel D. "Reading Children's Literature Multiculturally." *Reflections of Change: Children's Literature Since 1945*. Ed. Sandra Beckett. Westport, CT: Greenwood, 1997. 113-22.

Hahn, Songsuk. "Accidents and Contingencies of Love." *Adoption Matters: Philosophical and Feminist Essays.* Ed. Sally Haslanger and Charlotte Witt. Ithaca: Cornell UP, 195-218.

Hansen, Maia. "Skin City." *The Real Las Vegas: Life Beyond the Strip.* Ed. David Littlejohn. New York: Oxford UP, 1999. 217-42.

Haraway, Donna. "A Manifesto for Cyborgs: Science, Technology, and Socialist Feminism in the 1980s." *The Haraway Reader*. New York: Routledge, 2004. 7-45.

Harvey, David. *The Condition of Postmodernity: An Enquiry into the Origins of Cultural Change.* Oxford: Blackwell, 1990.

Hausbeck, Kathryn. "Who Puts the 'Sin' in 'Sin City' Stories?: Girls of Grit and Glitter in the City of Women." *The Grit Beneath the Glitter: Tales from the Real Las Vegas.* Ed. Hal K. Rothman and Mike Davis. Berkeley: U of California P, 2002. 335-46.

Hearn, Lafcadio. *Exotics and Retrospectives.* 1898. New York: Little Brown, 1907.

Hearn, Lafcadio. *In Ghostly Japan.* 1899. Boston: Little, Brown, 1908.

Hearn, Lafcadio. *A Japanese Miscellany.* 1901. London: Kegan Paul, 1918.

Hearn, Lafcadio. *Kwaidan: Stories and Studies of Strange Things.* 1904. Boston: Houghton Mifflin, 1930.

Heberle, Mark A. *A Trauma Artist: Tim O'Brien and the Fiction of Vietnam.* Iowa City: U of Iowa P, 2001.

Heller, Joseph. *Catch-22.* New York: Simon and Schuster, 1961.

Hersey, John. *Hiroshima.* 1946. New York: Alfred A. Knopf, 1985.

Herzog, Tobey C. *Tim O'Brien.* New York: Twayne, 1997.

Hitchcock, Alfred, dir. *Dial M for Murder*. Hollywood: Warner Home Video, 1954.

Ho, Yun Seok, dir. *Winter Sonata*. Seoul: KBS Television Series, 2002.

Hollingworth, Christopher. *Poetics of the Hive: The Insect Metaphor in Literature*. Iowa City: U of Iowa P, 2001.

Homans, Margaret. "Adoption Narratives, Trauma, and Origins." *Narrative* 14.1 (2006): 4-26.

Hooker, Richard. *M*A*S*H.* New York: William Morrow, 1968.

Horkheimer, Max, and Theodor W. Adorno. *Dialectic of Enlightenment*. 1944. Trans. John Cummings. New York: Herder and Herder, 1972.

Horner, Avril, and Sue Zlosnik. *Gothic and the Comic Turn*. New York: Palgrave Macmillan, 2005.

Hughes, William, and Andrew Smith. "Introduction: Bram Stoker, the Gothic and the Development of Cultural Studies." *Bram Stoker: History, Psychoanalysis and the Gothic*. Ed. William Hughes and Andrew Smith. New York: St. Martin's, 1998. 1-11.

Ibuse, Masuji. *Black Rain*. Trans. John Bester. Tokyo: Kodansha International, 1970.

Inglis, Fred. *The Promise of Happiness: Value and Meaning in Children's Fiction.* Cambridge: Cambridge UP, 1981.

Ishiguro, Kazuo. *An Artist of the Floating World.* 1986. New York: Vintage, 1989.

Ishiguro, Kazuo. *Never Let Me Go*. New York: Knopf, 2005.

Ishiguro, Kazuo. *A Pale View of Hills.* 1982. New York: Vintage, 1990.

Ishiguro, Kazuo. *The Remains of the Day.* 1989. New York: Knopf, 1990.

Ishiguro, Kazuo. *The Unconsoled.* New York: Knopf, 1995.

Ishiguro, Kazuo. *When We Were Orphans.* New York: Knopf, 2000.

Ito, Robert. "Stuck in Asia, Dreaming of Hollywood." *New York Times* 11 Feb. 2007: AR15+.

Jakobson, Roman. *Fundamentals of Language*. Trans. Morris Hale. The Hague: Mouton, 1956.

Jasper, David. *The Sacred Desert: Religion, Literature, Art, and Culture.* Malden: Blackwell, 2004.

Jen, Gish. *Mona in the Promised Land.* New York: Vintage, 1996.

Jia, Sidao. *Cu zhi Jing* (Book on Crickets). Taipei: Yi wen yin shu guan, 1966.

Jia, Zhangke, dir. *Still Life* (*Sanxia haoren*). Shanghai: Shanghai Film Studios, 2006.

Jia, Zhangke, dir. *The World* (*Shijie*). Perf. Zhao Tao and Chen Taisheng. Zeitgeist Films, 2004.

Johnson, Kay. "Chaobao: The Plight of Chinese Adoptive Parents in the Era of the One-Child Policy." *Cultures of Transnational Adoption.* Ed. Toby Alice Volkman. Durhan, NC: Duke UP, 2005. 117-41.

Joslin, Lyndon W. *Count Dracula Goes to the Movies: Stoker's Novel Adapted, 1922-2003.* Jefferson: McFarland, 2006.

Kadohata, Cynthia. *The Floating World.* New York: Viking Books, 1989.

Kafka, Franz. *The Metamorphosis.* 1915. Trans. Michael Hofmann. New York: Penguin, 2011.

Kaplan, Robert. *The Nothing That Is: A Natural History of Zero.* Oxford: Oxford UP, 2000.

Kaplan, Steven. *Understanding Tim O'Brien.* Columbia: U of South Carolina P, 1995.

Kawajiri, Yoshiaki, dir. *Ninja Scroll.* 1993. Toho. 1995.

Keller, Nora Okja. "A Bite of Kimchee." *Comfort Woman.* New York: Penguin, 1997. 7-11.

Khoo, Tseen-ling. *Banana Bending: Asian-Australian and Asian-Canadian Literatures.* Montréal: McGill-Queen's UP, 2003.

Kilgour, Maggie. *From Communion to Cannibalism: An Anatomy of Metaphors of Incorporation.* Princeton: Princeton UP, 1990.

Kilgour, Maggie. "Vampiric Arts: Bram Stoker's Defence of Poetry." *Bram Stoker: History, Psychoanalysis and the Gothic.* Ed. William Hughes and Andrew Smith. New York: St. Martin's, 1998. 47-61.

Kim, Elaine H. *Asian American Literature: An Introduction to the Writings and their Social Context.* Philadelphia: Temple UP, 1982.

Kim, Eleana. "Wedding Citizenship and Culture: Korean Adoptees and the Global Family of Korea." *Cultures of Transnational Adoption.* Ed. Toby Alice Volkman. Durhan: Duke UP, 2005. 49-80.

Kim, Kichung. "Unheard Voices: The Life of the *Nobi* in O Hwi-mun's *Swaemirok.*" *Korean Studies* 27 (2004): 108-37.

Kim, Ki-duk, dir. *3-Iron.* Hollywood: Sony Pictures Classics, 2004.

Kim. Ki-duk, dir. *Bad Guy.* Parsnippany: Lifesize Entertainment, 2001.

Kim, Ki-duk, dir. *The Bow.* Paris: TFM Distribution, 2005.

Kim, Ki-duk, dir. *The Isle.* Los Angeles: Empire Pictures, 2000.

Kim, Ki-duk, dir. *Real Fiction.* Seoul: Saerom Entertainment, 2000.

Kim, Ki-duk, dir. *Samaritan Girl.* New York: Tartan Video USA, 2004.

Kim, Ki-duk, dir. *Spring, Summer, Fall, Winter, and . . . Spring.* Hollywood: Sony Pictures Classics, 2003.

Kim, Kyu Hyun. "Horror as Critique in *Tell Me Something* and *Sympathy for Mr. Vengeance.*" *New Korean Cinema.* Ed. Chi-Yun Shin and Julian Stringer. New York: New York UP, 2005. 106-16.

Kim, Ronyoung. *Clay Walls*. 1987. Seattle: U of Washington P, 1990.

King, Stephen. *Cell*. New York: Scribner, 2006.

Kingston, Maxine Hong. *The Woman Warrior: Memoirs of a Girlhood Among Ghosts*. New York: Knopf, 1976.

Kirby, William, and William Spence. *An Introduction to Entomology*. New York: Longman, Brown, Green and Longmans 1846.

Kobayashi, Masaki, dir. *Kwaidan*. Morton Grove: Criterion, 1964.

Kobayashi, Yoshinori. *Taiwan Lun* (On Taiwan). 2000. Taipei: Avanguard, 2001.

Kojiki. Trans. Donald L. Philippi. Princeton: Princeton UP, 1969.

Kristeva, Julia. *Powers of Horror: An Essay on Abjection*. Trans. Leon S. Roudiez. New York: Columbia UP, 1982.

Kurosawa, Akira, dir. *Dream*. Burbank: Warner Bros.,1990.

Kyoka, Izumi. "The Holy Man of Mount Koya." *Japanese Gothic Tales*. Trans. Charles Shiro Inouye. Honolulu: U of Hawaii P, 1996. 21-72.

Lederer, William J. and Eugene Burdick. *The Ugly American*. New York: Norton, 1958.

Lee, Chang-rae. *Aloft*. New York: Riverhead, 2004.

Lee, Chang-rae. *A Gesture Life*. New York: Riverhead, 1999.

Lee, Chang-rae. *Native Speaker*. New York: Riverhead, 1995.

Lee, Leo Ou-fan. *Voices from the Iron House: A Study of Lu Xun*. Bloomington: Indiana UP, 1987.

Lee, Min Jin. *Free Food for Millionaires*. New York: Warner Books, 2007.

Legge, James F., ed. and trans. *The Chinese Classics. The She King*. Taipei: Wenshije Publisher, 1972.

Leighton, Kimberly. "Being Adopted and Being a Philosopher: Exploring Identity and the 'Desire to Know' Differently." *Adoption Matters: Philosophical and Feminist Essays*. Ed. Sally Haslanger and Charlotte Witt. Ithaca: Cornell UP, 2005. 146-70.

Lesnik-Oberstein, Karin. "Essentials: What is Children's Literature? What is Childhood." *Understanding Children's Literature*. Ed. Peter Hunt. London: Routledge, 1999. 15-29.

Levi, Primo. *Survival in Auschwitz*. 1959. Trans. Stuart Wolf. New York: Collier, 1986.

Li, Han Hsiang, dir. *Butterfly Lovers* (*Liang Shanbo yu Zhu Yingtai* or *The Romance of Liang Shanbo and Zhu Yingtai.)* Hong Kong: Shaw Brothers Studio, 1963.

Li, Shizhen. *Bencao gangmu* (*Compendium of Materia Medica*). Beijing: Foreign Language, 2006.

Liem, Deann Borshay, dir. *First Person Plural*. San Francisco: NAATA, 2000.

Lifton, Betty Jean. *Journey of the Adopted Self: A Quest for Wholeness*. New York: Basic Books, 1994.

Lifton, Robert Jay. *Death in Life: Survivors of Hiroshima*. New York: Basic Books, 1967.

Lifton, Robert Jay. *Thought Reform and the Psychology of Totalism*. New York: Norton, 1961.

Lim, Genny. *Paper Angels. Unbroken Thread: Anthology of Plays by Asian American Women*. Amherst: U of Massachusetts P, 1993.

Lipsitz, George. "The Possessive Investment in Whiteness: Racialized Social Democracy and the 'White' Problem in American Studies." *American Quarterly* 47.3 (1995): 369-87.

Littlejohn, David. "Introduction: The Ultimate Company Town." *The Real Las Vegas: Life Beyond the Strip.* Ed. David Littlejohn. Oxford: Oxford UP, 1999. 1-40.

Lone, John, dir. *Paper Angels*. New York: The American Playhouse, PBS, 1982.

Louie, David Wong. *The Barbarians Are Coming.* New York: Berkley, 2000.

Lowe, Lisa. *Immigrant Acts: On Asian American Cultural Politics*. London: Duke UP, 1996.

Lowenstein, Adam. *Shocking Representation: Historical Trauma, National Cinema, and the Modern Horror Film.* New York: Columbia UP, 2005.

Lu, Sheldon H. *Chinese Modernity and Global Biopolitics: Studies in Literature and Visual Culture.* Honolulu: U of Hawaii P, 2007.

Lu, Xun. [Zhou Shuren]. "Diary of a Madman." 1918. *Selected Stories of Lu Hsun*. 1960. Trans. Yang Hsien-yi and Gladys Yang. Peking: Foreign Language Press, 1978. 7-18.

Lu, Xun. [Zhou Shuren]. "Medicine" 1919. *Selected Stories of Lu Hsun*. 1960. Trans. Yang Hsien-yi and Gladys Yang. Peking: Foreign Language Press, 1978. 25-33.

Lu, Xun. [Zhou Shuren]. "The New Year's Sacrifice" 1924. *Selected Stories of Lu Hsun*. 1960. Trans. Yang Hsien-yi and Gladys Yang. Peking: Foreign Language Press, 1978. 125-43.

Lu, Xun [Zhou Shuren]. *Selected Stories of Lu Hsun*. 1960. Trans. Yang Hsien-yi and Gladys Yang. Beijing: Foreign Language P, 1978.

Lu, Xun. [Zhou Shuren]. "The True Story of Ah Q." 1921. *Selected Stories of Lu Hsun*. 1960. Trans. Yang Hsien-yi and Gladys Yang. Peking: Foreign Language Press, 1978. 65-112.

Luckhurst, Roger. *"The Angle Between Two Walls": The Fiction of J.G. Ballard.* New York: St. Martin's, 1997.

Luckovich, Mike. Editorial cartoon. *Atlanta Journal-Constitution* 15 Aug. 2007.

Lung, Yingtai. "Zhushi yige gudu de reibian" ("Gazing at an Ancient Capital's Metamorphosis"). *World Journal* 27 July 2006: A12.

Lynch, David, dir. *The Elephant Man*. Hollywood: Paramount, 1980.

Ma, Sheng-mei. *The Deathly Embrace: Orientalism and Asian American Identity*. Minneapolis: U of Minnesota P, 2000.

Ma, Sheng-mei. *Diaspora Literature and Visual Culture: Asia in Flight.* London: Routledge, 2011.

Ma, Sheng-mei. *East-West Montage: Reflections on Asian Bodies in Diaspora*. Honolulu: U of Hawaii P, 2007.

Ma, Sheng-mei. "*The Great Dictator* and *Maus*: 'The Comical' Before and After the Holocaust." *Proteus* (Special Issue on Holocaust Studies) 12.2 (1995): 47-50.

Ma, Sheng-mei. *Immigrant Subjectivities in Asian American and Asian Diaspora Literatures*. Albany: State University of New York P, 1998.

Ma, Sheng-mei. "Mourning with the (As a) Jew: Metaphor, Ethnicity, and the Holocaust in Art Spiegelman's *Maus*." *Studies in American Jewish Literature* 16 (1997): 115-29.

Maddin, Guy, dir. *Dracula: Pages from a Virgin's Diary.* New York: Zeitgeist Films, 2003.

Mailer, Norman. *The Naked and the Dead.* 1948. New York: Rinehart, 1948.

Marshall, Rob, dir. *Memoirs of a Geisha.* Hollywood: Sony Pictures, 2005.

Marx, Karl. *Capital: A Critique of Political Economy.* 1867. Trans. Samuel Moore and Edward Aveling. New York: International Publishers, 1967.

Marx, Leo. *The Machine in the Garden: Technology and the Pastoral Ideal in America.* 1964. Oxford: Oxford UP, 2000.

Mendoza, Lunita. "China: Mobile Superpower." *Asia Unplugged: The Wireless and the Mobile Media Boom in the Asia-Pacific*. Ed. Madanmohan Rao and Lunita Mendoza. London: Response, 2005. 373-83.

Meng, Zhaolian. *Qiannian qiuxing huacishuai* (*On Crickets for a Thousand Autumns*). *Zhongguo suwenhua congshu* (Chinese Folk Culture Series). Jinan: Shangdong Education Publisher, 1999.

Meyer, Michael. *The Last Days of Old Beijing.* New York: Walker and Company, 2008.

Miyazaki, Hayao. "I Understand NAUSICAA a Bit More than I Did a Little While Ago." Interview with Ryo Saitani. *comicbox.co.jp (2005):* <http://www.comicbox.co.jp/e-nau/e-nau.html>.

Miyazaki, Hayao, dir. *Nausicaa of the Valley of the Wind.* Hollywood: Walt Disney, 1984.

Miyazaki, Hayao, dir. *Spirited Away*. Hollywood: Buena Vista, 2001.

Miyazaki, Hayao, dir. *Totoro*. Hollywood: Twentieth Century Fox, 1988.

Mizejewski, Linda. "Stardom and Serial Fantasies: Thomas Harris's *Hannibal*." *Keyframes: Popular Cinema and Cultural Studies.* Ed. Matthew Tinkcom and Amy Villarejo. London: Routledge, 2001. 159-70.

Möller, Hans-Georg. "Zhuangzi's 'Dream of the Butterfly': A Daoist Interpretation." *Philosophy East and West* 49.4 (1999): 439-50.

Mori, Kyoko. *The Dream of Water.* New York: Fawcett Columbine, 1995.

Mori, Kyoko. *Polite Lies: On Being a Woman Caught between Cultures*. New York: Henry Holt, 1997.

Mori, Kyoko. *Shizuko's Daughter*. New York: Fawcett Juniper, 1993.

Mori, Kyoko. *Stone Field, True Arrow*. New York: Picador, 2001.

Morison, Robert S. "Death: Process or Event?" *Science* 173 (20 August 1971): 694-98.

Mukherjee, Arun P. "Canadian Nationalism, Canadian Literature, and Racial Minority Women." *Testing the Limits: Postcolonial Theories and Canadian Literature.* Ed. Diana Brydon. *Essays on Canadian Writing* 56 (1995): 78-95

Mulvey-Roberts, Marie. "*Dracula* and the Doctors: Bad Blood, Menstrual Taboo and the New Woman." *Bram Stoker: History, Psychoanalysis and the Gothic*. Ed. William Hughes and Andrew Smith. New York: St. Martin's, 1998. 78-95.

Murayama, Milton. *All I Asking for Is My Body.* Honolulu: U of Hawaii P, 1975.

Na, Hye-sok. "Kyonghui." *Korea Studies* 26.1 (2002): 61-86.

Nakata, Hideo, dir. *Ringu*. Tokyo: Toho Company, 1998.

Nakazawa, Keiji. *Barefoot Gen: A Cartoon Story of Hiroshima.* 1972-73. Philadelphia: New Society Publishers, 1987.

Nakazawa, Keiji. *Barefoot Gen: The Day After.* 1972-73. Philadelphia: New Society Publishers, 1988.

Nakazawa, Keiji. *Barefoot Gen: Life After the Bomb.* 1972-73. Philadelphia: New Society Publishers, 1989.

Nakazawa, Keiji. *Barefoot Gen: Out of the Ashes.* 1972-73. Philadelphia: New Society Publishers, 1994.

Nazareth, Peter. *In the Trickster Tradition: The Novels of Andrew Salkey, Francis Eberjer and Ishmael Reed.* London: Bogle L'Overture, 1994.

Nelson, Victoria. *The Secret Life of Puppets.* Cambridge, MA: Harvard UP, 2001.

Neuman, Kurt, dir. *The Fly*. Hollywood: Twentieth Century Fox, 1958.

Ng, Fae Myenne. *Bone*. New York: Hyperion, 1993.

Nguyen, Viet Thanh. *Race and Resistance: Literature and Politics in Asian America.* New York: Oxford UP, 2002.

O'Brien, Tim. *Going After Cacciato*. 1978. New York: Broadway, 1999.

O'Brien, Tim. *If I Die in a Combat Zone, Box Me up and Ship Me Home.* New York: Laurel, 1979.

Oe, Kenzaburo, ed. *The Crazy Iris and Other Atories of the Atomic Aftermath*. 1984. New York: Grove, 1985.

Oldendburg, Ray. *The Great Good Places.* New York: Marlowe, 1989.

Ozeki, Ruth L. *My Year of Meats.* New York: Penguin, 1998.

Park, Chanwook, dir. *Cut* segment of *Three Extremes.* Santa Monica: Lionsgate Films, 2004.

Park, Chanwook, dir. *Oldboy*. New York: Tartan Video USA, 2003.

Park, Chanwook, dir. *Sympathy for Lady Vengeance*. New York: Tartan Video USA, 2005.

Park, Chanwook, dir. *Sympathy for Mr. Vengeance*. New York: Tartan Video USA, 2002.

Park, Chul-Soo, dir. *301/302.* New York: Arrow Releasing, 1996.

Pinedo, Isabel Cristina. "Postmodern Elements of the Contemporary Horror Film." *The Horror Film*. Ed. Stephen Prince. New Brunswick: Rutgers UP, 2004. 85-117.

Polanski, Roman, dir. *Chinatown.* Hollywood: Paramount, 1974.

Pu, Songling. *Liaozhai zhiyi* (*Strange Tales from a Chinese Studio*). 1766. Trans. John Minford. New York: Penguin, 2006.

Punter, David. *Modernity.* New York: Palgrave Macmillan, 2007.

Rickels, Laurence A. *The Vampire Lectures*.Minneapolis: U of Minnesota P, 1999.

Ritzer, George. *The Globalization of Nothing.* Thousand Oaks: Pine Forge, 2004.

Rivlin, Gary. "Las Vegas Caters to Asia's High Rollers." *New York Times* 13 June 2007: 1-2 <http://www.nytimes.com/2007/06/13/business/13vegas.html>.

Roberts, Dmae. *Mei Mei: A Daughter's Song*. Radio documentary. Salt Institute for Documentary Studies, 1989: <http://www.prx.org/pieces/49659-27-mei-mei-a-daughter-s-song>

Robinson, Katy. *A Single Square Picture: A Korean Adoptee's Search for Her Roots*. New York: Berkley, 2002.

Roman, Annette. Introduction. *Adolf: Days of Infamy*. By Osamu Tezuka. San Francisco: VIZ Media, 1996.

Rosenfeld, Alvin H. *Imagining Hitler.* Bloomington: Indiana UP, 1985.

Rothman, Hal. *Neon Metropolis: How Las Vegas Started the Twenty-First Century.* London: Routledge, 2002.

Said, Edward W. *Orientalism.* New York: Pantheon, 1978.

Sakamoto, Kerri. *One Hundred Million Hearts.* Orlando: Harcourt, 2003.

Say, Allen. *El Chino.* Boston: Houghton Mifflin, 1990.

Say, Allen. *The Feast of Lanterns.* New York: Harper and Row, 1976.

Say, Allen. *Grandfather's Journey.* Boston: Houghton Mifflin, 1993.

Say, Allen. *Home of the Brave.* Boston: Houghton Mifflin, 2002.

Say, Allen. *The Ink-Keeper's Apprentice.* 1979. New York: Houghton Mifflin, 1994.

Say, Allen. *The Lost Lake.* Boston : Houghton Mifflin Co., 1989.

Say, Allen. *The Sign Painter.* Boston: Houghton Mifflin, 2000.

Say, Allen. *Stranger in the Mirror.* Boston: Houghton Mifflin, 1995.

Say, Allen. *Tea with Milk.* Boston: Houghton Mifflin, 1999.

Say, Allen. *Tree of Cranes.* Boston: Houghton Mifflin, 1991.

Say, Allen. Interview with Stephanie Loer. *houghtonmifflinbooks.com* (2007): <http://www.houghtonmifflinbooks.com/authors/allensay/questions.shtml.>

Schodt, Frederik L. *Dreamland Japan: Writings on Modern Manga.* Berkeley, CA: Stone Bridge, 1996.

Selden, George. *The Cricket in Times Square.* New York: Yearling, 1960.

Shapiro, Jerome F. *Atomic Bomb Cinema.* London: Routledge, 2002.

Shaviro, Steven. "Fire and Ice: The Films of Guy Maddin." *North of Everything: English-Canadian Cinema since 1980.* Ed. William Beard and Jerry White. Edmonton: U of Alberta P, 2002. 216-21.

Shi, Nai-an, and Lo Guan-zhong. *The Tiger Killers: Part Two of The Marshes of Mount Liang.* Trans. John Dent-Young and Alex Dent-Young. Hong Kong: The Chinese UP, 1994.

Shi, Nai'an, and Luo Guanzhong. *All Men Are Brothers.* Trans. Pearl Buck. Kingston, RI: Moyer Bell, 2004.

Shih, Shu-mei. *The Lure of the Modern: Writing Modernism in Semicolonial China, 1917-1937.* Berkeley: U of California P, 2001.

Shimizu, Takashi, dir. *Ju-On.* Perf. Yûrei Yanagi and Chiaki Kuriyama. Horizon Entertainment, 2000.

Shimizu, Takashi, dir. *Ju-On: The Grudge.* Hollywood: Sony Pictures Entertainment, 2004.

Shin, Jeeyoung. "Globalisation and New Korean Cinema." *New Korean Cinema.* Ed. Chi-Yun Shin and Julian Stringer. New York: New York UP, 2005. 51-62.

Sinyard, Neil. *Graham Greene: A Literary Life.* New York: Palgrave, 2003.

Smith, Lillian. *The Unreluctant Years: A Critical Approach to Children's Literature.* Chicago: American Library Association, 1991.

Snodgrass, W.D. *The Fuhrer Bunker.* Brockport: Boa Editions, 1977.

Snyder, Gary. *Riprap and Cold Mountain Poems.* San Francisco: North Point, 1990.

Song, Cathy. "Chinatown." *Picture Bride.* New Haven: Yale UP, 1983. 61-64.

Spiegelman, Art. Introduction. *Barefoot Gen.* By Keiji Nakazawa. San Francisco: Last Gasp of San Francisco, 2003.

Spiegelman, Art. *Maus: A Survivor's Tale. Part I: My Father Bleeds History*. New York: Pantheon, 1986.

Spiegelman, Art. *Maus: A Survivor's Tale. Part II: And Here My Trouble Began*. New York: Pantheon, 1991.

Spielberg, Steven, dir. *Saving Private Ryan.* Hollywood: Dreamworks, 1998.

Spooner, David. *The Insect-Populated Mind: How Insects Have Influenced the Evolution of Consciousness.* Lanham: Hamilton P, 2005.

Steiner, George. *The Portage to San Cristobal of A.H.* New York: Simon and Schuster, 1981.

Stoker, Bram. *Dracula*. 1897. New York: Norton, 1997.

Stoker, Bram. *The Lair of the White Worm.* 1911. London: Jarrolds, 1966.

Stone, Oliver, dir. *Platoon.* Hollywood: MGM, 1986.

Styron, William. *Sophie's Choice*. New York: Random House, 1979.

Suzuki, Koji. *The Ring.* 1991. Trans. Robert B. Rohmer and Glynne Walley. New York: Vertical, 2003.

Swift, Jonathan. "A Model Proposal." 1729. London: W. Bickerton, 1730.

Tajiri, Rea, dir. *Strawberry Fields*. Los Angeles: Vanguard Cinema DVD, 1997.

Takahata, Isao, dir. *Grave of the Fireflies.* Central Park Media, 1988.

Takao, Okawara, dir. *Godzilla and Mothra: The Battle for Earth*. Tokyo: Toho, 1992.

Takashi, Miike, dir. *Box* segment of *Three Extremes*. Santa Monica: Lionsgate Films, 2004.

Tan, Amy. *The Hundred Secret Senses*. New York: Putnum, 1995.

Tan, Amy. *The Joy Luck Club*. New York: Putnam, 1989.

Tang, Xiaobing. *Chinese Modern: The Heroic and the Quotidian.* Durham: Duke UP, 2000.

Tanizaki, Junichiro. *Sasameyuki* (*The Makioka Sisters*). 1946-48. Trans. Edward G. Seidensticker. New York: Knopf, 1957.

Tanizaki, Junichiro. *Some Prefer Nettles*. Trans. Edward G. Seidensticker. 1928. New York: Vintage, 1995.

Tanizaki, Junichiro. "Terror." *Seven Japanese Tales.* Trans. Howard Hibbett. New York: Wideview, 1963, 85-94.

Tannahill, Reay. *Flesh and Blood: A History of the Cannibal Complex*. New York: Stein and Day, 1975.

Telnaes, Ann. Editorial cartoon. *CWS/NYTS. New York Times* 8 Aug. 2007.

Teshigahara, Hiroshi, dir. *Woman in the Dunes.* Chatsworth: Image Entertainment, 1964.

Tezuka, Osamu. *Adolf: 1945 and All That Remains*. Trans. Yuji Oniki. 1985. San Francisco: Cadence, 1996.

Tezuka, Osamu. *Adolf: Days of Infamy*. Trans. Yuji Oniki. San Francisco: Cadence, 1996.

Tezuka, Osamu. *Adolf: An Exile in Japan*. Trans. Yuji Oniki. San Francisco: Cadence, 1996.

Tezuka, Osamu. *Adolf: The Half-Aryan*. Trans. Yuji Oniki. San Francisco: Cadence, 1996.

Tezuka, Osamu. *Adolf: A Tale of the Twentieth Century*. Trans. Yuji Oniki. San Francisco: Cadence, 1995.

Thomas, D.M. *The White Hotel*. New York: Viking, 1981.

Thompson, G. Richard. *The Gothic Imagination: Essays in Dark Romanticism*. Pullman: Washington State UP, 1974.

Thompson, Stith. *Tales of the North American Indians.* Bloomington: Indiana UP, 1929.

Thoreau, David Henry. *Walden and Civil Disobedience*. New York: Penguin, 1983.

Tötösy de Zepetnek, Steven. "From Comparative Literature Today Toward Comparative Cultural Studies." *Comparative Literature and Comparative Cultural Studies.* Ed. Steven Tötösy de Zepetnek. West Lafayette: Purdue UP, 2003. 235-67.

Tötösy de Zepetnek, Steven. "Literary Theory, Ethnic Minority Writing, and the Systemic Approach." *Ethnic Minority Writing and Literary Theory.* Ed. Joseph Pivato. *Canadian Ethnic Studies / Etudes ethniques au Canada* 28.3 (1996): 100-06.

Tötösy de Zepetnek, Steven. "The Importance of Cultural Dialogue: A Case Study of Ethnic Minority Writing and Cultural Participation in Canada." *Cultural Dialogue and Misreading.* Ed. Mabel Lee and Meng Hua. Honolulu: Hawaii UP, 1997. 367-76.

Tötösy de Zepetnek, Steven. "The New Humanities: The Intercultural, the Comparative, and the Interdisciplinary." *Globalization and the Futures of Comparative Literature*. Ed. Jan M. Ziolkowski and Alfred J. López. Thematic Section *The Global South* 1.2 (2007): 45-68.

Tötösy de Zepetnek, Steven, Asma Sayed, and Domenic A. Beneventi. "Selected Bibliography of Work on Canadian Ethnic Minority Writing." *CLCWeb: Comparative Literature and Culture* (*Library*): <http://docs.lib.purdue.edu/clcweblibrary/canadianethnicbibliography>.

Tsutsumi Chunagon Monogatari: A Collection of Eleventh-Century Short Stories. Trans. Umeyo Hirano. Tokyo: Hokusaido, 1963.

Twitchell, James B. *The Living Dead: A Study of the Vampire in Romantic Literature.* Durham: Duke UP, 1981.

Uribayashi, Tadamichi. *Picture Letters from the Commander in Chief.* New York: VIZ Media, 2007.

Van Ash, Cay, and Elizabeth Sax Rohmer. *Master of Villainy: A Biography of Sax Rohmer*. London: Tom Stacey, 1972.

Verrier, Nancy Newton. *The Primal Wound: Understanding the Adopted Child.* Baltimore: Gateway, 1993.

Volkman, Toby Alice. "Embodying Chinese Culture: Transnational Adoption in North America." *Cultures of Transnational Adoption*. Ed. Toby Alice Volkman. Durham: Duke UP, 2005. 81-113.

Wachowski, Andy, and Laurence Wachowski. *The Animatrix.* Script. Hollywood: Warner Home Video, 2003.

Wachowski, Andy, and Larry Wachowski, dirs. *The Matrix*. Burbank: Warner Bros., 1999.

Wachowski, Andy, and Larry Wachowski, dirs. *The Matrix: Revolutions*. Burbank: Warner Bros., 2003.

Wah, Fred. *Diamond Grill.* Edmonton: NeWest, 1996.

Walas, Chris, dir. *The Fly II*. Hollywood: Twentieth Century Fox, 1989.

Walpole, Horace. *The Castle of Otranto*. 1764. New York: Oxford UP, 1982.

Walton, Priscilla L. *Our Cannibals, Ourselves*. Urbana: U of Illinois P, 2004.

Wang Chen-ho. *Mei-kuei Mei-kuei Wu-ai-ni* (*Rose, Rose, I Love You*). 1984. Trans. Howard Goldblatt. New York: Columbia UP, 2000.

Wang, David Der-wei. *The Monster That is History: History, Violence, and Fictional Writing in Twentieth-Century China.* Berkeley: U of California P, 2004.

Wang, Wayne, dir. *Chan is Missing*. New York: New Yorker Films, 1981.

Wang, Wayne, dir. *Dim Sum: A Little Bit of Heart.* Hollywood: Orion, 1985.

Wang, Wayne, dir. *The Joy Luck Club*. Hollywood: Hollywood Pictures, 1993.

Wang, Xiaoshuai, dir. *Beijing Bicycle* (*Shiqi sui de danche*). Hollywood: Columbia TriStar, 2001.

Webster, Harvey Curtis. "The World of Graham Greene." In *Graham Greene: Some Critical Considerations.* Ed. Robert O. Evans. Lexington: U of Kentucky P, 1963. 1-24.

Welles, Orson, dir. *The Lady from Shanghai.* Hollywood: Columbia Pictures, 1948.

Wiesel, Elie. *Night*. 1956. Trans. Stella Rodway. New York: Bantam, 1982.

Williams, Amie. "Looking into a Dry Lake: Uncovering the Women's View of Las Vegas. A Film Journal." *The Grit Beneath the Glitter: Tales from the Real Las Vegas.* Ed. Hal K. Rothman and Mike Davis. Berkeley: U of California P, 2002. 291-303.

Witt, Charlotte. "Family Resemblances: Adoption, Personal Identity, and Genetic Essentialism." *Adoption Matters: Philosophical and Feminist Essays.* Ed. Sally Haslanger and Charlotte Witt. Ithaca: Cornell UP, 2005. 135-45.

Wong, Sau-ling Cynthia. "Denationalization Reconsidered: Asian American Cultural Criticism at a Theoretical Crossroads." *Amerasia Journal: Double Issue on Thinking Theory in Asian American Studies* 21.1-2 (1995): 1-27.

Wong, Sau-ling Cynthia. *Reading Asian American Literature: From Necessity to Extravagance.* Princeton: Princeton UP, 1993.

Wu, William F. *The Yellow Peril: Chinese Americans in American B Fiction, 1850-1940.* Hamden: Archon, 1982.

Yamamoto, Hisaye. *Seventeen Syllables and Other Stories.* Latham: Kitchen Table/ Women of Color Press, 1988.

Yamauchi, Wakako. *Songs My Mother Taught Me: Stories, Plays, and Memoir*. New York: The Feminist Press, 1994.

Yeats, W.B. "Among School Children." *The Collected Poems of W.B. Yeats.* By W.B. Yeats. New York: Macmillan, 1959. 212-14.

Yi, Mun-yol. *The Poet* (*Shiin*). 1992. Trans. Chong-hwa Chung and Brother Anthony of Taize. London: Harvill, 1995.

Yngvesson, Barbara. "Going 'Home': Adoption, Loss of Bearings, and the Mythology of Roots." *Cultures of Transnational Adoption*. Ed. Toby Alice Volkman. Durham: Duke UP, 2005. 25-48.

Yue, Gang. *The Mouth that Begs: Hunger, Cannibalism, and the Politics of Eating in Modern China*. Durham: Duke UP, 1999.

Yuji, Oniki. Introduction. *Adolf: An Exile in Japan*. By Osamu Tezuka. Trans. Yuji Oniki. San Francisco: Cadence, 1996.

Zanger, Jules. "Metaphor into Metonym: The Vampire Next Door." *Blood Read: The Vampire as Metaphor in Contemporary Culture*. Ed. Joan Gordon and Veronica Hollinger. Philadelphia: U of Pennsylvania P, 1997. 17-26.

Zhang, Yang, dir. *Xizao* (*Shower*). Hollywood: Sony Pictures, 1999.

Zhang, Yimou, dir. *Happy Times*. Hollywood: Sony Pictures, 2001.

Zhang, Yimou, dir. *Ju Dou*. Santa Monica: Santa Monica: Miramax, 1990.

Zhang, Yimou, dir. *Raise the Red Lantern*. Hollywood: Orion, 1991.

Zhang, Yimou, dir. *Red Sorghum*. New York: New Yorker Films, 1987.

Zhang, Yimou, dir. *The Story of Qiu Ju*. Hollywood: Sony Pictures, 1992.

"Zhang Yimou and his 'Five-Tiger Generals.'" *The People's Daily* 25 Aug. 2007: 1.

Zhuangzi. "*Qiwu lun*." ("On Leveling All Things") *Zhuangzi*. Taipei: Shang wu yin shu guan, 1968.

Index